Ethics in
Public Service

Originally published in the
Edinburgh University Press
Series

PUBLIC ADMINISTRATION
IN THE 1990s

General Editor
MICHAEL HUNT
Sheffield City Polytechnic

Ethics in
Public Service

Edited by
RICHARD A. CHAPMAN

Carleton University Press
Ottawa, Canada
1993

© Edinburgh University Press 1993

ISBN 0–88629–191–7 (paperback)

Originally published in the UK by
Edinburgh University Press
22 George Square, Edinburgh

Published in Canada by Carleton University Press

Printed and bound in the UK

Carleton Public Policy Series 10

Canadian Cataloguing in Publication Data

Main entry under title:

  Ethics in public service

(Carleton public policy series; 10)
Includes bibliographical references and index.
ISBN 0–88629–191–7

  1. Public administration — Moral and ethical aspects.
2. Civil service ethics.   I. Chapman, Richard A.   II. Series

JF1525.E8E84   1992   172'.2   C92–090537–4

Distributed by: Oxford University Press Canada,
                  70 Wynford Drive,
                  Don Mills, Ontario,
                  Canada. M3C 1J9

                  (416) 441–2941

Acknowledgements:

Carleton University Press gratefully acknowledges the
support extended to its publishing programme by the
Canada Council and the Ontario Arts Council.

Contents

Acknowledgements

This book is the product of a conference of the International Political Science Association Research Committee on the Structure and Organization of Government (SOG). Planning the conference began in 1987 and the conference was held in 1990, in the impressive venue of Durham Castle (which houses University College, the oldest college in the University of Durham). All the participants are grateful to the Master and Staff of the College for ensuring that the accommodation and the domestic arrangements were to such a high standard, to the University for its hospitality, and also to Mr Alan Piper, for giving participants a memorable guided tour of the castle.

From the outset it was decided that the conference would be small, with participants all playing active roles. It was also intended that the conference papers would be revised for publication as a book. Eight leading international experts in public service ethics were invited to present papers on themes currently attracting particular attention. The plans for the conference were announced through the SOG Newsletter, and this attracted a small number of participants. In addition, we invited some distinguished public servants to join us, thus ensuring that our discussion did not overlook practical perspectives. The Joseph Rowntree Charitable Trust awarded a grant towards the expenses and we wish to express our thanks to the Trust for this assistance. Edinburgh University Press encouraged us from the outset. We were particularly pleased that representatives of both the Trust and the Press were able to participate in the conference. Later, it was agreed that the book would be published in the new series *Public Administration in the 1990s*, being edited by Mr Michael Hunt, and we wish to acknowledge his sympathetic support and advice.

All the conference participants had roles to play: there were no free-riders. Participants preparing papers consulted widely during the conference. All the papers were revised, not only after the conference sessions, but also again after further comments had been sought from the conference discussants and the editor. During the conference, at a special session devoted to publication plans, it was agreed, after discussion, that more attention should be given to certain aspects not covered in the conference papers, and this led to the contributions from Professor Paul Finn and Dr Barry O'Toole. A cooperative team spirit emerged, and the project has benefited accordingly. Consequently, all the contributions have been specially written for this book, none has been published elsewhere, and all have been revised after extensive discussion and consultation.

The authors of the individual chapters accept full responsibility for what they have written. All, however, wish to express their thanks to the other conference participants. We have all benefited from this collegial process of discussion and consultation.

RAC
Durham, November 1991

Notes on Contributors

PROFESSOR COLIN CAMPBELL S J is University Professor in the Martin Chair of Philosophy and Politics at Georgetown University, Washington DC. He also serves as Director of the Graduate Public Policy Programme at Georgetown. He has authored or co-authored five books, including *The Superbureaucrats, Governments Under Stress* and *Managing the Presidency*. He has published five edited collections, including *The Bush Presidency*. He has served as President of the Canadian Study of Parliament Group, co-chairman of the International Political Science Association Research Committee on the Structure and Organization of Government and co-editor of *Governance: an International Journal of Policy and Administration*.

PROFESSOR RICHARD A. CHAPMAN is Professor of Politics, University of Durham. He previously taught at Carleton University and the Universities of Leicester, Liverpool and Birmingham; before that he was a civil servant. He was Chairman of the Public Administration Committee of the Joint University Council 1977–81. His most recent book is *Ethics in the British Civil Service* (Routledge, 1988).

SIR BRIAN CUBBON GCB was Permanent Secretary at the Home Office from 1979 to 1988. Before that he was Permanent Secretary at the Northern Ireland Office from 1976 to 1979. After Cambridge University and National Service he entered the civil service in 1951, joining the Home Office. He was Principal Private Secretary to James Callaghan in 1968–9 and again in 1971–5, when he was concerned with European Community matters.

PROFESSOR PAUL FINN is Head of the Division of Philosophy and Law, Research School of Social Sciences, the Australian National University. His books and articles are concerned in the main with the standards of conduct to be expected of public officials and of persons in commercial and professional relationships. In cooperation with governments in Australia he is currently conducting a national project entitled 'Integrity in Government'.

DR MICHAEL W. JACKSON is an Associate Professor in the Department of Government, University of Sydney, Australia, where he teaches ethics in the Master of Business Administration and the Master of Public Policy degrees. He has run ethics programmes for government and business. His most recent book (with Christopher Hood) is *Administrative Argument* (Gower, 1991).

PROFESSOR KENNETH KERNAGHAN is Professor of Politics and Management at Brock University, St Catharines, Ontario, Canada. He taught previously at the University of Waterloo and Carleton University and worked for the Canadian government on an executive exchange programme. He has been President of the Institute of Public Administration of Canada, Vice-President of the International Association of Schools and Institutes of Administration, Editor of the learned journal *Canadian Public Administration* and Chairman of the Academic Advisory Committee of the Ontario Council on University Affairs. He is currently Editor of the *International Review of Administrative Sciences*. His most recent books include *Public Administration in Canada: A Text* and *The Responsible Public Servant*.

PROFESSOR LENNART LUNDQUIST is Professor of Political Science, University of Lund, Sweden. He was previously Professor of Public Administration, Aalborg Centre, Denmark, 1975, and Professor of the Study of Politics, University of Copenhagen, Denmark, 1975–86. Since 1985, he has been the Editor of *Statsvetenskaplig Tidskrift* (the Swedish Political Science Review). Lately, he has been working on problems of democracy and ethics in relation to public administration. Three of his books are in English: *Means and Goals in Political Decentralization* (1972), *The Party and the Masses* (1982) and *Implementation Steering* (1987).

DR BARRY J. O'TOOLE is Lecturer in Public Sector Management at the University of Loughborough, where he is also Director of the ERASMUS linked European Business Degree Programme. He has written widely on civil service trade unionism, including his book, *Private Gain and Public Service: The Association of First Division Civil Servants* (Routledge, 1989). In addition, he is Editor of *Public Policy and Administration*, the journal of the Public Administration Committee of the Joint University Council.

PROFESSOR GUY PETERS is Maurice Falk Professor of American Government and Chair of the Department of Political Science at the University of Pittsburgh. He was co-founder of the International Political Science Association Research Committee on the Structure and Organization of Government and of its journal *Governance*. His publications include *Comparing Public Bureaucracies, The Politics of Taxation* and *The Politics of Bureaucracy*.

PROFESSOR GEORGE SZABLOWSKI is with the Department of Political Science, York University, Canada. Before that he practised Law in Montreal. He holds BCL and Ph.D degrees from McGill University and is co-author of *The Superbureaucrats: Structure and Behaviour in Central Agencies*. Currently he is on leave studying the EC policy of accession and its implementation in relation to East-Central Europe.

What ought to be done?

Conference Participants

Sir Lawrence AIREY
formerly Inland Revenue

Mrs Vivian BONE
Edinburgh University Press

Professor Colin CAMPBELL SJ
Georgetown University USA

Professor Richard A. CHAPMAN
University of Durham

Sir Brian CUBBON
formerly Home Office

Professor Graeme DUNCAN
Newcastle Upon Tyne Polytechnic

Professor Paul FINN
The Australian National University

Mr Michael HUNT
Sheffield City Polytechnic

Dr Michael JACKSON
University of Sydney, Australia

Mr Peter JONES
Council of Civil Service Unions

One

Introduction

RICHARD A. CHAPMAN

Ethics in government refers to moral standards in the public service. It is not concerned simply with what the constitutional structure of government ought to be, nor with the nature and quality of measurable services carried out to meet the requirements or obligations of statutes, although these are most certainly relevant. It is, of course, concerned with those elements of structure and organization that determine their quality and the acceptability of their standards, but it also extends more generally to the quality of government and its administration. It therefore has implications for the professional standards of all engaged in government whether they be politicians or officials. It also has important implications for citizens. Consequently, it is one of most important subjects within the scope of the study of politics. Moreover, it is a subject that has, in recent years, consistently received a great deal of public interest and discussion, often stimulated by cases which have received widespread publicity.

At a theoretical level, ethics in this context may encompass what government ought or ought not to do in given circumstances. It therefore reflects the standards or values of society: but what is acceptable in one place or at one time may differ from what is acceptable in another place or a different time. Ordinary citizens in western style democracies expect governments to abide by the rules and values of society in much the same ways as they are expected to abide by them themselves. In this context the subject may consequently be concerned with the implications for governmental structure and organization of concepts like justice, fairness and equality. All these are qualities of special relevance in considering processes of government in democratic political systems. This is not to say that these concepts have no relevance in other political systems. Nevertheless, for reasons of practicality this book concentrates on the experience of a few modern democracies, rather than trying to consider the relevance of ethics in public service from a world-wide perspective. For a number of reasons, a selection had to be made, and one of the criteria adopted was that the resulting publication, though drawing on the advantages of comparative approaches, should not duplicate the work of others in recent years. For the wider view, see for example Dwivedi (1978), and Kernaghan and Dwivedi (1983).

At the administrative level, the subject may be primarily concerned with the standards of the officials – not simply when they are carrying out instructions from higher authority but also when they are making judgments that have implications for their professional standing. Of course, many of these issues have as much relevance to the behaviour of politicians in public service as they have to the behaviour of officials. But, again, all aspects of ethics in public service could not be included in this project, and the line was drawn so that the main focus was on the problems of administrators rather than the problems of politicians. Consequently, the questions considered here have a great deal to do with areas which are receiving so much attention at the present time – discretionary decisions in official work and the constraints on officials when giving advice to ministers and when acting in their names. Although it is not widely recognized, these topics have as much relevance for the structure and organization of government as they have for ideology and theory.

From the perspective of a liberal democracy, ethical behaviour in government should reinforce the democratic process by ensuring that representatives and officials respect the rights of citizens and uphold those values which have been agreed as essential to a particular democracy. Responsible behaviour by all persons engaged in public service should be measured against these expectations, but it is not always easy to ensure that officials in public service are sensitive to these values or that they are sufficiently self-questioning in their daily decision-making and / or in the execution of policies.

In recent years there has been considerable public discussion of these matters in liberal democracies. This discussion has become increasingly sophisticated and increasingly aware that issues of ethics in public service are not just concerned with such topics as the impropriety of partisan behaviour by appointed officials, or personal gain from official knowledge (both of which are examples of matters that are, indeed, important in official conduct, but which can in many cases be controlled by legal requirements). Contemporary discussions now appreciate that ethics in public service encompasses many issues which have arisen because of the increasing complexities of modern government and which can be as difficult for some officials to resolve now as they always have been. In some cases the complexities of modern government have made them more difficult to resolve.

The intention of this book is therefore to focus attention on some of these aspects of ethics in public service. It begins with Sir Brian Cubbon's reflections on how he saw the subject from his long career in the British civil service. Sir Brian stresses the civil servant's duty as a professional and emphasises the importance of accountability within a democratic political system. In his official career he did not personally encounter officials being anxious about policy and propriety, but other facets of ethics in public service were nevertheless of deep concern to him and he provides a unique insight into an ex-Permanent Secretary's interpretation of this topic, including a valuable list of matters of individual conscience which arose out of his working experience.

This is followed by two chapters which deal with ways of promoting ethical behaviour. Kenneth Kernaghan, who played an important role in the development of the Statement of Principles regarding the conduct of public employees in Canada (Kernaghan, 1987), argues that while written ethical rules are important, they are insufficient means of promoting public service ethics: certain ethical issues are more amenable than others to management by ethical rules. His contribution draws attention to the relationship of ethics to values and includes a thought-provoking list of the purposes of promoting ethical behaviour. As with Cubbon, Kernaghan's chapter refers to the limitations of written rules, and to important questions of accountability. From this chapter it is evident that codes have an important role to play in promoting ethical behaviour within modern systems of government, but so also have other means. One of the other means, and one that is often raised during discussions in universities and in schools and institutes of administration, is the extent to which ethics can be taught through training courses. This is the subject of Michael Jackson's chapter. Jackson argues that what is important is not so much the development of a textbook definition of ethics, but the ability to identify ethical implications in daily situations. He believes ethics can be taught, but in this context he means that officials can be stimulated to recognise ethical issues, their comprehension of ethics can be deepened, enabling them to sustain ethical analysis, and their attention can be drawn to exemplary instances of ethical analysis. His chapter is firmly grounded in his extensive experience of developing courses on ethics in numerous public administration career development programmes in Australia and in the Master of Public Policy programme at the University of Sydney and the master of Business Administration programmes at the University of Sydney and at Macquarie University.

Next, Guy Peters asks what principles, in addition to legal principles, should be applied in making choices within public sector bureaucracies. He highlights the moral nature of choices that are made according to other criteria, and draws attention to the moral dimension of public policy-making. He then explains his main concern in this chapter, which is the moral implications of making rules which determine the outcome of particular cases, because they can be a major factor contributing to tragic consequences in individual cases. These choices, that have to be made by administrators within the normal constraints of working in the public service and in the absence of consultation with others (including elected representatives), can result in administrators being uncomfortable for ethical reasons about the outcome of policy decisions.

Peters' chapter is complemented by George Szablowski's chapter on administrative discretion where the rights of individuals may be affected. He highlights the importance for officials of safeguarding human rights when implementing government policies. He discusses the need for administrators to examine the interests of individual citizens, stresses the moral and professional responsibility of officials to engage in legal and policy analysis to determine whether a specific violation of human rights is justifiable, and offers proposals for action by officials to enhance the protection of human rights.

Sweden provides a contrast to the experience of most other countries, particularly those where contemporary political systems have been influenced by anglo-saxon traditions. Sweden has a quite different tradition, which includes an alternative approach to accountability, with freedom of the press and the protection of whistle-blowers. This removes from controversy significant areas of conduct, particularly those associated with ministerial responsibility which are often debated in other countries. However, this does not mean that public servants in Sweden do not encounter issues that require them to question their values and those of the organization. Lennart Lunquist therefore explains the practical options available to Swedish officials when they are dealing with matters which they feel should be publicly known. Enshrining for citizens wide opportunities to know about public sector activities means that moral dilemmas for officials do not disappear, but instead are expressed in different ways. Officials in Sweden have loyalties to the law, to superiors, to citizens and to subordinates and peers as, indeed, officials do in other countries, though the problem may not be appreciated in quite the same way in other political systems. These loyalties place somewhat different demands on Swedish officials in their different circumstances, and they can come into conflict. What, then, asks Lundquist, does the bureaucrat do? The opportunities in Sweden are outlined and the lesson emerges from this chapter that ethical dilemmas can exist in Sweden as elsewhere, thought the issues may be presented differently. This Swedish experience has important lessons for officials facing comparable problems elsewhere.

The chapters by Richard Chapman and Colin Campbell focus, from different perspectives, on other problems associated with the constraints of the political environment within which the ethical problems of officials develop. In Britain some of these problems arise from the country's peculiar, so-called 'unwritten' constitution. This means that the relationship between civil servants and the Government is different from anywhere else and involves prerogative power, ministerial responsibility (and the behaviour of ministers) and the accountability of officials. In Britain some of these features can themselves become the focus for officials experiencing moral dilemmas, though in other circumstances they can reduce the scope for such dilemmas. Chapman's chapter concludes that, in Britain, there may be reform proposals worth considering, to enhance the standards of public service, but as long as current societal values persist, changes in structure and organization will never eliminate the scope for moral dilemmas. It is nevertheless in the interests of the system of government to recognise that these problems will continue, to educate citizens about such aspects of their system of government, and to consider measures to safeguard the rights and interests of officials.

These questions are raised from another perspective when Colin Campbell considers how constitutional and administrative systems may foster ethical behaviour among officials. He draws a distinction between those who emphasise accountability to superiors and those who emphasise recognising complexities in life and who do not find all situations fitting neatly into hierarchical modes when resolving conflicts of conscience. In particular, differences in interpreting accountability are highlighted by the new approaches of public choice and managerial theories of bureaucracy, which emphasise value for money and the development of agencies. Campbell also sees genuine problems arising when officials are requested, by their superiors, to act in ways they believe to be unethical, or when officials become aware of improper behaviour by their political masters. There is therefore a continuing need to consider how accepted requirements for accountability can be maintained while preserving the capacity of officials to act as moral agents in complex situations.

On a number of occasions at the conference, Paul Finn argued that the discussions had not given sufficient attention to the ways public officials were already constrained by the law, which carries its own discipline for public officials and can therefore contribute to resolving ethical problems. The experience of particular countries may be different in a variety of respects, but in his chapter Finn makes two important points: that, in the experience of most of the countries from which the conference participants came, officials *are* personally responsible in law as well as being hierarchically accountable to ministers; and that proposed reforms, intended to minimize problems of conscience for public service officials, including innovations like codes of conduct, must be consistent with the requirements of the law and not in opposition to it.

One of the subjects occurring frequently in contemporary discussions of public service ethics is the role of trade unions and implications for their members. Barry O'Toole has therefore provided a valuable overview of this aspect of the topic, from British experience. Trade unions have introduced a new factor in the debate about ethics because they are concerned not only with protecting the financial interests and working conditions of their members, but also with standards of professional conduct in public life. As O'Toole explains, unions have made important contributions in reacting to the standards of conduct of politicians; and they have also drawn attention to some of what they conceive as the ethical consequences of policies, right up to the increasing influence of the very latest phenomenon in this context, the ethics of consumerism.

The issue of ethics in public service may be as old as public service itself, but new experiences will always arise. This is because the structure and organisation of governments are not static; ideologies, values and policies also change from time to time; and, above all, public servants are human beings who are chosen by approved processes of staff selection, are conditioned by socialization and training, and develop professional standards and ways of doing things according to the rules. Moreover, they are employed for their abilities and qualities which are important factors in the development of public service ethics. This perspective was expressed well by Marshall E. Dimock nearly half a century ago when he wrote:

The busy executive needs ... a philosophy [of administration] ... because it is the indispensable tool of decision making, and the administrator's life is filled with daily decisions, some small and relatively insignificant, others large and momentous ... If the decision cannot be related to a grand-strategy philosophy it will have to be related to something else. All too often the alternative is rules and procedures when not understood in their ultimate significance result in behavior by rote ... I believe that administrators ought to be individuals, not cogs, because the secret of success is individual ... [and] An ultimate test of a good administrative system is whether it communicates spirit and a rounded feeling of widespread satisfaction. (Dimock, 1958, pp. 5, 6, 2, 4)

The alternative Dimock indicates may be more extreme than is usual in actuality, but the message is still worth pondering. Problems arise because public servants are individuals. They may be servants, but they are professionals: they need to be educated, selected and trained; they must act according to the law, whatever political system they serve; they are hierarchically accountable – in democratic systems, ultimately to elected representatives; and their duties often involve the development as well as the implementation of policies. In the practical experience of a complex modern world officials will always encounter moral dilemmas; often they are real, but sometimes they are imagined (and they are no less serious when imagined). The tasks facing those with overall responsibility for the public service include understanding the nature of such problems, devising procedures to mini-mise them, and ensuring that those that cannot be resolved are dealt with as satisfactorily as possible and in accordance with the standards and values of society.

Dimock, Marshall E. (1958), *A Philosophy of Administration*, New York and Evanston: Harper and Row.

Dwivedi, O.P. (1978), *Public Service Ethics*, Brussels: International Institute of Administrative Sciences.

Kernaghan, Kenneth (1987), 'The Statement of Principles of the Institute of Public Administration of Canada: the rationale for its development and content', *Canadian Public Administration*, 30, pp. 331–51.

Kernaghan, Kenneth and Dwivedi, O.P. (eds) (1983), *Ethics in the Public Service: Comparative Perspectives*, Brussels: International Institute of Administrative Sciences.

Two

The Duty of the Professional

BRIAN CUBBON

I retired exactly two years ago. After one month of leisure, in the deep trough of redundancy, Professor Chapman invited me with some blandishment to address this conference on ethics in public service. On the advice of Professor Chapman, I started writing this talk with a blank sheet of paper. I am not steeped in the academic literature on this subject. But I do not start with an open mind. I applaud the open scholarship of the organisers of this conference in asking me to speak without knowing what I might say.

In this talk I shall set the scene in which a British senior civil servant operates, take a passing swipe at some current hobby-horses, and end with an account of some of the things which troubled me as I went about my duties. What this leaves you with by way of ethics I fear you may find insubstantial. I doubt also whether the other expression in the title of the conference – 'public service' – is all that useful. One of my limitations is that I come from a special kind of public service. The higher civil service in Britain has a distinctive and limited perspective of what is commonly called public service. Even so, can one phrase comprehend the Whitehall operator, an official at a DSS local office, a nurse, a train driver, and a privatised bus driver? Like all Sellars and Yeatman expressions denoting A Good Thing (e.g. morality, justice and ethics), it is a propaganda expression of limited definitional utility. It is right that public officials should be constantly reminded that they are giving a service to the public, but many civil servants join the civil service, and stay in it, not so much for reasons of altruism, but more for security and the unequalled importance and interest of the job.

Nor should we talk of public service as though there is a master/servant relationship between the public and the government official. The Government is the master of its servants: a theme I return to later.

Emphasis on 'service' also clouds the essential coarseness of acts of government. I prefer to describe the business I was in as the exercise of power within a democratic system. It is salutary to remember that all government is the exercise of power by public authority to the detriment of someone – granting or refusing planning permission, discriminating where there is a choice, taking time to give a decision, collecting Income Tax and giving people less social security benefit than they want.

This exercise of power is made acceptable because the people who exercise it are democratically accountable. Accountable in parliament; at a general election; and through media investigation and questioning morning, noon and night. This media accountability – the Daily Ballot Box – intensified dramatically during my career, rightly and naturally with the enlargement of the areas in which governments exercise power. It is the guarantee of our freedoms.

It is no good pretending that power and accountability are easy bedfellows. If they are, something is wrong. Conflict and tension between them are of the essence of democratic government. We freely use phrases like 'democratic government' as though there was some absolute blue print for democratic government, when the in-built tension between the two words means that the phrase is merely defining a subject for debate.

Total democracy is inconsistent with sober and stable administration: the mob is fickle. The exercise of power can be prejudiced operationally by total openness or reduced to inaction by the requirement for an absolute majority on every issue. But power will always be abused without exposure and the brutal threat of democratic rejection.

Each country squares these circles in its own way. In Britain, we rely not on a formal constitution, but on traditional institutions, in a state of some tension, which we also institutionalise. Our system entrenches tension and adversariality, like duelling, as a civilised and pragmatic way of settling issues. Adversariality is built into our refusal to have proportional representation at elections, our criminal trial procedures, our television interviews and the Prime Minister's twice weekly questioning in the House of Commons.

But not in front of the children, not at any rate all the time. We soften the edges, for mass consumption, by comfortable references to 'checks and balances', by the role attributed to the Monarchy and by a good British helping of hypocrisy and deception. People do not want conflict all the time. They want, in Bagehot's terms, a dignified as well as an efficient system of democracy.

Cabinet government is a good example. I once heard a critic of Mrs Thatcher call with equal vehemence for cabinet government and open government. But the cabinet system of collective responsibility depends crucially on deception. A minister whose view has not prevailed in a cabinet committee must embrace and defend the committee's conclusion as if he agreed with it. Each minister must tell the same story in public, whatever he has said in private. 'If we do not hang together, we are sure to hang separately.' This applies not only to cabinet business. Handling the media is the daily preoccupation of all ministers, even on the tiniest detail of departmental business, because the interests of government, any government, are often in total collision with the aim of the media to reveal all.

This scrappy, scrapping world is the setting for the extraordinary relationship between ministers and senior civil servants. Despite the use of special advisers and party committees, a departmental minister is still crucially dependent for his personal success on an apolitical civil service – on individual officials who owe him no political allegiance. The implied arrangement is that we, with our experience, will help you, ministers, make the system work in pursuance of your political aims, and you tell us about everything you think and do and listen to us. That is the heart of the special minister–civil servant relationship in this country. (There is a lot of interest these days in how the executive arm of government is organised – agencies, nationalised industries, privatisation, etc.: but that is peripheral to the key relationship between ministers and headquarters civil servants.)

In polite company, we wrap up our role by using the dignified phrase 'policy advice' to describe the contribution of officials, constantly emphasising that policy is for ministers to decide. Policy-making is not a satisfactory term for describing the daily role of ministers. I suspect that it was invented by civil servants to flatter ministers into thinking that ministers' contributions are more coherent and rational than they really can be. Ministers think in terms of ideas and prejudices and headlines, rather than policies.

Furthermore 'advice' suggests a distancing of the two roles. In practice, civil servants take part in a dialogue with ministers which is often about the political and media handling of the matter as well as the merits. Would it not be better, minister, to get some bad news out of the way, just before some better news? A department is essentially a marriage between the professionalism and experience of its individual officials and the policy ideas and political skills of its transient ministers. The role of officials is advisory only in the sense that ministers have the last word both before and *after* a decision. (I took the view that even if an official acts totally within proper authority, if the minister subsequently thinks the official was wrong, he was wrong.)

In the intimacy of this arranged marriage, we see ministers in the raw: naked and unashamed. Loyalty to them is natural. We see them warts and all. Often selfish, vain, ambitious, unreasonable and sometimes personally unpleasant: but at the same time conscientious, honourable and courageous. I would apply these last three adjectives to every minister I have worked with.

Nevertheless, the senior civil servant must remain professional, and become neither a courtier nor an obstruction. One of my predecessors, John Anderson, was Permanent Secretary of the Home Office in 1924 when Joynson-Hicks arrived as Home Secretary. Despite his kill-joy policies, Jix was himself a genial person. The first thing he did was to breeze into Anderson's room, thump him on the back and exclaim 'Well, I hope you are going to like your new Home Secretary.' Anderson replied: 'Sir William, it is no part of my duty either to like or to dislike Home Secretaries.'

We have a special expertise in making this unique system work. Making the system work is a profession in itself. Our system of government defies all management models. Where else would you have a board of directors consisting mainly of marketing men conducting all the key operations themselves, with the thinking at a much lower level in the organisation?

In making the system work we act as an apolitical and objective ballast when ministers are in full sail. We widen the *objective* base on which are made what must inevitably be *political* decisions. We present arguments and reality to the fevered ambitions and fears of politicians. We concentrate on 'what *can* happen', *not* 'what *ought* to happen'.

So – in a 'can' world rather than an 'ought' world – where do ethics come in?

At this stage you may hope that having acknowledged the imperfections and warts of the present system, I am bound to endorse the various ideas for policing the exercise of Government power: whistle-blowing, codes, etc. I am afraid not.

But first: a government health warning. I have had for a great many years, a vested interest in preserving the existing system. Because the role of the senior civil servant is unique, he is not easily employable elsewhere. Nevertheless, I reject absolutely any duty or licence for a civil servant in this country to indulge in whistle-blowing, in the sense of going outside the government machine if he thinks that there is malpractice by ministers. In a system where adversariality, and conflict, is of the essence, you have to be on one side or the other. As a civil servant you are on the side of power. Your loyalty to ministers is absolute. You are there for that purpose. If you feel that the system is being abused, you must look, and be able to look, to your professional head, the head of the civil service, to take a professional view and if necessary put the point to the Prime Minister knowing that *in extremis* the head of the civil service can resign. If you are still desperately upset, you may feel, as a *citizen* that you must leave, but as a *civil servant* your only duty is to the government of the day. (Note that in saying that your only duty is to the government of the day, I do not add wish-washy words like 'for all practical purposes'. The duty is absolute so long as the present constitutional arrangements are unthreatened, and it is not for civil servants to subvert them.)

It is the system and not individuals which guarantees propriety in government. Ministers have to reveal all, in total trust, to officials who owe them no political allegiance, and listen to what they say and continue to depend on them after the decision has been taken. This is a powerful guarantee of propriety. A single act of disloyalty can weaken that trust and thereby the very safeguards that the system provides.

I do not favour the idea of a code of ethics, in the sense of guidelines which stand separately from the management of the day. In this country either you have legal requirements and obligations, enforceable by the courts, or you do not. The danger about codes is that they can be used in a sloppy way to enforce restrictions by bluff, and so can be flouted. They also tend to deal with the last horse that bolted.

Take for example the 'rules' for business appointments on retirement under which a senior civil servant is expected to obtain approval for *any* employment he takes up within two years of retirement. The rules are a sort of code. They have no force of law, and are backed by no legal sanction, but it is clear that 'the machine' will not help in future anyone who flouts them. The 'rules' can also be futile and ineffective. I meekly put in an application under the 'rules'. In order to discover whether I put some Home Office business in the way of a prospective employer in the expectation of future employment I was asked to list all Home Office contracts in recent years (well over a million). I was *not* asked whether my prospective employer might think that I have been in a position to do him a favour over a possible prosecution under the Official Secrets Act. The disadvantage of stable doors, and maybe codes, is that they are wooden and inflexible. (I recognise that less senior civil servants, at the sharp end of public administration, need careful and precise guidance and direction about how they should behave. Any code here is for management to determine.)

I reject, as having anything to do with ethics, the continuing controversy about protection of official information and the alleged secretiveness of our system of government. It is simply all part of the in-built tension between orderly government and democratic scrutiny. It is a serious question and the issues are rightly debated, but they are political issues rather than ethical issues. Why is it that confidentiality is all right, but secrets are not?

Of course, it is good fun to analyse the practice of successive administrations in these matters and construct cathartic concepts about 'dirty hands', etc. But these are conventions, not principles. And conventions, like statistics, are primarily useful in political argument in order to refute those produced by the other side. The principle lies in the fact that a free debate takes place, backed by the existence of the ballot box.

The most difficult issues which troubled me personally during my period as Permanent Secretary were of a different order. And if ethics is concerned with matters of individual conscience, I think it right to mention a random selection, in no particular order, to see whether they fall within your view of ethics.

One concern was about the representational role of civil servants. These days, at parliamentary select committees and in dealing with outside interests, a civil servant is engaged in representation and often negotiation, where will-power and belief in the ministerial decision has to be evident if he is to do his job well. Over time, this brainwashes the objectivity away.

Secondly, in order to counter the morning, noon and night pressures of the media, I felt it a duty to push ministers as far as possible from the short term into the medium term and look at what might be called strategy.

Thirdly, as an accounting officer, I had a special duty in relation to ensuring value for the taxpayer's money which is totally neglected by ministers, parliament and the media. Everyone laps up simple statements about how many roads are to be built or how many police officers are to be recruited, without pinning the government down on what is the planned effect on crime or the expected increase in traffic flow.

Fourth, I was at all times concerned to ensure that officials were seen to be loyal to ministers. My personal performance indicator was to maintain a *total* absence of leaks from the Department. (I mentioned this in the one interview I ever gave to a journalist – just before I retired. He wrote a good piece but of course did not mention it.)

More generally, I had to ensure that this improbable marriage of ministers and officials, of two utterly different cultures, worked. It was my job to produce coherent effort between the Department and ministers. If there was incoherence, or friction, or lack of understanding, it was my fault. Ministers thought that I spent all my time making sure that they understood the views of officials. Officials believed that I was always getting them to recognise the political circumstances which required ministers to take a different view from theirs.

Fifth, I was concerned about maintaining the total integrity and incorruptibility of my staff. Was it right that I should go to the Derby every year as a guest of the Jockey Club when a minor works manager would be disciplined if a contractor took him to the dogs?

Sixth, I worried whether the Home Office was sufficiently detached and objective on policy matters. If the Home Office has a departmental view on anything, and a departmental view is much less common than is supposed, it is that for the last thirty years the prison population has been too high.

It is entirely right that individuals should hold this view. A good minister will not mind hearing it, and even welcome it out in the open (or at any rate, round his office table!). But in the early 1980s I was concerned that in our thinking, analysis and proposals we should recognise that that view was essentially subjective, and could not be made politically viable.

Seventh, I worried, in retrospect, about whether I and my staff had shown sufficient imagination in controlling crime, in spotting police malpractice or in devising anti-terrorist measures which would have saved lives.

Eighth, and perhaps the most personal responsibility of all, I worried greatly about the appointments, promotions and careers of the key Home Office staff who would, by their own ability and sense of duty, continue to uphold these same standards of professionalism and objectivity.

Finally, I am bound to say that I do not recall that I was ever confronted by a civil servant in the Home Office who was inconsolable on a matter of policy or propriety. Sometimes, at election time, a garbled message from the minister's office might excite questions about what a civil servant could properly be asked to do. They were quickly resolved. In twelve years as a Permanent Secretary, with both political parties, there was no question of propriety, and this includes financial propriety, when ministers did not readily accept my view.

I have left a lot out: fairness, ability, humanity, legality, and each day I did or said something which I hope demonstrated my attachment to one of these virtues.

The question I pose is whether the *personal* preoccupations I have listed are matters of ethics. Or have I slipped into talking about duty? I prefer myself to talk about the civil servant's duty as a professional: hence my title. He is a professional in an imperfect system, which he still manages to make work, against heavy odds at some times.

It is this sense of the professionalism of the civil servant that has come under threat in recent years. Ministers are powerful and demanding. As I stated earlier, a senior civil servant must not become a courtier. He must be his own man.

We live in an age of total accountability, and accountability, as practised today, can undermine the nature of professionalism. We live in an age where institutions are thought to be elitist, uncritical of themselves and conservative (and they often are). We live in an age where people in public positions are there to be cut down to size rather than trusted. But the professionalism of an apolitical civil service remains one of the distinctive features of our system of government. It would be a different system of government if we did not have it. I therefore talk about professional duty rather than ethics: a professional duty to sustain, and not imperil, the system I have described.

Three

Promoting Public Service Ethics: The Codification Option

KENNETH KERNAGHAN

At the end of the 1970s, the conclusion was drawn that 'from an international perspective, the 1970s may be described as the "ethics decade" in the historical development of the study and practice of public administration' (Kernaghan, 1980, p.207). There is now considerable evidence to suggest that the 1970s – and the 1980s – have been part of an 'ethics era' in the evolution of public administration. The historical pattern of relatively brief cycles of rise and decline in public and governmental concern about public service ethics has been disrupted by the current period of enduring concern. The sustained focus on public service ethics during the past two decades is in large part a result of continuing revelations and allegations of unethical behaviour involving both public servants and politicians. It is also, however, a result of broad societal concern about ethical behaviour in general; this concern extends beyond public organisations to business and professional organisations as well. Thus, for example, greatly increased attention is now being paid to ethical issues and reforms in business firms and in the medical profession and to the teaching of ethics in business and medical schools.

A central theme of this enduring and widespread interest in ethics is the best means of promoting ethical behaviour. The primary focus of this chapter is on the use of codes of ethics to foster ethical behaviour in the public service. This chapter is concerned with the management of ethics rather than the ethics of management; it examines the means by which political executives and public service managers can promote ethical behaviour rather than the extent to which these persons act ethically. Two major arguments are presented. The first is that written ethical rules in general and codes of ethics in particular are an important but insufficient means of promoting public service ethics. The second argument is that certain ethical issues are more amenable than others to management by ethical rules. In this chapter the links between ethics and values are explained as a basis for examining arguments for and against written ethical rules and for assessing the utility of these rules compared to other means of pursuing ethical behaviour. Illustrative references are drawn from Australia, Britain, Canada and the United States.

ETHICS AND VALUES

The term *public service ethics* (or administrative ethics) refers here to principles and standards of right conduct in the administrative sphere of government. Ethics is concerned not only with distinguishing right from wrong and good from bad but also with the commitment to do what is right or what is good. The concept of ethics is inextricably linked to that of *values*, that is, enduring beliefs that influence the choices we make from among available means and ends.

Since public servants are actively involved in politics in the broad sense of the authoritative allocation of values for society, the values which they bring to their decisions are centrally important in the development, implementation and evaluation of public policy. There is an enormous range of values by which public servants' attitudes and actions are influenced. These include social, political, personal and administrative (or organisational) values. Many values (for example, wealth, success) have relatively little direct connection with ethics; but many other values (for example, fairness, honesty) are in essence concerned with what is right or good and can be described as *ethical values*. The critical link between ethics and values is that ethical standards and principles can be applied to the resolution of value conflicts or dilemmas. Consider the challenge of applying ethical principles to the reconciliation of such administrative values as efficiency, effectiveness, accountability, neutrality and responsiveness. For example, public servants may seek to resolve a clash between the values of accountability to political superiors and responsiveness to the public by reference to such ethical principles as truth telling or promise keeping.

Public servants have traditionally been advised that responsible administrative behaviour requires that they adhere to a number of generally worded rules or commandments. These commandments include such succinct advice as: Act in the public interest! Be politically neutral! Do not disclose confidential information! Protect the privacy of citizens and employees! Provide efficient, effective and fair service to the public! Avoid conflicts of interest! Be accountable! (Kernaghan and Langford, 1990) In contemporary governments, several difficulties arise from these commandments. First, it is not easily apparent to public servants – or indeed to anyone else – precisely what these general rules mean in practice. For example, what exactly does it mean to be politically neutral? Second, even when the meaning of the rules is clear, there is disagreement as to whether the rules themselves are appropriate. For example, there is much difference of opinion as to what benefits public servants should accept from persons with whom they conduct official business. Third, the rules sometimes clash with one another. A public servant cannot, for example, always be both accountable and efficient. There is a need to provide structures and processes to clarify and interpret the current meaning of the traditional rules. There is a need also for mechanisms to ensure a vigorous and continuing dialogue among public servants as to the ethical principles and standards to be applied in the face of competing values.

THE ETHICAL DIMENSION OF PUBLIC ADMINISTRATION

Compared to the political, legal, technical and financial dimensions of public administration, the ethical dimension has been sorely neglected; it is much more pervasive than is commonly recognised, even by many public administration scholars. Much of the recent public and media concern about public service ethics has centred on conflicts of interest and, to a lesser extent, on issues of political partisanship, public comment and confidentiality. Among the many questions currently being posed in these areas are the following: What kind of gifts or entertainment should public servants accept from someone with whom they do business? Under what circumstances is moonlighting acceptable? Is an apparent conflict of interest as serious as an actual conflict? To what extent should public servants participate in partisan political activity? To what extent should public servants criticise government policies and programmes in public? Under what circumstances, if any, are public servants justified in leaking government documents?

The effective management of these issues is generally acknowledged to be essential to public trust and confidence in government. Consequently, over the past two decades governments have responded to public concern about these issues by unleashing an unprecedented torrent of statutes, regulations and guidelines bearing on ethical conduct. However, these high-profile issues constitute only a small proportion of the total field of ethical problems. Many other ethical issues of enormous importance receive comparatively little public and scholarly attention. These are issues which relate less to the use of public office for private, personal, or partisan gain and more to ethical and value conflicts and dilemmas that arise in the performance of administrative duties. Among these issues are the following: Under what circumstances, if any, should public servants lie to the public? Should public servants implement zealously a policy which they think is misguided? Do public servants owe their ultimate loyalty to their political superior? To the public? To their perception of the public interest? To their conscience? Is it appropriate to bend the rules to assist a member of the public who is especially needy or especially deserving? Is the public interest the same thing as the interest of the government of the day? What level of risk should a public servant take with the public? Where should the balance be struck between a representative public service and an efficient and effective public service?

It is notable that these issues, compared to issues like conflict of interest and confidentiality, have not only received less public attention but are also less amenable to management by the use of written ethical rules. Thus, the effective management of these issues requires that ethical rules in general and ethical codes in particular be supplemented by other means of promoting ethical behaviour.

APPROACHES TO PROMOTING ETHICAL BEHAVIOUR

Given the pervasiveness of ethical issues in public service, more attention needs to be focused on their management. Among the questions to be considered are these: Are written ethical rules the best means of promoting ethical behaviour? Or should we require that both existing and aspiring public servants take courses on ethics and values? To what extent can – or should – public servants be expected to model their ethical behaviour on that of their political superiors and administrative colleagues? These questions highlight three means of preserving and promoting ethical behaviour among public servants, namely written rules, including codes of ethics; pre-service education and in-service training and development; and reliance on the role model provided by hierarchical superiors and associates. The following discussion will deal primarily with written rules but will include reference to the other approaches as well.

The utility of these various approaches depends on the objectives being sought. Given the widely acknowledged importance of childhood socialisation for moral development, it is unlikely that the use of any one, or any combination, of these techniques will bring about dramatic 'born again' conversions to ethical behaviour. What then are the objectives of these efforts to promote ethical behaviour? Among the central objectives are these: (1) to promote public trust and confidence in the ethical performance of public servants; (2) to decrease and, if possible, to eliminate, unethical practices by discouraging and punishing them; (3) to legitimise the imposition of sanctions for unethical behaviour; (4) to sensitise both current and aspiring public servants to the ethical and value dimensions of bureaucratic decisions; (5) to reduce uncertainty as to what constitutes ethical and unethical behaviour; (6) to develop skills in the analysis of ethical and value issues; (7) to assist public servants to resolve ethical and value dilemmas; and (8) to promote moral development. While written rules can contribute to the accomplishment of all of these objectives, we shall see that other approaches are likely to be more effective than written rules in achieving some or these objectives.

VIRTUES AND LIMITATIONS OF CODES OF ETHICS

A *code of public service ethics* is a statement of principles and standards about the right conduct of public servants. It normally contains only a portion of a government's rules on public service ethics and is, therefore, a more narrow term than *ethical rules*, which includes statutes, regulations and guidelines. As explained in the next section, the form, content and administration of ethical codes differ significantly from one government to another. Indeed, we shall see that much of the dispute over the utility of codes of ethics arises from the fact that such a wide variety of instruments are described as codes. The situation is further complicated by the fact that public servants may be subject not only to their government's code of ethics but also to codes developed for their profession (for example, law, engineering) and to codes developed by professional associations of public servants

(Institute of Public Administration of Canada, 1986; American Society for Public Administration, 1984).

Even the most vigorous advocates of codes of ethics for public servants acknowledge that codes are not a panacea for unethical behaviour. There is, however, much disagreement as to how useful codes actually are. The arguments presented below relate specifically to the use of ethical codes for public servants as opposed to ethical codes in general. Certainly the distinctive political, legal and administrative environment of government makes the drafting of a public service code a significantly different task than drafting a code for a business enterprise. It is generally recognised that taxpaying citizens expect higher standards of ethical performance from public servants than from businesspersons; certain practices, especially in the conflict of interest sphere, are acceptable in the business community but are proscribed in the public service.

Perhaps the most common complaint made by critics of public service codes is that the broad ethical principles contained in many codes of ethics are often difficult to apply to specific situations. For example, what precisely does it mean in practice to 'put loyalty to the highest moral principles and to country above loyalty to persons, party, or Government department' (United States, 1958)? A second and related concern is that codes of ethics, even if they contain detailed provisions, are difficult to enforce; indeed many codes contain no provision for their enforcement. Third, given the considerable size and complexity of government, it is difficult to draft a code that can be applied effectively and fairly across all departments and agencies. Fourth, codes can affect adversely the individual rights and private lives of persons whose ethical behaviour is beyond reproach. Consider the effect on individual privacy of the requirement in some governments that public servants disclose not only their own financial interests but also those of their spouses and dependent children. Some codes explicitly acknowledge the danger of undue interference with legitimate personal activities. The Australian *Guidelines*, for example, note that 'where personal behaviour does not interfere with the proper performance of official duties, and where it does not reflect on the integrity or standing of the Service, it is of no interest or concern to the employing authority' (Australia, 1982). Fifth, as noted earlier, certain ethical and value issues (for example determining what measure of risk to the public is acceptable) are not easily amenable to management by ethical rules in general or ethical codes in particular. Sixth and finally, codes are ineffective in dealing with systemic corruption where 'the organization professes an external code of ethics which is contradicted by internal practices' and where 'internal practices encourage, abet and hide violations of the external code' (Caiden, 1983, p.67).

Advocates of public service codes acknowledge that codes alone are not sufficient to ensure ethical behaviour but contend that codes can effectively promote the first five objectives outlined in the previous section of this chapter and make a modest contribution to achieving the others (Kernaghan, 1975, pp.4–7). Moreover, they argue that many of the critics' concerns can be overcome by careful drafting and effective administration of codes. What form does this argument take?

THE CONTENT, FORM AND ADMINISTRATION OF CODES

In most governments, ethical rules have traditionally been scattered throughout various statutes, regulations and guidelines rather than being contained in a single document. During the past two decades, however, many governments have adopted codes of ethics which contain not only new ethical rules but also a consolidation of some of the existing rules. For example, the United States Ethics in Government Act of 1978, among other things, codified and supplemented all the rules previously contained in law or executive order. These various codes differ significantly from one another in both content and style because in the drafting process different balances and choices are made between such competing considerations as comprehensive coverage and selective coverage, generality and specificity, and legislative and administrative measures. Each of these sets of considerations is discussed below.

CONTENT

Given the pervasiveness of ethical issues in the public service, where should the balance be struck between *comprehensive* coverage of ethical issues and more *selective* coverage? Governments usually cover those areas where they have – or anticipate – problems, especially problems which are likely to receive media attention and cause political embarrassment (for example, the unauthorised disclosure of government information). Moreover, as noted earlier, some ethical problem areas (for example, conflicts of interest) are more amenable to treatment by written rules than other problem areas (for example, a clash between the ethical values of truth telling and promise keeping). No doubt these considerations account in large part for the fact that many public service codes in the United States focus on or deal solely with conflicts of interest.

The lack of consensus as to what problem areas should be covered in a code of ethics and indeed as to what constitutes a genuine ethical problem can be demonstrated by reference to Britain's *Pay and Conditions of Service Code* and the *Establishment Officers' Guide*. The coverage of these documents is broader than many documents that are labelled codes of ethics in that they contain a relatively detailed treatment of political partisanship, the disclosure of official information and several varieties of conflict of interest. Yet the *Guide* itself asserts that it has never 'been thought necessary to lay down a precise code of conduct because civil servants jealously maintain their professional standards' and a British expert on ethics observed in 1988 that the *Code* and the *Guide* 'say nothing about professional or ethical considerations' (Chapman, 1988, p.305). More recently, however, the *Code* now includes a summary of the Armstrong Memorandum (on the duties and responsibilities of civil servants in relation to ministers) and also the new provisions on official information arising from the Official Secrets Act 1989.

FORM

The tension between *generality* and *specificity* in the form of a code of ethics can be demonstrated by distinguishing between two polar types of codes – the *Ten Commandments model* at one pole of a continuum and the *Justinian Code model* at the other (Kernaghan, 1975, p.11) The Ten Commandments model contains a small number of general precepts which are expressed in broad terms. It is often difficult to apply these precepts to concrete cases and normally no provision is made for the code's administration. The Justinian Code model tends to provide comprehensive as opposed to selective coverage in that it makes specific provision for a wide range of ethical problems and either includes or refers to existing statutes, regulations and other ethical rules. While this type of code usually provides for its administration, it is a lengthy and complicated document which few public servants are likely to refer to regularly and which is unlikely to be an effective instrument for sensitising public servants to ethical issues. The ten-part *Code of Ethics for Government Service* adopted by the United States in 1958 exemplifies the Ten Commandments model whereas Australia's *Guidelines on Official Conduct* (Australia, 1982) are located towards the Justinian Code pole of the continuum. Canada's Conflict of Interest Code (Canada, 1985) lies near the middle of the continuum, but it covers only one problem area. This is well illustrated by the revised form of the Armstrong Memorandum (1987), which was worked out in conjunction with the unions and as a result was a better balanced and more generally accepted document than the original, 1985 version.

There is considerable variation from one country to another – and from one government to another within a single country – as to whether ethical rules in general or codes in particular take the form of legislative or administrative measures. While codes of ethics are widely perceived as applying to the 'grey area' of proper conduct not covered by law, many so-called codes take the form of statutes. At the state level in the United States, for example, 'by far the most popular method of enacting codes is through statutory provisions' (Hays and Gleissner, 1981, p.50). Moreover, some non-statutory codes supplement their provisions with reference to statutes or sections of statutes bearing on ethical conduct. The United States relies more on legislation to regulate public service ethics than do Australia, Britain or Canada. For example, there is in the United States a Council on Government Ethics Laws – a professional organisation which provides various means for exchanging information on significant developments and trends in governmental ethics, elections, campaign finance and lobby *laws*. It is notable, however, that in Canada the federal Task Force on Conflict of Interest (Canada, 1984, p.87) recommended that a code of ethical conduct (of the Ten Commandments variety) be enshrined in a statute which would be supplemented by procedural rules in the form of regulations made under the statute and by supplemental codes of rules and procedures devised to meet the unique needs of specific departments and agencies.

Statutory codes tend to foster a greater measure of rigidity in the interpretation, application and revision of ethical rules. If these codes provide for their enforcement in the regular courts, they permit the exercise of less administrative discretion in the management of ethical conduct than codes which take the form of administrative measures. Resort to the courts is usually necessary in respect of such serious ethical offences as bribery and corruption, but in most areas of ethical behaviour a strong case can be made for administrative management of ethical rules. Many ethical offences that deserve some penalty are not serious enough to require resort to the courts. Moreover, managers may turn a blind eye to ethical offences if the punishment is too severe.

It is notable that statutory codes and other rules that deal solely or primarily with conflicts of interest touch only a small part of the large field of public service ethics. Nevertheless, there is a widespread tendency, especially in the United States, for governments, the public and the media to identify ethical behaviour with the avoidance of conflicts of interest. This practice obscures the scope and importance of other ethical issues in public administration, many of which cannot be effectively managed by written rules, no matter what their form.

ADMINISTRATION

The content and form of codes of ethics affect significantly their administration, especially in respect of enforcement. It is widely held also that codes will be more credible among public servants and therefore easier to administer if there is widespread public service involvement in their formulation. A sense of ownership and commitment to codes can be achieved through widespread consultation on their content and form, even with members of the public. Indeed, the process of developing a code – and of revising it – may be as important as the final product in sensitising public servants to the ethical and value dimensions of their decisions. Widespread publicity about the content and the application of the code among both the public and public servants is an essential element of effective administration. Publicity helps to promote public trust and confidence in government and reminds public servants of the ethical standards to which they are expected to adhere.

The diversity in the form and content of codes of ethics is matched by a similar diversity in the mechanisms for their enforcement. Some governments, especially state governments in the United States, have established ethics commissions to advise governments on ethical issues or to enforce ethics laws, or both (Hays and Gleissner, 1981, pp.52–3; Burke and Benson, 1989, p.97)[1]. A persuasive argument can be made for the creation of an ethics office or commission headed by an ethics counsellor who can serve as an advisor and a mediator for public servants facing difficult ethical questions. Canada's federal Task Force on Conflict of Interest recommended the establishment of an Office of Public Sector Ethics headed by an Ethics Counsellor to perform advisory, administrative, investigative and educational functions (Canada, 1984, pp.208–13) The creation of such an office is likely to enhance the credibility of the government's ethical regime and to promote consistency in the interpretation of ethical rules across the government.

IS THERE AN IDEAL CODE?

The ideal content, form and administration of a code of ethics are very much in the eye of the beholder, but there is growing recognition that a two-part or three-part code may be the most efficacious in overcoming the criticisms of codes outlined earlier. The first part would contain a brief statement of general principles along the lines of the Ten Commandments approach. The second part would supplement these principles by an explanation or illustrations of what the principles are intended to mean in practice. Alternatively, this elaboration could be interspersed with the principles. This two-part approach is often found in professional codes of ethics (for example, for engineers and lawyers) and was adopted by the International City Management Association in its *Code of Ethics with Guidelines* (1987). For example, section 11 of the Code reads as follows:

> 11. Handle all matters of personnel on the basis of merit so that fairness and impartiality govern a member's decisions pertaining to appointments, pay adjustments, promotions and discipline.
>
> *Guideline*
> *Equal Opportunity.* Members should develop a positive program that will ensure meaningful employment opportunities for all segments of the community. All programs, practices and operations should: (1) provide equality of opportunity in employment for all persons; (2) prohibit discrimination because of race, color, religion, sex, national origin, political affiliation, physical handicaps, age, or marital status; and (3) promote continuing programs of affirmative action at every level within the organization.
>
> It should be the member's personal and professional responsibility to actively recruit and hire minorities and women to serve on professional staffs throughout their organization.

In the case of codes drafted by governments as opposed to professional organisations, this second part could include reference to relevant ethical rules contained in statutes, regulations and other official documents. Also for government codes, a third part could be added which would tailor the general principles and their commentary to the particular needs of individual departments. Consider the problem of dealing with the conflict of interest issue for the government as a whole and, for example, for employees in a customs department. A three-part code could contain (1) a general principle advising against using one's public office for private gain; (2) supplementary commentary explaining the various types of conflicts of interest and referring to related rules in other documents; and (3) information and advice pertinent to the special problems of conflicts of interest in the customs area.

An alternative to combining general ethical principles with elaborative guidelines is to formulate a statement of what may be described as 'mid-level bridging principles' (Bayles, 1984, p.110), that is, principles which serve as a bridge between broad fundamental principles and specific rules and decisions. This was the approach taken by the Institute of Public Administration of Canada for its *Statement of Principles* (Kernaghan, 1987). For example, on the issue of accountability, the Statement reads as follows:

> *Accountability.* Public employees are accountable for the quality of their advice, for carrying out their assigned duties and for achieving policy and program objectives within the framework of law, prevailing constraints, direction from their superiors, and the limits of the authority and resources at their disposal.
>
> Public employees are accountable on a day-to-day basis to their superiors

for their own actions and the actions of their subordinates. They owe their primary duty, however, to their political superiors. They are indirectly account-able to the legislature or council and to the public through their political superiors. Public servants also have a responsibility to report any violation of the law to the appropriate authorities.

ALTERNATIVES AND COMPLEMENTS TO CODIFICATION

Both the advocates and opponents of codes of ethics are, empirically speaking, on thin ice because of the scarcity of hard data on the efficacy of ethical rules as well as on the comparative efficacy of other approaches to promoting ethical behaviour. In a 1979 survey of 650 *business* firms, the vast majority of respondents stated that their codes were 'helpful in ensuring praiseworthy business conduct' (Bowman, 1981, p.61). And in a 1976 survey of business executives, most respondents favoured ethical codes but felt that 'codes alone would not substantially improve business conduct' (Brenner and Molander, 1977, p.59). This author's own research and experience suggest that these findings are generally applicable to the public sector also; codes are useful but insufficient.[2]

Even when ethical rules are painstakingly codified and careful provision is made for their enforcement, these rules cannot cover effectively the whole range of ethical and value issues that arise in public service. For example, the United States Ethics in Government Act of 1978 'synthesizes and simplifies what had theretofore been many disparate and overlapping rules for government behaviour', but 'it still concentrates upon the negative and shows little regard to the nuances of govern-ment decision making, the realities of human relationships, or the importance of human motivation'. Indeed, 'all of the effort to anticipate and block every avenue of potential wrongdoing creates a monstrous task of detection and enforcement but does little to build the kind of attitudes and morale that develops the real backbone of sensitive ethical performance' (Stahl, 1983, p.26). Clearly, other paths to promoting ethical behaviour must be explored. Aside from codes of ethics, the main approaches mentioned earlier were the influence of role models and reliance on education and training. Each of these approaches complements codes of ethics in fostering the several objectives outlined early in this paper.

SENIOR PUBLIC SERVANTS AS EXEMPLARS

A 1982 survey of federal public service executives in the United States found that the behaviour of one's superiors (followed by the behaviour of one's peers in the organisation and society's moral climate) was perceived as the most significant factor in influencing subordinates to act unethically (Schmidt and Posner, 1986, p.452). In the same survey respondents indicated that when confronted with an ethical dilemma in performing their job, they usually consult other persons in the following order: their spouse – 26.9 per cent; no one (work it out myself) – 21.7 per cent; boss (superior) – 20.6 per cent; colleagues (other people at my level) – 12.8 per cent (Schmidt and Posner, 1986, p.453). Thus, they are most significantly influenced by the ethical performance of their superior but are most likely to discuss ethical issues with their spouse. In the 1976 survey of business executives mentioned above, respondents indicated that the behaviour of their superiors and, to a much lesser extent, formal company policy are the major factors influencing executives to make unethical decisions (Brenner and Molander, 1977, p.59).

These data suggest that the influence of administrative superiors, both in public and business organisations, is extremely important in promoting ethical behaviour. In the context of the British civil service, Richard Chapman contends that 'the approved high standards of professional conduct at all levels in the ... service depend largely on the controls and influence exercised by outstanding civil servants who may be called leaders' (Chapman, 1988, p.307). Sir Edward (later Lord) Bridges, the leader on whom Chapman's work focuses, provides an exemplar of ethical behaviour. He served as Secretary to the Cabinet from 1938 to 1946 and as Permanent Secretary of HM Treasury from 1945 to 1956. It was said of him that 'his personal code of professional ethics was a very serious matter for him ... His standards and his rules became known by example, not by precept' (Winnifrith, quoted in Chapman, 1988, p.308).

Senior public servants in other countries have similarly been celebrated as role models of exemplary ethical behaviour. It is notable, however, that most of these officials served at a time when governments were much smaller and less complex than they are now. It is widely acknowledged that contemporary governments, and indeed many individual departments, are so large that the administrative heads of departments have personal contact with only a very small number of their subordinates. Thus, it is more difficult for the influence of the most senior officials to filter down the administrative pyramid. Current bureaucratic leaders do, of course, exercise an important influence on the ethical – or unethical – behaviour of their immediate subordinates who can in turn pass the message down the hierarchy. Moreover, the efficacy of a code of ethics can be promoted by bureaucratic leaders who live by its precepts – who translate the precepts into action. But it is unrealistic to argue that the role model provided by bureaucratic leaders can serve as the sole means of promoting ethical behaviour in the public service. Like a code of ethics, ethical leadership is necessary but insufficient.

ETHICS EDUCATION AND TRAINING

Public service executives and managers can also demonstrate their commitment to high ethical performance by ensuring that public servants at all levels of the hierarchy are sensitised to ethical and value issues – and to the means of dealing with them – through formal staff development courses.

Some scholars are pessimistic about the usefulness of both ethical rules and training for promoting ethical behaviour. While no one is likely to learn morality in training courses, such courses can *improve* ethical behaviour by sensitising participants to the importance of enduring ethical principles and can help develop skills for analysing the application of such principles to ethical and value issues. Moreover, as noted earlier, there are many rules of varying degrees of clarity and specificity regarding the responsible behaviour of public servants. Training courses can foster *understanding* of what these rules mean in practice and can stimulate formal changes in rules that are unrealistic. The value of training courses is particularly evident at the induction stage: what is learnt at entry often conditions a whole career.

Codes of ethics can serve a useful complementary purpose in training courses by articulating the rules of appropriate behaviour and providing a framework for discussion of ethical issues. Training courses provide opportunities for applying a code to the resolution of specific issues and for consulting those affected by a code on its appropriate content and form. In addition, these courses can provide an intellectual basis and stimulus for a continuing dialogue on ethical issues. Given the complexity of ethical issues, combined with the need for exemplary role models in the senior ranks of the public service, training courses are especially important for top-level officials; such courses provide formal opportunities for these officials to articulate their values and assess the extent to which these values are shared by their colleagues.

There is increasing evidence to support the view that moral development can be effectively promoted through formal education as opposed to short training courses. James Rest, a leading researcher in this field, asserts that the psychological literature shows that 'dramatic and extensive changes occur in young adulthood (the 20's and 30's) in the basic problem solving strategies used by the person in dealing with ethical issues' and 'deliberate educational attempts (formal curriculum) to influence awareness of moral problems and to influence the reasoning/judgment process can be demonstrated to be effective' (Rest, 1988, p.23). These findings provide an important part of the rationale for a substantial ethics component in public administration programmes for university students. In this context, it is notable that the American Society for Public Administration, in concert with the National Academy of Public Administration and the Government Ethics Centre, has approved a Resolution on Ethics Education which asserts that 'university programs preparing people for careers in public service ... should provide explicit curriculum coverage for all students that enables and encourages them to act ethically'. In particular, programmes should, among other things,

> – Train students 1) to recognize and focus on ethical problems; 2) to develop and refine appropriate methods of moral reasoning; and 3) to be sensitive to the nuances and ambiguity of ethical situations.
>
> – Encourage students 1) to see public service as a noble calling and a public trust, deserving commitment to the highest standards of honor and personal integrity; 2) to appreciate the ethical dimension in decision making (just as they appreciate the political and managerial dimensions); and 3) to accept the multiple and sometimes conflicting obligations of public service.

Rest notes that 'with over 100 studies now evaluating the effectiveness of moral education programs, there is more documentation for moral education programs than for most academic courses, especially courses in the Liberal Arts. It is ironic then that many people who believe in the value of Liberal Arts believe that moral education is a waste of time' (Rest, 1988, p.24).

CONCLUDING OBSERVATIONS

It is evident that the objectives of efforts to promote ethical behaviour outlined early in this paper will be better achieved through a combination of codes, exemplary role models and staff development than through codes alone. For example, the leadership of senior officials can sensitise public servants to the ethical and value dimensions of their decisions and training and education can help to develop skills in the analysis of ethical issues. Yet codes which are carefully drafted and vigorously administered can be very effective in promoting ethical behaviour. Moreover, in situations where public servants have neither exemplars to emulate nor access to training courses, ethical rules in general and codes in particular may be the only means available to promote ethical behaviour. The fact remains, however, that effective use of all three approaches is much more likely to make ethical behaviour an integral part of the culture – or ethos – of the public service.

In addition to the three approaches discussed above, there are measures of a less focused nature that can help to foster sensitivity to ethical and value issues in the public service. Among these measures are mechanisms to facilitate public participation in government decision-making (e.g. through advisory boards), to ensure that this participation is based on adequate information (e.g. 'sunshine laws' which open up government decision-making procedures to public scrutiny), and to promote greater participation in decision-making by the public servants themselves (e.g. by decentralising decision-making authority).

The role of political executives is extremely important in creating a milieu in which public servants are encouraged to adhere to high ethical standards. Political executives can not only serve as exemplars, in much the same way as bureaucratic leaders, but they can also support training courses in ethics and the formulation of appropriate rules. The negative public image of government officials created by the involvement of political executives in unethical behaviour can have an unfortunate spillover effect on the public's perception of public servants and, indeed, on the commitment to ethical behaviour of the public servants themselves.

Reliance on personal ethical standards is not an adequate means of ensuring that public servants will make ethical decisions. Moreover, the suggestion that contemporary public services can rely for ethical guidance simply on *unwritten* rules in the form of traditions, conventions, understandings and practices is naïve, and even dangerous (Kernaghan, pp.5–6). As explained earlier, a dominant rationale for written rules – and indeed for ethics education and training as well – is that there is much uncertainty as to what the traditional rules are and what they mean in the day-to-day operations of the public service. It must be acknowledged, however, that on rare occasions none of the mechanisms for promoting ethical behaviour offers relief from ethical quandaries. On such occasions 'difficult decisions facing public employees can ultimately be resolved only by resorting to individual conscience' (Institute of Public Administration of Canada, 1986).

ACKNOWLEDGEMENT

The author wishes to thank Peter Jones, Secretary of the Council of Civil Service Unions, for commenting on an earlier draft of this chapter.

NOTES

1. For a detailed proposal for a general counsel to deal with whistle-blowing issues in the public service, see the Ontario Law Reform Commission's *Report on Political Activity, Public Comment and Disclosure by Crown Employees* (Toronto: Ministry of the Attorney General, (1986), pp.327–52).
2. This conclusion is based not only on substantial research in this field but also on my experience as a public service manager, twenty-five years of close contacts with public servants, my drafting of public service codes of ethics, and considerable experience in organising and facilitating workshops on ethics and values for public service executives and managers.

American Society for Public Administration (1984), *Code of Ethics* and *Implementation Guidelines*.

Australia (1982), *Guidelines on Official Conduct of Commonwealth Public Servants*, Canberra: Australian Government Publishing Centre.

Bayles, Michael D. (1984), 'Moral theory and application', *Social Theory and Practice*, 10, pp.97–120.

Bowman, James (1981), 'The management of ethics: codes of conduct in organizations', *Public Personnel Management*, 10, pp.59–66.

Brenner, Steven N. and Molander, Earl A. (1977), 'Is the ethics of business changing?', *Harvard Business Review*, 55, pp.57–71.

Burke, Fran and Benson, George (1989), 'Written rules: state ethics codes, commissions and conflicts', *State Government*, 62, pp.195–8.

Caiden, Gerald (1983), 'Public service ethics: what should be done?' in Kenneth Kernaghan and O.P. Dwivedi (eds), *Ethics in the Public Service: Comparative Perspectives*, Brussels: International Institute of Administrative Sciences.

Canada, Task Force on Conflict of Interest (1984), *Ethical Conduct in the Public Sector*, Ottawa: Supply and Services.

Canada, Treasury Board (1985), *Conflict of Interest and Post-Employment Code for the Public Service*, Ottawa: Supply and Services.

Chapman, Richard (1988), *Ethics in the British Civil Service*, London: Routledge.

Hays, Steven W. and Gleissner, Richard R. (1981), 'Codes of ethics in state government: a nationwide survey', *Public Personnel Management*, 10, pp.48–58.

Institute of Public Administration of Canada (1986), *Statement of Principles Regarding the Conduct of Public Employees*.

Kernaghan, Kenneth (1975), *Ethical Conduct: Guidelines for Government Employees*, Toronto: Institute of Public Administration of Canada.

Kernaghan, Kenneth (1980), 'Codes of ethics and public administration: progress, problems and prospects', *Public Administration*, 58, pp.207–23.

Kernaghan, Kenneth (1987), 'The Statement of Principles of the Institute of Public Administration of Canada: the rationale for its development and content', *Canadian Public Administration*, 30, pp.331–51.

Kernaghan, Kenneth and Langford, John (1990), *The Responsible Public Servant*, Toronto: Institute of Public Administration of Canada and Halifax: Institute for Research on Public Policy.

Rest, James R. (1988), 'Can ethics be taught in professional schools? The psychological research', *Ethics: Easier Said Than Done*, 1, pp.22–6.

Schmidt, Warren H. and Posner, Barry Z. (1986), 'Values and expectations of federal service executives', *Public Administration Review*, 46, pp.447–54.

Stahl, O. Glenn (1983), 'Public service ethics in the United States', in Kenneth Kernaghan and O.P. Dwivedi (eds) *Ethics in Public Service: Comparative Perspectives*, Brussels: International Institute of Administrative Sciences.

United States (1958), *The Code of Ethics of Government Service*, 85th Congress, 2nd session, Concurrent Resolution 175.

Four

How Can Ethics Be Taught?

M.W. JACKSON

INTRODUCTION

In 1976 the Australian public service was made the subject of a thoroughgoing study by the Royal Commission on Australian Government Administration chaired by H. C. Coombs. The findings of this commission made ethics its first recommendation (Coombs,1976, p.25). But there is precious little that bears on ethics in the voluminous research that accompanied the report. The same gap between recommendations concerning ethics and research into ethics is also evident in a more recent commission of inquiry into corruption in the state of Queensland (Fitzgerald, 1989).

More than 9,000 Commonwealth public servants were interviewed by researchers working for the Coombs Commission, but the primary focus of these interviewers was satisfaction with working conditions. The one item on the detailed interview schedule that focuses most explicitly on ethics asks if it would be moral for a public servant to comment in the media on working conditions, the administration of a government programme, or to speak against an incumbent government at a political rally. Some scholars have interviewed Commonwealth public servants, too, but ethics has not figured in their analyses (Higley, Deacon and Smart, 1979, pp.46–8ff. and Pusey, 1988).

Identified as a key issue in 1976, ethics was not explored in the Coombs report and it has not been probed by the little research that has been done among public servants in Australia. By 1987 an observer would have to be forgiven for thinking that ethics was no longer on the agenda. In that year the *Guidelines on Official Conduct of Commonwealth Public Servants* (Public Service Board, 1987) was published and widely distributed. The *Guidelines* emphasise following orders, subordination, and hierarchy. Those perplexed or troubled by their duties are advised to seek the advice of their superiors. The implicit argument is that the government of the day is democratically elected and so public servants simply must obey (Wilenski, 1979).

That such a conception of the relationship between the public service and politicians would appear under a Labor government is no surprise. High in the Australian Labor Party's cosmology is the belief that Labor governments have failed in the past because of the inertial resistance of the public service. Of course, Liberal–National party governments often feel themselves undermined by a public service that they perceive to favour the ALP (Weller, 1989). But that is but a manifestation of a feeling common to those parties in power.

The *Guidelines* allow public servants, in turn, a degree of participation in partisan politics, for example unpaid leave while running for office. Some wits have described it as a Faustian bargain: obedience in return for partisan liberty.

The importance of the *Guidelines* should be stressed. In some federal systems the constituent governments, like the Canadian provinces, serve as laboratories implementing and evaluating new ideas. In Australian politics the reverse has largely been the case. Innovation has been in the central government. (And innovations have as often as not been made by conservative governments.)

Of course no one is against ethics, and some people see it as a weapon to be used against political opponents when allegations of corruption occur. Such allegations are a frequent occurrence in any political system, and Australia is no exception. Nevertheless, Australians seldom admit that there is political corruption (Robinson, 1988, p.12). But in the main, integrity and honesty – taken as ethical qualities – are regarded as weaknesses in Australian politics, at least among the men (Dodson, 1990, p.4).

There is no doubt that in the last generation the image of public service has been tarnished. Instances of malfeasance and allegations of corruption have been made at every level of government. An increasingly well-educated public can be expected to insist on the highest standards of responsibility and accountability in government.

The first step in teaching ethics in public administration is to develop the recognition of the ethical dimension of administration and policy. The perception of ethics comes no more naturally than perception of anything else. If public servants are to respond to the demand for ethics, then ethics should be taught. Why? Because good people do not always make good decisions (Janis, 1979).

Consider an analogy. Technically competent people, say engineers, do not always make technically competent decisions. They make technically competent decisions if and only if they follow systematic strategies in analysis and action. (Even then mistakes can be made.) The same is true for ethics. Morally good people can make morally bad decisions, if they fail to think through the ethics of the matter. It was Max Weber (1947, pp.122–3) who argued that in political life evil can come from good. A 'morally bad' decision for these purposes is one that a person would subsequently say was a morally bad decision. (This definition avoids the pit of the relativism of judgment.) Good people can make bad decisions. Management education and training is premised on this assumption, and it applies to ethics. Systematic analysis can decrease the number of bad decisions. This, too, is a premise of management education and training that applies to ethics.

If the ethical aspects of public administration and policy are perceived, then further goals include the development of the capacity to analyse these dimensions. Ethical analysis involves an understanding of the origins, implications, explanation, and consequences of the components of a situation. It requires the toleration of ambiguity and the search for the variety of legitimate points of view. At the end of the day, ethics education and training needs to encourage people to adopt systematic strategies to capture and articulate the ethical implications of public administration and policy.

The purpose of this chapter is to concentrate on techniques for focusing attention on ethics in teaching and learning. It begins by identifying the basic obstacles that have to be dealt with to start a degree course or to develop a workshop on ethics.

BASIC PROBLEMS ENCOUNTERED IN PROVIDING COURSES ON ETHICS

There are a number of problems in providing courses on ethics. The first is the foundation assumption that ethics can be taught. There is a school of thought according to which we learn the ethics of our lifetime at a paternal knee. If we do not learn virtue then, we will never learn it. The second obstacle is the assumption that ethics permeates everything we do and so need not be singled out for attention in a course or session exclusively devoted to it.

These may be considered in reverse order. To argue that there is no need for singling out ethics for attention because it is implicit throughout public service education is an argument against putting ethics on the syllabus. While it is certainly true that ethics is an element in much else, is that a sufficient reason for not focusing on it? Let us consider an analogy. Micro-economics is a constituent of nearly all management activity. But no one argues from that fact to the conclusion that micro-economics should not be given special attention. Quite the reverse argument is made. Micro-economics is so pervasive that it must be singled out for measured attention. This is the analogy with ethics. Ethics is so pervasive in management activity that it must be analysed in its own right.

The purpose of management education and training is to reduce the complexities of management to constituent parts so that constituents can be examined. No one is against including ethics, but there are different ways to be for it. Furthermore, it is sometimes said that ethics is something that cannot be taught (Bok, 1976). The first task of the instructor is therefore one of presentation: how should ethics be introduced into the programme?

The course or the session can be described as the opportunity to reflect upon and pool the experience of the participants in order to bring out the ethical aspects. The instructor is not cast in the role as someone teaching ethics, but rather as someone who is structuring the opportunity for the participants to analyse their own experience.

In addition, a distinction can be made between subjects that are based on information and subjects that are based on experience. Examples of subjects based on information are mathematics and history. One cannot learn history or mathematics without the exposition of material. There are other subjects that are based on experience. Examples are aesthetics and ethics. One cannot appreciate these subjects without experience. A person who has never seen a painting will not grasp the importance of perspective and balance. Equally, a person who has never made an ethical decision, a decision about good and bad or right and wrong, will not appreciate the difference between a utilitarian and an deontological approach to ethics.

The conclusion to be drawn is that the experience that the participants bring to the subject is essential. This supposition coheres with the general tenets of management education in degree programmes. It is also stressed in mid-career staff development work.

However, the individuals who are sent on six week residential programmes in mid career want answers much more than questions. To return to the analogy with micro-economics: they want to learn some principles and procedures of micro-economic analysis. They do not want to learn the criticisms made of the assumptions of micro-economics, or of competing schools of thought.

The instructor may have to be prepared to admit the limits of ethical education and training. It does not suffice to make people good any more than the study of law makes all lawyers law-abiding. None the less, students often demand answers to ethical questions while attending courses and it is necessary to meet this demand in some way. Failure to do so means that the credibility of the ethics sessions suffers.

Once ethics is given a place on the education and training agenda, reference may be made to cultural or individual differences. When this is articulated it usually comes in the form of saying people disagree about what is right and wrong – from which it is concluded that there is no point in trying to analyse ethics.

Differences about the value of studying ethics, however, may be similar to other differences that have been important in the development of management education. For years, accounting was not regarded as sufficiently important or intellectual to earn a place in universities, but this is no longer the case. Indeed, many of the subjects taught in Master of Business Administration (MBA) or Master of Public Policy (MPP) programmes or included in staff development programmes were once regarded as irrelevant to management education. Moreover, the notion of management education itself was long decried. 'Good managers were born not made', was the thesis that delayed the foundation of business schools and retarded the development of their curricula (Chandler, 1977).

The same beliefs have bedevilled the development of schools of public affairs where public administration and policy are taught. A core of opinion maintains to this day that effective public service requires nothing more than diligence and common sense. As one seasoned observer noted some time ago:

> One of the difficult problems of schools of public affairs is to overcome the old fashioned belief – still held by many otherwise sophisticated people – that the skills of management are simply the application of 'common sense' by any intelligent and broadly educated person to the management problems which are presented to him. It is demonstrable that many intelligent and broadly educated people who are generally credited with a good deal of 'common sense' make very poor managers. The skills of effective management require a good deal of uncommon sense and uncommon knowledge. (Miles, 1967, p.350)

This observation certainly still applies where ethics is concerned. Even well into an ethics course or training programme a variant of this objection may arise. It is the feeling that ethics is vague. Once again this objection can be met directly by comparing ethical analysis to other kinds of analysis. Is ethical analysis any more vague than legal analysis? Is there not almost always room for argument over the interpretation of the law? Is it any more vague than the practice of accounting where there is argument over what and how to count assets and income?

The apparent vagueness of ethics may be related to the vagueness of other important decisions in an individual's private life. Important decisions are complex, as ethical matters are, and as a result it is difficult to isolate and analyse the factors that go into them. For example, the decision to marry, to have children, how to educate them, which house to buy and so on do not lend themselves to cost benefit analysis or risk assessment. Yet these are important decisions. Furthermore, important but vague decisions like these are often made better if we talk them through with others: friends, relatives, colleagues, and the like. The same applies to ethical matters.

Three of the most obvious problems in promoting ethics education and training in the public service have now been identified. These are the thesis that ethics cannot be taught, that it should not be taught in a separate course, and the belief that it is all relative. This last problem raises two other problems: the desire for answers and the sense that ethics is vague and so irrational.

There is a fourth fundamental problem. That is the demand that will be voiced in the first moments of any session on ethics. It is the request for a definition of 'ethics'. An educator can try a couple of ways to meet this demand: Following Peter Singer (1979), something can be said about what ethics is not. Ethics is not specially limited to matters of sex, drugs and religion. We can know a person's religion without knowing very much at all about what kind of person that individual is. We will not know whether the person is trustworthy, loyal, constant, or the like. We can know something about a person's sexual preferences or activities without knowing what kind of person that individual is. The bottom line of ethics was well put by T.M. Scanlon (1982, p.16), who has written that ethics is finally the 'desire to be able to justify [our] actions to others on grounds they could not reasonably reject'.

Evidence for Scanlon's thesis is readily available. Few people readily admit to acting unethically. Even those who would deny that ethics has any meaning justify their actions. Stuart Henry (1978, pp.46–8) found, for example, that those who acted on the borderline of acceptable conduct invariably offered mitigating circumstances: low wages, special need, retribution for the practices of big business and government, and the time honoured assertion that 'everyone else does it' or would do it in the same situation. Henry described these as the effort to neutralise formal standards of behaviour. Someone selling stolen videos would never admit they were stolen, but would rather say that they had 'fallen off the back of a truck'. The use of such coded phrases serves to justify questionable actions.

An example of such a justification has recently been aired in Australian politics. Donald Frederick Lane, a former Queensland cabinet minister, admitted to the misuse of ministerial funds, and went on to say that 'his activities accorded with the custom of his Ministerial colleagues' (Fitzgerald 1989, p.172). Such an example makes apparent how important norms are in producing ethical conduct.

Some fundamental problems associated with ethics education can be dealt with in these ways; other problems can be circumvented. Indirection is often the best way to persuade sceptics rather than refutation. Taking the point made earlier that ethics is based upon reflection on experience, it may be possible to move directly into some ethical thinking on the grounds that once the participants have the chance to think through some concrete examples of ethics these fundamental problems can be better put in context. What is needed, after all, is not the recitation of a textbook definition of the word 'ethics' or a digest of the history of moral philosophy but some ability to identify ethical implications in daily situations.

TECHNIQUES IN ETHICS EDUCATION AND TRAINING

A variety of teaching techniques may be used to direct attention to ethical issues in management. The following examples relate to a stand-alone two-hour workshop in an executive development programme or the opening session in a series of workshops on ethics or a degree course in a MPP or MBA programme. The question 'Who are you to teach me ethics?' may be defused with some self-deprecation: 'Indeed, who am I to teach anyone ethics!' It may be helpful to start sessions with a few words about experience and reflection, then move as quickly as possible to involving the participants in the style of a workshop. Participants may be asked to list up to five words that they associate with the word 'ethics'. In order to make it challenging, when this programme was offered in the University of Sydney it was assumed that everyone associated the words 'morality', 'religion' and 'legality' and their derivatives with the word 'ethics'. These words were not to be listed by the participants.

The purpose of this exercise was to focus their minds on ethics, and also to show them that they did have ideas about what it means. In this respect the technique is effective. Participants have little trouble in generating a list. These can be collected and some of the words can be displayed to the group on a board or overhead projector. Among the words that participants may generate are: responsibility, accountability, conduct, honesty, loyalty, guidelines, principle, equity, fairness, and so on.

This technique has been found to work well in focusing the group and for opening discussion on ethics, but it is a little awkward to collect the responses and list the terms. In listing the terms participants assume that there is some hidden order to them. As it turns out there is.

Experience has shown that there are four categories of values in responses:

- Honesty
- Integrity
- Fairness
- Caring

In fact, responses most frequently mentioned fell under the headings of honesty, then integrity, then fairness, and finally caring. These categories are listed here in descending order of the frequency with which they are mentioned. A certain number of responses to this approach may be cynical: equating ethics with officiousness or a busybody or with self-righteous, holier than thou attitudes. It may be useful to treat these responses as seriously as other responses and attention may be directed to spelling them out.

While the word association technique works, it may be even better and more concrete to ask participants to think of the most ethical person they know. Then ask them to spell out four or five words that identify the characteristics of this person that are ethical; this seems to make it easier for people to list some words. With the abstract word association exercise, done in ten minutes in a session, there are always a few participants who simply are not able to list any words. Causing participants to think in terms of someone they know makes it easier for everyone. Furthermore, it also seems to reduce the free floating cynicism that the abstract word association invites, though it does not eliminate it.

Most people can think of someone they admire as a person and then can articulate some of the qualities of that person. The exercise is then made personal in a double sense: it focuses on someone in particular for each participant and it commits each participant to explaining the qualities of a person whom they admire.

Mindful of the latent relativism of people of middle years, after this exercise has been done the results may be predicted before examining them. That is, an overhead transparency may be taken to the session with the four values named above spelled out. This exercise has been used with more than twenty groups and every group has nominated the same kinds of values. Doing so partly legitimatises the response of each group and also points them to the consensus that exists concerning the importance of being honest, having integrity, being fair, and caring for others.

We may not know exactly what 'fairness' is but we know that it is important to be fair. We need to take some time to figure out what fairness means. And so on for the other categorical values.

Predicting the group's results after their pieces of paper have been collected but before they have been examined may seem showy but it does serve a purpose. Most participants are so focused on their own responses to the question that they do not think about what other people might put. But it is essential that the realisation that others have similar values is driven home. While it will be patently obvious to the workshop leader, time must be devoted to allowing the participants to see it.

The question about the most ethical person is followed by three short follow-up questions. (This pattern of questioning is derived from that used by the Josephson Institute for the Advancement of Ethics.) These are the following:

2. Would the people who know you well say that you are an ethical person? Yes or no.
3. Are the people you work with more or less ethical than people in general? More or less.
4. Are the people in your profession more or less ethical than people in general? More or less.

Once again the results of these questions can be predicted after the participants have answered them. From over twenty groups there has never been less than 85 per cent of the respondents saying 'Yes, those who know me would say that I am an ethical person'. To be among the righteous is a common experience in ethics education and training. In predicting that result, the workshop leader can challenge its veracity. 'Other people would not think of you as the most ethical person they know! They probably would not think of you at all.' Part of the aim here is to get attention by being provocative. The conclusion is that there is a discrepancy between the way we see ourselves and the way others see us. The question then is what is the cause of this discrepancy.

How do we judge ourselves? In judging ourselves we know our intentions and so we take them into account. When we judge other people, how do we do it? We judge other people by their ... actions. Every time this approach has been used the sentence has always been finished by some of the participants. The gap between intentions and actions produces the discrepancy.

The same point applies regarding (3) work mates and (4) professional colleagues. We judge them favourably because we understand a good deal of the intentions that go into their actions. Consequently, we tend to rate them highly, more highly than an outsider would do. Experience with this exercise has shown that 75 per cent of individuals say that their workmates and colleagues are more ethical than people in general.

The conclusion from these three supplementary questions is that our judgments of others should be modified by a consideration of intentions. In addition, to make our actions a true reflection of ourselves we have to try to close the gap between intention and action, and also to communicate our intentions. In judging others we have to be mindful of their intentions and in projecting ourselves to others in our actions we have to spell out our intentions. Communication is the means to cross the gap. The gap between intention and action may be narrowed but it will never be closed and so communication plays a part. There is a kind of golden rule here that if we want others to appreciate our intentions we have to consider their intentions. This discussion can also return to the earlier comment that to know a person's religion is not to know what kind of individual the person is.

There are a number of ways to go from here. Bearing in mind the four categories of values set forth above one might use a proprietary game like *Where do you draw the line?* This game brings out the distinctions we make in judgment by using a series of very short cases where roughly equivalent material factors are at stake, say $10. There might be, for example, four instances of the theft of $10 for four different reasons by four different kinds of people. A typical group will judge different situations quite differently, even when the theft of $10 is at stake in each of them. The exercise is useful to show how fine grained our judgments can be as we use the four kinds of values identified in practical situations. Fairness may mean different things in different situations, and so, too, may honesty, integrity and caring. It may be that the four kinds of values do not always cohere. The caring response may not be the fair response and so on. It is very often true that 'it does depend' upon circumstances.

The coherence of the four values can be handled in many ways. For instance, the group may be presented with a list of words, all at once or a few at a time, and asked to characterise the list.

THE A-LIST

- Rules
- Adjudicate
- Right(s)
- Decision
- Responsibility
- Conduct
- Fairness
- Logic
- Reason
- Duty
- Task
- Code
- Guidelines
- Equity
- Deliberate
- Rationality
- Consistency
- Obligation
- Principle
- Justice
- Impartiality

Participants can be asked, 'If you had to say, would you say that the words on the A-list are warm or cold? Hard or soft? Objective or subjective? Thinking or feeling? Male or female?

The B-list is then presented:

THE B-LIST

- Acceptance
- Mollify
- Appease
- Sustain
- Abide
- Accommodate
- Responsive
- Conciliation
- Propitiate
- Concede
- Acquiesce
- Intuition
- Exception
- Reconcile
- Pacify
- Allay
- Tolerate
- Confer
- Support
- Maintain
- Concession

Again participants are asked, 'If you had to characterise the B-list would you say that it is warm or cold? Hard or soft? Objective or subjective? Thinking or feeling? Male or female?

While some discussion of the words on each list must be expected, the purpose of contrasting the lists is to raise the question of the consistency of the four values identified.

The values of honesty, integrity and fairness fit well with the A-list, but less well with the B-list. On the other hand, the words that fall into the caring category fit better with the B-list. The point may be made that the indexes of books in moral philosophy and ethics are replete with the words of the A-list, while those of the B-list are hardly to be found in this scholarly literature. Provided that the participants have been stimulated by the lists the stage is now set, if the time is available, as it would be in a course in a degree programme, to turn to the works of Aristotle, Immanuel Kant, John Rawls, Lawrence Kohlberg and Carol Gilligan.

In a stand-alone workshop session there are a number of well-prepared cases with discussion questions that can be used at this point, breaking the group up into syndicates. In a subsequent plenary session the syndicates can compare notes. This technique corresponds to that which generally prevails in management education and training. Participants are comfortable with it.

Wherever possible participants may be asked to prepare naïve cases. That is, as preparation for the session they are asked to state an ethics problem they have or might have at work. They are instructed to protect their own anonymity as they see fit. At the very least these cases give the workshop leader a good idea of the way participants perceive ethics before the session, which is why they are termed naïve cases. Moreover, with the permission of the authors some of these cases may be read aloud for group discussion.

In the plenary discussion of the prepared cases and the participants' cases the leader may note how the participants' discussion of the cases draws on the four value categories noted above. Apart from moderating the discussion the leader needs to pause the discussion now and again to make this point

Experience has shown the need to leave the participants with something tangible from the session; this is especially so in executive development groups. There are a couple of techniques that may be used to accommodate this demand for answers rather than questions. Towards the end of the session the leader may review the discussion, and propose an ethics contract with each participant. This contract can be drawn in one of several ways. If time permits it can be done at the session. Participants may be invited to write out an ethics goal for themselves that they would like to meet in the next six months. If time does not permit, the leader might have a form stating the terms of the contract together with an envelope for the participants to take away and to post to the leader at their own convenience. The terms of the contract that would appear on this form are simple. Each participant writes a practical goal. The leader will hold the goals in sealed envelopes and post them back to the participants in six months' time. At that time, in a covering letter the leader can invite the participants to redraft their goal or devise another way and submit it as a new contract. One of the side effects of this technique is that the leader makes clear a willingness to stay in touch with participants after the session.

CONCLUSION

In a short workshop or at the beginning of a degree course the chief goal is to accustom participants to thinking in terms of ethics by making them comfortable with the term, linking it to other people and words with which they are more comfortable. In a course in a degree programme the goals grow from this point.

The goals stated for a course in a typical degree programme include the recognition of ethical issues, a deepened comprehension of ethics, sustained ethical analysis, and contact with exemplary instances of ethical analysis (Steinfels, 1977; Fleishman and Payne,1980; Worthley,1981; Rohr, 1989).

The principal conclusion drawn from experience in ethics education and training is that ethics can be taught. Reflection on our experience and the experience of others broadens our horizon. Thinking about people whom we admire occasions thought about what it is about them that we admire, and why. This is the beginning of ethical analysis. Once a course on ethics gets started there is no shortage of material to use. The initial challenge to the instructor is to motivate participants to take ethics seriously.

Though we seldom use the word 'ethics' it inheres in our social life. If it does not, our life is that much less social (Ignatieff, 1984, pp.138–42). To fail to use the words of ethics is to risk the erosion of the meanings of those words from our minds. Without the words to express feelings the feelings themselves may be lost.

ACKNOWLEDGEMENT

The author wishes to thank Charles Raab, University of Edinburgh, for his comments on an earlier draft of this chapter.

Bok, Derek (1976), 'Can Ethics be Taught?', *Change*, October, pp.26–30.

Chandler, Alfred (1977), *The Visible Hand: The managerial revolution in American business*, Cambridge, MA: Harvard University Press.

Coombs, H. C. (1976), *Royal Commission on Australian Government Administration, Report*, Canberra: Australian Government Publishing Service.

Dodson, Louise (1990), 'Women politicians set for leadership', *Australian Financial Review*, 18 January, p.4.

Fitzgerald, T. G. (1989), *Report of the Commission of Inquiry into Possible Illegal Activities and Associated Police Misconduct*, Brisbane: Government Printer.

Fleishman, Joel and Payne, Bruce (1980), *Ethical Dilemmas and the Education of Policymakers*, Hastings on Hudson: The Hastings Center.

Henry, Stuart (1978), *The Hidden Economy: The context and control of borderline crime*, London: Martin Robertson.

Higley, John, Deacon, Desley and Smart, Don (1979), *Elites in Australia*, London: Routledge & Kegan Paul.

Ignatieff, Michael (1984), *The Needs of Strangers*, London: Chatto & Windus.

Janis, Irving (1979), *Groupthink*, Boston: Houghton Mifflin.

Miles, Rufus (1967), 'The search for identity of graduate schools of public affairs', *Public Administration Review*, 27, pp.343–56.

Public Service Board (1987), *Guidelines on Official Conduct of Commonwealth Public Servants*, Canberra: Australian Government Publishing Service.

Pusey, Michael (1988), 'Our Top Public Servants under Hawke', *Australian Quarterly*, 60, 1, pp.109–22.

Robinson, Peter (1988), 'Tunnel vision is undermining our perception of corruption and sleaze', *Australian Financial Review*, 16 February, p.12.

Rohr, John (1989), 'Ethics in public administration', in Lynn, Naomi and Wildavsky, Aaron (eds), *Public Administration: The state of the discipline*, Chatham: Chatham House, pp.97–123.

Scanlon, T.M. (1982), 'Contractualism and Utilitarianism', in Sen, Amartya and Williams, Bernard (eds), *Utilitarianism and Beyond*, Cambridge: CUP, pp.103–28.

Singer, Peter (1979), *Practical Ethics*, Cambridge: CUP.

Steinfels, Peter (1977), *The Place of Ethics in Schools of Public Policy*, Hastings on Hudson: The Hastings Centre.

Weber, Max (1947), *From Max Weber*, London: Kegan Paul.

Weller, Patrick (1989), *Malcolm Fraser. P.M.*, Sydney: Penguin.

Wilenski, Peter (1979), 'Ministers, public servants and public policy', *Australian Quarterly*, 51, 2, pp.31–45.

Worthley, John (1981), 'Ethics and public management: education and training', *Public Personnel Management Journal*, 10, 1, pp.41–7.

Five

Tragic Choices: Administrative Rulemaking and Policy Choice

B. GUY PETERS

Perhaps the central feature of administrative life is the necessity to make choices. At the highest levels of the public bureaucracy these are choices about 'policy', or general rules intended to apply across a range of cases. In the lower echelons of the bureaucracy the choices are more often about individual cases, including who is eligible to receive either the benefits or the sanctions available from government. At both of these levels of bureaucracy, and at all the levels in between, the decisions taken by administrators are guided by laws and by the rules of the organisation within which the individual works. This chapter will argue that other types of principles must be applied to those decisions, in addition to the principles contained in law. Such alternative principles are applied conventionally by using evaluation techniques such as cost-benefit analysis, which apply the criterion of utility-maximisation to public decisions. The economic criteria contained in cost-benefit analysis are important, but are only a few among many which must be considered when making public policies.

It will be argued that highlighting the essentially moral nature of the choices required in public administration may improve the quality of decision-making. This is especially true given the uncertainties involved in many policy areas, and the extremely serious consequences which may befall individuals and/or society if the risk calculations are incorrect. Further, such ethical criteria should be used as a central component in the design of public policies, and more conscious consideration should be given to those design features in making policy. It has been argued that most policy-making in industrialised democracies occurs through incremental rather than systematic choice (Braybrooke and Lindblom, 1963), but the focus here is on a more systematic examination of values (see Goodin, 1982). That is, policy-makers should be more cognisant of the need to construct policies with some prior consideration of the options for intervention and of their valuative nature.

Furthermore, administrative decision-makers are acting on behalf of other citizens in a context of substantial uncertainty. The responsibility they have as agents of others places special claims on their actions (Hampshire, 1978), and the uncertainty makes the task harder. Some of that uncertainty is the result of insufficient understanding of the basic causal linkages at work in policy areas, and of having multiple and conflicting views about those causal mechanisms. This inadequate understanding is compounded by the absence of an adequate under-standing of the dynamics of the various instruments available to the public sector to influence the economy and society. Governments and policy analysts have employed a large variety of policy 'tools' for a number of years, but often have done so without understanding the efficiency and utility of those tools, or their possible subsidiary effects. Thus, when government intervenes in society, it does so under risk and uncertainty (Rubenstein, 1975), with the distinct possibility that some of its actions may produce more harm than they prevent (Sieber, 1981).

Thus, caution may appear to be called for when government intervenes, but at the same time governments and their agents are paid to solve problems and timidity may produce an even greater range of undesirable results. The failure to act can be as devastating as, or sometimes more devastating than, acting incorrectly. The advantages of inaction appear primarily political. First, tax money need not be used for a poorly conceived programme, and, second, political leaders do not become associated with an obvious programme failure. In addition, just because a programme is poorly conceived, that does not prevent clients and providers from becoming attached to it, and thereby making adoption and implementation of a better programme more difficult in the future (Hogwood and Peters, 1983). The logic of incrementalism is that mistakes are correctable, but those corrections are generally easier to make theoretically than they are in practice.

On the other hand, a failure to act may be equally unwise politically, and governments may find themselves in the awkward position of having to respond to a perceived (or real) crisis, no matter what the cost. This necessity of intervention may arise because of the emergence of a severe problem with no ready solution available through private mechanisms. Instead of a measured reaction, the feeling of urgency may create a 'war' type programme (poverty, cancer, drugs) even if the root causes are not understood, and the problem may be more amenable to small-scale than large-scale solutions (Schulman, 1980). In a decision setting in which both action and inaction have their social costs, and in which those social costs may not be knowable in advance, what is government to do?

TYPES OF CHOICES

This chapter draws its title from an important book on policy choice written by Guido Calabresi and Phillip Bobbitt just over a decade ago (1978). That book was concerned with the choices that individuals in positions of authority have to make that almost certainly will have tragic (that is, loss of life) consequences for other people. The decision-making situation was further constrained because of the scarcity of resources, so that choosing to save one person's life would, by definition, require someone else to lose his or her life. The particular example used throughout the book was the allocation of exotic life-saving technologies such as (then) kidney machines or (now) liver transplants. The two authors considered a variety of techniques – selling access to the technology, lotteries, first-come first-served, etc., – that might be used to make such awful allocations, and examined the ethical and practical implications of each technique. Calabresi and Bobbitt settled on the 'aresponsible jury' as the most effective and ethically defensible mechanisms for making these difficult choices. These juries are organisations with the power to make binding choices without any explanation of the rationale underlying the choices. The two authors recognised that their choice of allocative method was to some degree determined by cultural as well as formal ethical preferences, but believed that this method could produce, on average, the best outcomes.

As well as the difficult choices among individuals described above, Calabresi and Bobbitt also discussed the question of budgetary allocations among programmes that might have differential consequences for saving lives. These choices they referred to as 'first order' tragic consequences, while the individual level decisions were referred to as 'second order' tragic consequences. Thus, the need to make the second order decisions arises as a consequence of the first-order decisions; we have to make allocations of kidney machines among patients because previous budgetary decisions did not permit enough kidney machines to be purchased to service all patients who might require dialysis. Calabresi and Bobbitt argued that there might never be sufficient scarce resources – time, money, personnel – to meet all legitimate demands for expensive medical services, so that the second order tragic choices might always arise. The question in the first order case is whether one should allocate sufficient resources for an average demand for the services, for some observed peak demand, or for the highest possible demand. There are no easy ethical or economic answers to that question.

Taken to more general level, there are never sufficient societal resources for governments to be able to protect all people from all dangers, so that allocative choices with tragic consequences are almost inevitable for governments. Many industrialised democracies have gone a great distance in attempting to protect their citizens from all manner of social and economical threats, but even these wealthy countries have limited resources. Further, they must determine, probably according to efficiency criteria, where the points of diminishing returns are reached for protective programmes (see Leonard and Zeckhauser, 1986). That is, where does one more life saved from a potential threat, for example carcinogens, become too costly to justify? While that economic logic has substantial appeal to the citizen in the role of taxpayer, its appeal may be lessened when he or she considers him/herself as the consumer of the risks not being protected against. This view of allocation in regulatory policy was advanced by Schelling's seminal work in the field (1968), and has become the dominant approach to the problem, despite possible ethical objections. For civil servants in particular, their commitment to the 'public good' and the values of public service may override any utilitarian calculations in determining appropriate public policies (O'Toole, 1990).

As noted above, Calabresi and Bobbitt argued for the aresponsible jury as the most appropriate mechanism for making second order tragic choices. Their argument was that the need to justify allocative decisions, if made through a more responsible mechanism, would strain both the values of the individual decision-makers and the bonds of the society which required the members of the jury to make those difficult decisions. There is also the danger of a 'Guinness effect' (Hanson, 1982) if the criteria for selection are made known widely. Potential candidates may manipulate their cases (assuming variables like age or gender are not dominant) to enhance the probability for selection. This was seen by many to be an unseemly scramble to save one life at the expense of others, although in essence that conflict among individuals is inherent in tragic choices.

For first order tragic choices, the decisions are made through more responsible institutions, but still somewhat removed from the public. The budgetary process is complex and there is relatively little direct public access, except the opportunity to vote out, at the next election, the people who constructed the budget. Further, the decisions made are often not visible as choices among life-saving capacities except to those most knowledgeable about the programme. Finally, as will be pointed out below, the politics of constructing the budget tends to produce 'multi-organizational sub-optimization', with money rarely being allocated to produce a Pigovian optimum – in these cases with the probabilities of loss of life being made equal among all causes – to the extent possible with the finite means available to the public sector.

The description of tragic choices provided above is a description of decision-making *in extremis*. Few civil servants face such obvious life and death situations in their normal professional lives, although some do. Individuals employed in medical services, protective services and the military may well be forced to make such decisions, often very quickly and without the assistance of 'aresponsible juries', or any other means to diffuse responsibility and provide advice. Other public administrators may face these decisions only in a probabilistic sense, as when drug regulators choose clinical trials for a drug presumed to work for a dread disease rather than choosing to take a chance and make it available immediately. This choice has to be faced in reality for the distribution of drugs for AIDS, and it is certainly a potential for other types of diseases. Although they are not directly facing the average civil servant, the concept of tragic consequences is a useful heuristic device to use in exploring some more general questions about administrative decision-making. If nothing else, this concept forces the decision-maker, or the policy analyst, to confront the allocative nature of almost all policy choices, and to consider the possible severe consequences of actions or inactions.

This chapter will apply some of the logic associated with tragic choices to decision-making within the public bureaucracy. Certainly some administrative decision-making appears very similar to the individual-level choices among beneficiaries or victims of second-order choices, but we will be more interested here in administrative rule-making. We are interested in the rules which would be developed to make individual level decisions, and the criteria which might be applied when making those rules. These rules establish the general parameters for subsequent decisions which may have tragic consequences for individuals. Further, we will concentrate our attention on regulatory interventions, and the allocation of risks, in areas such as health and safety, rather than the direct provision of services in health or income support.

TRAGIC CHOICES IN PUBLIC ADMINISTRATION

The argument here concerning decision-making in administrative positions is that it is likely to be neither first nor second order tragic choices, but instead an important linkage between those two choices. Few administrators are in positions to make decisions about the overall allocation of public funds among competing purposes, although they certainly argue for their own budgets and some may advise the political leaders who do make the final choices. Likewise, most civil servants are not cops on the beat who must make life and death decisions quickly, although decisions made by social workers, unemployment office clerks, public health officials and the like can have dire consequences for individuals. Rather than either of the above, the majority of administrative decision-making involves generating the rules and procedures which guide the application of broad policy statements to individual cases. These decisions therefore constitute the linkage between the macro-allocation of budgets and any micro-decisions about which specific individuals are to receive which benefits, and how much benefit, from the public sector.

Members of the civil service often are responsible for making policies which ramify and interpret broad policy statements; the process of 'regulation writing' and secondary legislation is well-known in almost all industrialised democracies (Bryner, 1987, West, 1985, Davis, 1976). Parliaments have neither the time not the information required to make detailed rules, and leave those to the bureaucracy. In addition, even when they themselves do not construct the rules, civil servants are central advisors to those who do, and hence may have a determinant role in the nature of the rules promulgated. Therefore we should understand the logic of constructing rules for allocation in an administrative setting, as well as the logic involved in their implementation. The rules devised by public administrators are rarely so specific as would be first order tragic choices, but they do define the classes of individuals who will be eligible for benefits or who would be 'eligible' to receive certain dangerous sanctions. As such, these rules will determine who gets what in a more impersonal sense than the usual meaning of tragic choices, but if the rules made are applied as intended, they will have the same direct consequence for individuals.

The differences between administrative rulemaking and other types of rulemaking should not imply that the consequences of those administrative choices may be any less severe than either the first or second order tragic choices discussed above. It is only that the proximity to individuals will differ, and the extent of certainty will also differ. First, the decisions made about general rules for allocating risk among the population are less proximate than second order choices, but substantially closer to the ground than first order choices. Therefore these decisions contain some notion of what types of people are likely to be the consumers of risk. Consider, for example, decisions about siting potentially dangerous facilities such as nuclear power plants and maximum security prisons. Deciding the rules by which these are to be placed, and by the demographic and geological characteristics that make a site 'safe' or not, involves making decisions about which people (by residence) are to bear the risk produced by generating broader social benefits. If there are accidents, the officials making the allocative rules will not be able to predict the names of the victims, but they would be able to predict the residences of most of the victims, and with that perhaps their socio-economic status. These choices have little to do with the individual worth of the individuals, as they might in normal tragic choices, but are purely statistical choices based on other criteria.

The other variable to be considered in administrative decision-making with potential tragic properties is that of the uncertainty involved in the environment of decision-making. It is hoped that the rules made by an agency will be sufficient to prevent any serious accidents or loss of life, but in all probability the rules will not be that strict. If they were, it is likely that regulated industries or individuals would complain about regulatory 'unreasonableness' (Bardach and Kagan, 1982) and attempt to receive some relief. This fundamental uncertainty about the world into which public interventions are thrust, and the need to assess the value (economic and otherwise) of those interventions, presents a substantial problem for decision-makers developing regulatory regimes. It also presents a problems for the consumers of the risk to understand what their personal and political stakes in the strictness of the regulations are.

One aspect of Yehezkel Dror's analysis of policy-making provides one approach to these questions, albeit from a different tack than that usually used in regulatory analysis. Dror is interested in what he identifies as 'policy gambling', or the extent to which uncertainty of conditions and the uncertainty about the connections between potential interventions by governments and outcomes for individuals may make all policy-making in reality a gamble (Dror, 1983). Further, unlike with most gambling, it is virtually impossible to calculate the odds of any particular outcome, and therefore impossible to determine what risks are being undertaken by government, and by individual citizens through the policy. Thus, Dror terms the interventions 'fuzzy gambling' because they have many of the indeterminate properties of fuzzy sets in mathematics. This is an interesting analogy, but runs the risk of accentuating the potential irresponsibility of decision-making in these difficult circumstances. If policy-making really is a gamble, and a fuzzy gamble at that, then public decision-makers are justified in either adopting a *laissez-faire* attitude and under-regulating, or adopting a very strict set of regulations against all possibilities and over-regulating. As noted above, either outcome is potentially harmful to society, but uncertainty will prevent estimating which option is most harmful.

When considering administrative rulemaking from the perspective of tragic choices, it is also important to understand that these regulations may be used to guide the individual level, second order decision-making about tragic choices. These rules constitute a way to provide guidance for decision-makers faced with extremely difficult life or death decisions, and also a way to diffuse moral responsibility for those decisions. For example, supportive care protocols in hospitals are administrative rules (usually promulgated without the procedural protections described below) which inform physicians that they may legally and morally withdraw extraordinary technological supports for life. These protocols provide the physician with guidance for writing 'DNR' (Do Not Resuscitate) on a chart, and absolve him or her from the need to develop the personal criteria for choice in those situations. Those personal criteria could prove difficult to select, and may, perhaps, be ultimately indefensible – legally or morally (see Glover, 1977). Since these rules may be used to absolve their implementors from moral responsibility, a strong moral component in their formulation appears necessary.

RULEMAKING FOR POLICY CHOICE

From the perspective of policy design, this discussion of administrative policy-making is an exercise in meta-rulemaking. Dror (1968) characterised the process of meta-rulemaking as making rules about making rules. In this context, we are concerned with general guidelines for the selection of criteria to be applied to rules made in an administrative setting. These meta-rules obviously will contain a very significant substantive element; they will have to define the criteria which can be used to define classes of individuals (risk consumers within the regulatory framework discussed here) in ways that other relevant actors can understand and apply. In addition, the rules will have to specify the benefits or deprivations for which those consumers are at risk. In some instances these restrictions can be extreme, as with the 'Delaney Amendment' preventing any substance having known carcinogenic properties (in humans or animals) from being added to food, no matter how slight those effects may be determined to be in the laboratory. Most administrative rulemaking, however, does preserve some room for discretion on the part of the implementors of the policies.

The criteria to be applied to rulemaking, however, can also have a strong ethical and evaluative element. Most discussions of administrative ethics are couched in procedural terms, but it is necessary to examine the ethical implications of those potential administrative decisions, and the effects they could have on citizens. This involves understanding the evaluative elements associated with policy decisions and settling on a number that appears reasonable across a range of individual rules. This evaluative element in meta-rulemaking is closely related to the increasing volume of research on policy design (Linder and Peters, 1984; Ingraham, 1987; Bobrow and Dryzek, 1987), and on fashioning the most appropriate instruments for policy interventions (Hood, 1986; Linder and Peters, 1989; Salamon, 1989).

The process of meta-rulemaking also contains a strong procedural element. Indeed, in most political systems that procedural element has dominated the substantive and ethical elements in administrative rulemaking processes. Lacking, as noted above, any degree of certainty about the real impacts of policy, government decision-makers will instead concentrate requirements on the manner in which the rules are made. This is an attempt to ensure that the public believes that the rules which finally emerge from the process are fair, and that they will consent to them once adopted (MacLean, 1986). This consent is especially important in the distribution of risk and the possibility of 'tragic choices' in that context. If the rules chosen by government are to result ultimately in someone losing his or her life or having his or her health severely damaged while others will be protected from those harms, then at a minimum those rules and the processes by which they are formulated should conform to common societal judgments about fairness.

Generating consent in complex administrative rulemaking is, of course, a very difficult undertaking. It is difficult to know to what the citizen might be giving his or her consent; the connection between the known level of statistical risk and an individual outcome is often very tangential and difficult to prove (Hirshleifer and Shapiro, 1983). Further, it is difficult to involve most of the population in thinking about their acceptance of risk, much less involving them procedurally in decision-making. An increased awareness may occur for people mobilised politically concerning 'NIMBY' (Not In My Back Yard) facilities, where the social risk is clearly visible and concentrated, but is less likely to occur when the risk is diffused across the entire society. Because of this, elaborate procedures have been developed in some societies to generate *de facto* consent – if citizens, having been given fair warning and an opportunity to participate, do not chose to do so, then they must be willing to consume the potential consequences.

In addition to problems of consent, a strong political dimension involved in saving lives through public sector activity tends to confound and frequently override ethical, or even efficiency, criteria that might be included in meta-rules. Numerous studies of risk point to the disjuncture between actual and perceived risks, and perceived risks are more likely to receive funding than are real risks not perceived to be as threatening as they are in reality. Some deaths are merely 'normal accidents' (Perrow, 1984) that government cannot be expected to influence. This tendency to misallocate resources is compounded by the relative political popularity of agencies and programmes. For example, it has been estimated to cost $50,000 to save one life through the programme of the Consumer Product Safety Commission, but $12.1 million per life through the Occupational Safety and Health Administration (Graham and Vaupel, 1981). The budgetary allocations for these agencies do not reflect their relative efficiency at saving lives. The Consumer Product Safety Commission has been cut substantially, while OSHA has been doing reasonably well even under conservative administrations.

Even if a single model of saving lives through the public sector is adopted, for example the medical model, there may still be substantial disparities between real and perceived risks, and therefore between budget allocations. High profile diseases may receive greater allocations than the number of cases might warrant, compared to other diseases which have much higher incidences and death rates. Likewise, readily curable diseases may continue to produce deaths because they have become the 'orphans' of the medical profession and generate no interest in research. Finally, there is the 'mountain climber problem', in which identifiable lives (the climber stranded on the mountain) can exact huge expenditures while those expenditures put to another use (traffic safety, eradication of smoking, etc.) might actually save hundreds or thousands of lives rather than one. In other words, although most people in government are in favour of saving lives (and reducing risks of other negative outcomes) there are numerous barriers to either the ethical or the efficient allocation of public resources.

This leads to a consideration of some of the rules which are applied, or which might be applied, in rulemaking situations. These we will divide into procedural and substantive, although that distinction may well become artificial in practice. The discussion, particularly in relation to the more substantive rules, will be concerned with their inclusion in a design framework; this is especially important when such a framework might include trade-offs among important values as a means of approaching the generation of better policies. As well as trade-offs between procedural and substantive values, such a framework should include trade-offs between a variety of substantive values.

PROCEDURAL RULES

The most familiar rules governing administrative policy-making are procedural. The assumption appears to be that if the rules are adopted in the proper manner, then they will be acceptable and achieve consent. For example, the Administrative Procedures Act (APA) in the United States specifies a variety of steps through which administrative rulemaking must proceed if the outcomes are to be acceptable to the courts. These include public notice of the intention to issue regulations, publication of draft regulations for 'notice and comment' by the public, adequate time for citizens to respond to the draft regulations, and publication of the final regulations (Freedman, 1980). In some agencies (e.g the Food and Drug Administration), and for some types of more encompassing rules, a formal rulemaking procedure with quasi-judicial hearings and more formal rules of evidence will be required (Verkuil, 1974). In addition, the courts have increasingly required 'hybrid' procedures with a written record (Gormley, 1989) to ensure that the process used to construct regulations is 'due'.

The requirements for openness to the public contained in the APA are extreme in comparison to those in most other democracies, but all countries require some procedural guarantees to assess the legality of administrative rulemaking. Interestingly, the requirements for substantive due process are not nearly as strict. For example, the primary requirement for rules issued by the federal bureaucracy in the United States is that they should not be 'arbitrary and capricious' (Berger, 1965). The courts have interpreted this requirement quite loosely, so that if the rulemaking organisation can find any evidence or logic on which to base a decision, even if the preponderant evidence lies in the opposite direction, they will be justified legally in issuing their rule. Likewise, organisations may be required to write an environmental impact statement, but it is not clear exactly how constrained they are to avert any environmental dangers identified therein. Thus, the legal requirements for the substance of due process in administrative rulemaking tends to be much more lax than the procedural requirements, which then places the burden more squarely on the administrators themselves to infuse the proper values into their decisions. That statement, of course, begs the question of what the 'proper values' are for public policies.

As well as the legal requirements for administrative decision-making being more stringent about procedure than about substance, the ethical standards and the codes of conduct proposed for civil servants also tend to be much clearer about *how* things are done than about *what* is done. For example, admonitions concerning truth telling (Bok, 1978), openness (Ponting, 1985), accountability (Day and Klein, 1987) and responsibility (Burke, 1986) in government all have much more to say about the interactions of administrators with citizens, and the interactions of administrators with other public officials and institutions, than they do about the substance of public policy. Clear distinctions between process and substance for all public questions are difficult to generate and defend, but the emphasis in most evaluative work does appear to be on procedures. Further, it should be noted that some 'mere' procedural questions will have important substantive impacts on citizens. Decisions about truth telling for example, will determine the information on which citizens will make choices, and therefore will strongly influence those final choices.

SUBSTANTIVE CRITERIA

The above assumption concerning an emphasis on procedural rules in the analysis of administrative decision-making may appear unjustified, given the number of more substantive standards which have been applied to public policy. On the one hand, most policy analysis (cost-benefit analysis, decision-theory) is built on the substantive concepts of economic efficiency and utility-maximisation. There are numerous practical (Mishan, 1988) and ethical (Kelman, 1981) problems associated with applying this criterion, but it is certainly one which is applied frequently. Further, if one accepts the premises upon which the analysis is built, this approach has the advantage of being readily operational and of providing decision-makers with a single answer. Using this method, a policy can be determined to be 'good' or 'bad', and its relative worth can be compared with other projects which would employ the same scarce public funds.

On the other hand, there are a number of ethical criteria which can be applied to public programmes, for example, 'justice', 'fairness' and 'individual autonomy'. These standards have the advantage of capturing readily common-sense ideas of 'good' policy, as well as capturing moral and ethical criteria very well. The problem is, however, that they are less operational than most economic criteria and subject to multiple and even conflicting interpretations. In a familiar example, Rawls's (1972) ideas about justice in social policy would be diametrically opposed to those of Nozick (1974). Other scholars attempt to reconcile those positions, and other competitive positions, through contracts and bargaining (Gauthier, 1986). Even without direct negotiation these differences can be resolved through Axelrod's

(1984) notion of 'tit-for-tat' rules and tacit bargaining. The difficulty which arises in this instance is that, unlike with the economic methodologies described above, there is no set of agreed-upon indicators that can be used to identify 'good' policy and make the participants in the process agree that the right thing has been done.

A second problem which arises in the application of substantive principles to policy issues is that, when they are applied, they tend to be applied one by one. In reality, however, most policy decisions involve a number of values which have to be traded off against each other. Few if any decisions are just about economic efficiency, or just about justice; those values must be considered in the light of each other, and practical as well as moral choices must be made about the policies to be adopted. Further, those trade-offs may have be considered in the light of other circumstances such as the probable severity of the social harm at stake in the particular decision. These trade-offs are not easy decisions in the more abstract world of the academy, and are certainly a difficult undertaking in the more rough and tumble world of real public policy-making.

Although it stands as a recognition of the political dimension of evaluation of public policy, as opposed to the strict 'economism' (Self, 1972) which usually dominates the field, the criterion of feasibility is often used excessively in evaluating public policies. Saying that, *a priori*, a policy is feasible or not is often a way of saying that the policy is acceptable or not according to some (unexamined) ethical or practical principle. Further, feasibility is often considered too narrowly to include only those things which have been adopted in the past, and hence often constitutes a mortmain on policy innovation and more creative designs (Majone, 1975). It should be remembered that feasibility, like most political concepts, is highly elastic in practice and that capable political entrepreneurs often can extend the boundaries of the feasible far beyond what is usually considered possible.

THE QUESTION OF DESIGN

A design orientation towards policy-making requires the identification of a causal mechanism which produces a particular outcome which is the object of policy-making. This is generally a negative effect which government is attempting to alleviate or ameliorate, although there may be instances in which governments attempt to build on positive outcomes. The identification of this causal mechanism is by no means an easy task, and often involves the social construction of the problem. Most problems faced by government do not come ready made with a label on them. Public administration may be involved in this exercise, because the organisation which is successful in identifying the problem is also likely to be successful in capturing it and the resources used to alleviate it.

A design orientation also requires the identification and assessment of the instruments government will use as it attempts to intervene successfully in the above situation. Such an evaluation will be concerned with the relative efficiency of the instruments available, and with their secondary effects on other important values. As with the patterns of causation of social problems, an assessment of instruments may also be socially constructed. Different organisations may rely on different instruments, and may select those instruments through habit and custom rather than through serious cogitation about their utility and impacts. Perhaps above all, a design orientation requires a consideration of the range of options available for intervention, and their relative utility in solving particular social problems.

Finally, following from the above discussion, a design approach involves the identification of important social values to be achieved through policy-making and ways of including those values into the assessment of policies. This approach is distinguished from other cogitative approaches to policy-making (Linder and Peters, 1989) by the specific concentration on choice among competing instrument alternatives, as well as the involvement of multiple value dimensions in the assessments. Those value dimensions will directly affect the selection of policy instruments, and will also indirectly influence the evaluation of external social conditions which will have initiated the policy process.

The involvement of those multiple evaluative dimensions in the assessment of policies and policy-making necessarily forces trade-offs. As noted, there is a tendency to treat values as parametric values rather than tradable values, but the concept of tragic choices points out that a value that is often considered ultimate and unbargainable is, in fact, bargained away in any number of circumstances. In addition, when risk of loss of life, rather than the actual identifiable loss of life, is the consequence of action, then the trade-offs become easier for governments to make. This willingness to trade-off lives is true even if the same number of lives (or perhaps more) may be at stake. Although loss of life may be the final dependant variable for a great deal of risk analysis, there are other social and political values which become involved as these issues are processed through the 'issue machine' (Braybrooke, 1974).

For example, a government may be able to reduce substantially or even eliminate risk to its population if it is willing to engage in large scale monitoring and enforce-ment activities. Those monitoring systems would certainly maximise one important value (risk reduction, loss of life), but would also tend to minimise another, that is the freedom of adults from paternalistic intervention by others (Dworkin, 1971). The question then becomes one of balancing these competing values within a context of both procedural constraints and real technological capacities to reduce or eliminate risk. Further, the degree of risk government attempts to eliminate may be a function of the magnitude and distribution of that risk. More extensive social harm may merit greater public intervention, and risk concentrated in limited geographical areas, or affecting specially regarded segments of the population (children, the elderly, etc.) may merit stronger monitoring and enforcement. Thus, developing programmes for coping with potential tragic choices requires attention to a variety of values and to a variety of situational factors.

The question which then arises is whether the public bureaucracy is suited to such nuanced decisions and to such contextual decision-making. To the extent that membership in any one organisation creates a 'trained incapacity' to respond in other than a single way to particular problems and issues, organisations and their members may not be especially suitable for this type of difficult decision-making.

Further, as an increasing number of civil servants have professional education and training, their capacity to take other than a narrow perspective on the trade-offs involved in making critical decisions may be lessened. These concerns do not imply any moral or intellectual weakness on the part of civil servants taking a decision, but only reflect the narrowing of vision and concerns which are inherent in organisational and professional life. This inherent narrowing of perspective, therefore, invokes a need not only for the design of policies, but also the design of institutions to confront the different values circling around any one policy decision. Such institutional design would probably be very different from the sub-division of government into sub-government which characterises most contemporary democratic systems, and would require a formalised means of involving a variety of interests in an institutional way in the formulation of policy.

CONCLUSION

As is often the case, this paper has raised as many questions as it has answered, It has demonstrated that the concept of tragic choices can be an important way of understanding the difficult decisions faced by people in government, including public administrators. The decision-making which public administrators become involved in is particularly difficult because it involves the generation of general principles for allocating risk. This is at once an impersonal exercise and one which will have very real consequences for individuals and for the society at large. The connection between statistical risks and individual life and death is not clearly identifiable, and the distribution of negative consequences is also quite unclear.

Procedural rules have been the primary mechanisms employed to permit public administrators to cope with these complex and awful responsibilities. The ways in which administrative rules and regulations are written is prescribed, and in general the public is given some rights to participate and express its views. If the public does not participate, or if the participation is one-sided, consent can still be assumed, although the public at large are uninformed or even hostile to the policies. This possibility then requires the application of other, more substantive values by the administrators themselves. Most public administrators are at home with some substantive policy issues, but may be uncomfortable with ethical or moral issues about policy. Further, they may be trained to believe that if the legal requirements for rule-making are fulfilled then the substantive issues also should be fulfilled. These assumptions may be incorrect, and require some consideration in the training of public servants, and in the structuring of their decision-making environments.

ACKNOWLEDGEMENT

The author would like to express his appreciation to Barry O'Toole, and other participants in the Durham conference, for their useful comments on this paper.

Axelrod, R. (1984), *The Evolution of Cooperation*, New York: Basic Books.
Bardach, E. and Kagan, R. (1982), *Going by the Book*, Philadelphia, PA: Temple University Press.

Berger, R. (1965), 'Administrative arbitrariness and judicial review', *Columbia Law Review*, 64, pp.55–98.

Bobrow, D. and Dryzek, J. (1987), *Policy Analysis by Design*, Pittsburgh: University of Pittsburgh Press.

Bok, S. (1978), *Lying: Moral choice in public and private life*, New York: Pantheon.

Braybrooke, D. (1974), *Traffic Congestion Goes Through the Issue Machine*, London: Routledge & Kegan Paul.

Braybrooke, D. and Lindblom, Charles E. (1963), *A Strategy of Decision*, New York: The Free Press.

Bryner, G. C. (1987), *Bureaucratic Discretion*, New York: Pergamon.

Burke, J. P. (1986), *Bureaucratic Responsibility*, Baltimore: Johns Hopkins University Press.

Calabresi G. and Bobbit, P. (1978), *Tragic Choices*, New York: Norton.

Davis, K. C. (1976), *Discretionary Justice*, Urbana, IL: University of Illinois Press.

Day, P. and Klein, R. (1987), *Accountabilities: Five public services*, London: Tavistock.

Dror, Y. (1968), *Public Policymaking Reexamined*, San Francisco: Chandler.

Dror, Y. (1983), 'Policy Gambling: a preliminary exploration', *Policy Studies Journal*, 12, pp.9–13.

Dworkin, G. (1971), 'Paternalism', in R. Wasserstrom (ed.), *Morality and the Law*, Belmont, CA: Wadsworth.

Freedman, J. O. (1980), *Crisis and Legitimacy*, Cambridge: CUP.

Gauthier, D. (1986), *Morals by Agreement*, Oxford: Clarendon Press.

Glover, J. (1977), *Causing Deaths and Saving Lives*, Harmondsworth: Penguin.

Goodin, R. E. (1982), *Public Theory and Public Policy*, Chicago: University of Chicago Press.

Gormley, W. (1989), *Taming the Bureaucracy*, Princeton, NJ: Princeton University Press.

Graham, J. and Vaupel, J. (1981), 'The value of life: what difference does it make?' *Risk Analysis*, 1, pp.85–95.

Hampshire, S. (1978), 'Public and private morality', in S. Hampshire (ed.), *Public and Private Morality*, Cambridge: CUP.

Hanson, B. L. (1982), 'Harnessing the Guinness effect', *Journal of Public Policy*, 2, pp.165–77.

Hirshliefer, J. and Shapiro, D. L. (1983), 'The treatment of risk and uncertainty', in R.H. Haveman and J. Margolis (eds), *Public Expenditure and Policy Analysis*, 3rd edn, Boston: Houghton Mifflin.

Hogwood, B. W. and Peters, B. Guy (1983), *Policy Dynamics*, New York: St Martin's.

Hood, C. (1986), *The Tools of Government*, Chatham, NJ: Chatham House.

Ingraham, Patricia W. (1987), 'Toward a more systematic analysis of policy design', *Policy Studies Journal*, 15, pp.611–28.

Kelman, S. (1981), 'An ethical critique of cost-benefit analysis', *Regulation*, (January) pp. 33–40.

Leonard, H. B. and Zeckhauser, R. (1986), 'Cost-benefit analysis applied to risks', in D. MacLean (ed.), *Values at Risk*, Totowa, NJ: Rowman & Allanheld.

Linder, S. and Peters, B. Guy, (1984), 'From social theory to policy design', *Journal of Public Policy*, 4, pp.237–59.

Linder, S. and Peters, B. Guy (1989), 'Instruments of government: perceptions and contexts', *Journal of Public Policy*, 9, pp.35–58.

MacLean, D. (1986), *Values at Risk*, Totowa, NJ: Rowman & Allanheld.

Majone, G. (1975), 'The feasibility of social policies', *Policy Sciences*, 6, pp.49–69.

Mishan, E. S. (1988), *Cost-Benefit Analysis: An informal introduction*, Boston: Unwin Hyman.

Nozick, R. (1974), *Anarchy, the State and Utopia*, New York: Basic Books.

O'Toole, B. J. (1990), 'T. H. Green and the ethics of senior officials in British central government', *Public Administration*, 68, 3, pp.337–52.

Perrow, C. (1984), *Normal Accidents: Living with high risk technologies*, New York: Basic Books.

Ponting, C. (1985), *The Rights to Know: The inside story of the Belgrano affair*, London and Sydney: Sphere.

Rawls, J. (1972), *A Theory of Justice*, Cambridge, MA: Harvard University Press.

Rubenstein, M. F. (1975), *Patterns of Problem Solving*, Englewood Cliffs, NJ: Prentice-Hall.

Salamon, L. M. (1989), *Beyond Privatisation: The tools of government action*, Washington DC: Urban Institute.

Schelling, T. (1968), 'The life you save may be your own', in S. Chase (ed.), *Problems in Public Expenditure Analysis*, Washington DC: The Brookings Institution.

Schulman, P. R. (1980), *Large Scale Policymaking*, New York: Elsevier.

Self, P. (1972), *The Econocrats*, London: Macmillan.

Sieber, S. (1981), *Fatal Remedies*, New York: Plenum.

Verkuil, P. (1974), 'Judicial review of informal rulemaking', *University of Virginia Law Review*, 60, pp.185–245.

West, William S. (1985), *Administrative Rulemaking: Politics and Processes*, Westport, CT: Greenwood Press.

Six

Administrative Discretion and the Protection of Human Rights: Public Servants' Duty to Take Rights Seriously

GEORGE J. SZABLOWSKI

In their routine daily activities, public officials of every description make discretionary decisions which affect the rights of individuals. Immigration officers grant resident status to some and deny it to others, prison wardens censor mail of selected inmates and prohibit them to communicate with the outside world, police officers place electronic tapping devices on private telephones of suspected law-breakers. Normally, these decisions are not taken arbitrarily or without valid grounds; and they are always made in the name of the public interest and in the furtherance of generally recognised and often desirable policy objectives. Invariably, these decisions are legal in the sense that, in each case, there is a statutory or an analogous authority on which the public officials rely and which permits, but does not require, a specific administrative action. However, almost inevitably all of these decisions are likely to infringe individual rights: they may force deportation of those who failed to obtain resident status, inflict severe isolation and deprivation on those in prison, or invade the privacy and confidentiality of some others.

From a traditional perspective, the role of public officials is limited to the exercise of the administrative or policy functions assigned to them. They are not to be concerned (at least, not seriously) with the effect of their discretionary actions on the rights of individuals. If the administrative or enforcement decision is legal and if it effectively implements a recognised policy objective, the resulting curtailment or denial of individual rights is seen as necessarily incidental and acceptable. The primary professional responsibility of the public service is to administer, not to protect human rights whatever they may be. Such a narrow and outdated perception of the public service role must be rejected. In this chapter, an attempt will be made to explore a new formulation of the public service responsibility in the exercise of administrative discretion: its duty to take rights seriously (Dworkin, 1978).

BRITAIN AND THE EUROPEAN CONVENTION ON HUMAN RIGHTS: AN UNCOMFORTABLE RELATIONSHIP

In 1966 Britain granted to its citizens and residents the right to lodge individual petitions before the European Commission of Human Rights in Strasbourg. It took nearly a decade for the legal profession to begin to use the Convention system regularly and effectively. Today, it is fair to say that British trained lawyers (practitioners and academics) are among the most frequent and successful advocates who handle human rights cases on behalf of individual applicants. Their professional skills and their commitment to international protection of human rights are well recognised in Strasbourg. Similarly, human rights as a field for academic study and discourse is flourishing in Britain. Since the appearance of Lord Scarman's *English Law: The new dimension* in 1974, the discourse continues to focus on the peculiarities inherent in British constitutional theory and practice and their inconsistency with the 'entrenched' approach to the human rights protection. In a recent publication aptly entitled 'The Sovereignty of Parliament – in Perpetuity?' Professor Bradley wrote:

> As regards the protection of human rights and liberties, the disabling effect of the sovereignty of Parliament seems to be uppermost. Indeed, the doctrine all too often appears to be a massive obstacle which stands in the way of any significant increase in the level of formal protection that is given to human rights in our constitutional law. Under the doctrine there are no individual rights or liberties that may not be curtailed or suspended by Act of Parliament. (Bradley, 1989, p.44)

Bradley admits that the European Convention on Human Rights provides a 'political and moral (but not legal) restraint upon Parliament'.

Clearly, the strict reading of the doctrine of parliamentary sovereignty is not only an obstacle domestically but also an embarrassment internationally. Its message to the Strasbourg institutions and to the European member states asserts that, notwithstanding the United Kingdom's legal obligations under the Convention, the British Parliament (which for all practical purposes is directed by the political party in power) reserves the right to legislate as it pleases, and if such legislation breaches the Convention, the British courts will uphold the breach. No wonder, then, that a leading practitioner of human rights law speaks of Britain's isolation from the other member states of the Council of Europe which share 'written constitutions, fundamental rights, and comprehensive systems of public law', and points to the failure of the British constitution 'to adapt to the changed needs of the nation' (Lester, 1989, p.368). One might add that Mrs Thatcher's Government representatives in the Council of Europe have steadfastly opposed major proposals for the improvement of the Convention system, such as the merger of the Commission and the Court, on the ground of incompatibility between a strengthened international human rights enforcement process and parliamentary sovereignty in Britain (Proceedings of the Second Seminar on International Law and European Law, 1986).

The procedural rules governing individual applications require that all domestic recourses must be exhausted before the Commission will accept a claim as 'admissible'. This requirement is in keeping with the original intent of the contracting member states that the Convention system of human rights protection would be merely auxiliary to the domestic protection of human rights. In the light of the constantly increasing volume of admissible applications before the Commission and cases referred to and pending before the Court, the growing importance of the European Convention system must be fully acknowledged (European Commission of Human Rights, 1984). 'Conceived as regional international organs with limited jurisdiction and even more limited powers, they [the Strasbourg institutions] have gradually acquired the status and authority of constitutional tribunals' (Buergenthal, quoted in Merrills, 1988, p.10). Furthermore, the decisions of the Commission and the Court (and the behind-the-scenes deliberations of the Committee of Ministers) are in fact bringing about changes in domestic law and practice of the member states. These changes, states Professor Merrills, would not be taking place without the Convention system. 'Governments know that policies and practices which appear to conflict with the Convention are likely to be challenged and draw the obvious conclusion' (Merrills, 1988, p. 2).

Currently, the European Convention on Human Rights enjoys the status of domestic law in fourteen of the now twenty-two member states (Drzemczewski, 1985). As of May 1992, the membership has increased to twenty-seven European states. This permits national courts to apply and enforce the Convention directly and satisfies Article 13 which obligates the member states to provide 'an effective remedy before a national authority' to 'everyone whose rights and freedoms ... are violated ... by persons acting in an official capacity'. In Britain (as well as in the Scandinavian countries and in the Republic of Ireland) on the other hand, the Convention has no force of domestic law and the rights protected in it are not enforceable by the national courts. This situation compels the European Court to rule (as in the *Silver* and *Abdulaziz* cases) that, in particular circumstances, Britain has failed to comply with the provisions of Article 13, even though the Convention does not impose on the member states a general obligation to incorporate it into their domestic constitutions (Bradley, 1989, p.44). However, in the recent and important case of *Soering* v. *UK* (1989) the European Court of Human Rights has held that it is not necessary in order to satisfy Article 13 of the Convention that it should be enforceable *per se* in domestic courts. It is enough that the substance of the Convention issue may be raised domestically by whatever means (in *Soering*, judicial review was found to be sufficient).

The use of administrative discretion in public decision-making is as frequent in modern government as it is necessary. In Britain it has become in recent years one of the most effective grounds for complaint under the European Convention, as well a source of official embarrassment. Three such cases, dealing with prison discipline, telephone tapping, and immigration, ultimately decided by the European Court of Human Rights, merit a more detailed scrutiny.

Silver v. *United Kingdom (1983)*

This case involved a number of administrative decisions made by prison authorities (governors) over a period of time to control, censor and prohibit private correspondence between inmates and outsiders. These decisions were based on discretionary authority granted to the prison governors by the Prison Act, Prison Rules passed as statutory instruments, and unpublished Orders and Instructions issued by the Home Secretary as guidelines and directives to the prison authorities.The discretionary authority (to censor or prohibit) was to be used to promote 'good order and discipline' and to 'prevent or discourage crime' in the prison. The only remedy available to the prisoners was an official complaint to the Board of Prison Visitors (and to the Home Secretary) or to the Parliamentary Commissioner for Administration. Judicial review (a possible option, in principle) was ruled out because 'the courts could not have found the measures in question to have been taken arbitrarily, in bad faith, for improper motives or *ultra vires*' (*Silver*, p. 34). It was acknowledged that the decisions made by the prison governors were in conformity with English administrative law.

The European Court of Human Rights ruled that British prison officials violated Article 8 of the European Convention ('Everyone has the right to respect for his private and family life, his home and his correspondence.'). This violation was not justifiable on the grounds of public policy (as 'necessary in a democratic society') because it was not made in accordance with the law. The law must be adequately accessible to the citizen and sufficiently precise to enable the citizen to regulate his/her conduct and predict the consequences of his/her actions. The scope of any discretion conferred by law on public officials must be indicated as far as possible. Clearly, the unpublished Orders and Instructions issued by the Home Secretary failed to meet these standards. Thus, when private correspondence was controlled for reasons which were not known or expected by the prisoners, this was not done in accordance with the law. In addition, the Court found that there was a violation of Article 6(1) ('... right to a fair and public hearing ... by an independent and impartial tribunal established by law') and Article 13 ('right to an effective remedy before a national authority'). A complaint to the Board of Prison Visitors, to the Home Secretary or to the Parliamentary Commissioner is not an effective remedy because the Board cannot enforce its decisions, the Home Secretary is insufficiently independent, and the Commissioner has no power to render binding decisions. Jurisdiction of the courts to exercise judicial review in this case was so limited as to be practically illusory. Consequently, the prisoners were denied fair and public hearing and an effective remedy. Since the *Silver* case, however, the European Court of Human Rights has held that, in some instances, individually ineffective domestic remedies may nevertheless cumulatively satisfy Article 13 (see *Leander* v. *Sweden*).

Following the publication of the Commission's report in 1980 (which contained the same conclusions as the Court's judgment of 1983), the UK government decided to bring its administrative practices on the control of prisoners' correspondence in Britain closer to the standards required under the Convention. It is not clear, however, whether complete compliance with the judgment has been implemented. The judgment disclosed a rather wide discrepancy between the practices acceptable under English law and the values advanced and protected under international human rights law. It also cast a strong doubt on the assumption steadfastly proclaimed by the UK government that 'the rights and freedoms enumerated in the Convention are in all cases already secured by domestic law in Britain' (Drzemczewski, p.178). Since the *Silver* case decision, the UK House of Lords has ruled that the Boards of Visitors' disciplinary hearings and Governors' disciplinary proceedings are subject to judicial review (*R.* v. *Deputy Governor of Parkhurst Prison*, 1988).

Malone v. *United Kingdom (1984)*

The Metropolitan Police decided to tap Malone's home telephone in order to obtain incriminating evidence about suspected handling of stolen goods. Subsequently, Malone was charged, tried and acquitted. He then brought a civil action in damages against the police claiming that the tapping of his telephone had been illegal. Apparently, the police had acted on the strength of an 'administrative warrant' of the Home Secretary which did not 'purport to be issued under the authority of any statute or of the common law' (*Malone*, p. 23). The civil action was dismissed by the trial judge on the ground that 'a warrant was not needed to make the tapping lawful; it was lawful without any warrant ... simply because there was nothing to make it unlawful' (*Malone*, pp.23, 26). The trial judge ruled also that in English law there was 'neither a general right of privacy nor ... a particular right of privacy to hold a telephone conversation in the privacy of one's own home without molestation', and moreover, 'the European Convention of Human Rights was not part of English law and it did not confer [on citizens] direct rights that could be enforced in the English courts' (*Malone*, p.24).

The European Court held unanimously (a rare occurrence indeed with nineteen judges on the bench) that the police had breached Article 8 ('right to respect for private and family life, home and correspondence') of the Convention. The Court found that the scope of the administrative discretion granted to the police lacked 'reasonable clarity', and that 'the minimum degree of legal protection to which citizens were entitled under the rule of law in a democratic society' (*Malone*, p.39) was not there. Such legal protection is especially important 'where the power of the executive is exercised in secret, and the risks of arbitrariness are evident' (*Malone*, p.40). Thus, the administrative practice of intercepting telephone communications for criminal law enforcement purposes was not 'in accordance with the law', even though it was clearly not illegal under English law. Again, the code of behaviour for public officials (in this instance, police officers and ministers) laid down by the international court was significantly different from the policy and efficiency dictated considerations acceptable under English administrative law and practice.

Obviously in response to the *Malone* decision, the United Kingdom Government decided to provide express statutory authority for the issuance of telephone tapping warrants. The Interception of Communications Act 1985 came into force in April 1986. The new statute leaves the discretion to issue warrants with the minister and creates a quasi-judicial tribunal to hear complaints about any improper issue of warrants; it also prohibits judicial review (Leigh, 1986). The effect of this change is to render the interception of communications by British police 'in accordance with the law', as required by Article 8 of the Convention. Whether this change meets also the substantive provisions of Article 8 ('respect for private and family life, home and correspondence') remains to be seen. In addition, it can be questioned whether the express statutory exclusion of judicial review is not in conflict with Articles 6(1) and 13 of the European Convention. Since *Malone*, however, the courts held that it was possible to obtain judicial review of the Home Secretary's decision to issue a warrant for telephone tapping prior to the 1985 Act coming into effect (*R.* v. *Secretary of State for Home Affairs ex parte Ruddock*, 1987).

Abdulaziz, Cabales and Balkandali v. *United Kingdom (1985)*

The plaintiffs in this case were wives whose husbands had been refused permission to remain permanently in the United Kingdom. The plaintiffs claimed that these decisions deprived them of 'family life'. The immigration officials acted pursuant to discretionary authority conferred on them by the Immigration Act and by the Home Secretary's rules which allowed the officials to accept the wives as permanent UK residents and to refuse the same status to their husbands. Permission to lodge an appeal before the Immigration Appeal Tribunal was denied because there was no 'arguable point of law'. The British Government cited the protection of the domestic labour market at a time of high unemployment and the maintenance of 'public tranquillity' as legitimate policy considerations sufficient, in its view, to justify the different treatment of wives and husbands. The *bona fides* of their marriages was not in question. The Government produced statistics in support of its contention that 'men were more likely to seek work than women, with the result that male immigrants would have a greater impact on the market than female immigrants' (*Abdulaziz*, p.500). This view was rejected by the plaintiffs, who accused the Government of ignoring the role of women in a modern economy.

The European Court of Human Rights found unanimously that there was a violation of Article 8 ('family life') and Article 14 (prohibition of discrimination on the ground of sex) taken together, and of Article 13 'effective remedy'). Clearly, the wives had been victims of discrimination on the ground of sex. 'A difference in treatment in the enjoyment of rights and freedoms protected by the Convention is discriminatory if ... there is no reasonable relationship of proportionality between the means employed and the aim sought' (*Abdulaziz*, p.472). The policy objective of protecting the domestic labour market was legitimate, but 'the respective impacts on the labour market of the immigration of husbands and wives was insufficient, [and disproportionate] to justify their different treatment' (*Abdulaziz*, p.472). The Court ruled also that English law did not provide an effective remedy against these discretionary decisions and awarded the plaintiffs 'just satisfaction' in the sum of nearly £30,000 representing legal costs and expenses incurred by the applicants.

DOMESTIC JUDICIAL REVIEW: AN INSUFFICIENT REMEDY

The rule of law, like parliamentary sovereignty, is a doctrine which many believe represents the very foundation of British constitutionalism. Whether it is an ideal, an ideology or an illusion, the doctrine has continued to attract scholarly attention since its now largely discredited, one-hundred-years-old, Diceyan formulation (Harden and Lewis, 1986; Hutchinson and Monahan, 1987). Professor Jowell's view that today the rule of law should be seen primarily as a 'principle of institutional morality' is highly relevant and suggestive, and will be further discussed in the last section of this chapter. Rule of law is also seen as the constitutional basis for judicial review of administrative discretion: the courts as guardians of legality invoke the rule when they 'strike down a decision or action which [they feel] is beyond the powers conferred by the statute' or when they 'insist on the imposition of the principles of procedural legality', for example a fair hearing, even 'where the statute is silent on the point' (Jowell, 1989, p.19). Does this clearly limited form of judicial review practised in Britain provide an adequate remedy against the infringement of human rights by official action?

In the parliamentary system of government, public policy of the state may be expressed in several categories of instruments:

1. Primary legislation (statute law).
2. Secondary or delegated legislation (statutory instruments, regulations, orders, by-laws, etc.) passed by various 'subordinate' bodies.
3. Decisions of the collective executive (Cabinet/Prime Minister) taken pursuant to prerogative authority or general authority to govern.
4. Decisions of public officials made under statutory authority on behalf and in the names of ministers at various levels of the bureaucratic hierarchy and in the numerous specialised sectors of the bureaucratic establishment. These decisions may be called discretionary when the statute permits alternative courses of action and leaves the choice to the officials.

Pursuant to the traditional doctrine of judicial review, only secondary legislation and decisions of public officials were reviewable by the courts. Since the *GCHQ* (*Council of Civil Service Unions* v. *Minister for the Civil Service*, 1985) case executive decisions based on the prerogative appear, at least in principle, to be also reviewable. Secondary legislation is reviewable to determine whether it fits, or is strictly consistent with, the enabling primary legislation. In other words, the 'subordinate' legislative bodies exercising delegated power have no discretion to go beyond the terms of reference established in the primary legislation (doctrine of *ultra vires*). Judicial review of statutory decisions taken by bureaucratic officials is justified on the ground that administrative discretion is always presumed to be limited by law and only the courts can determine conclusively the precise scope of the limitation.

Perceived as the guardians of legality, the courts are expected to answer the question of the jurisdiction and the question of the procedural sufficiency and propriety of the decision-making process that involved the use of discretion.

They are not expected, however, to assume the role of government officials and to take the substantive administrative or policy decisions themselves. In other words, at least in theory, judicial review should not be confused with an appeal on the merits, which is rarely available when decisions are based on statutory discretion. Recent judicial incursions into substance notwithstanding (Jowell and Lester, 1987), judicial review by its very nature cannot consistently provide an effective remedy against human rights violations committed by public officials acting under discretionary authority, especially when the violations are protected by clear statutory language. In Britain, the traditional doctrine still persists and it restrains the courts from reviewing statute law itself and making explicit trade-offs between state interests and individual rights, between policy/administrative preferences and human values (Lacey, 1989; Lester, 1989). However, in one area, that of directly enforceable Community rights, Section 2 of the European Communities Act 1972 requires the UK courts to give preference to Community Law over conflicting domestic legislation. Elsewhere, the traditional doctrine continues to legitimise legal/procedural values while permitting the courts to make implicit political choices (most obviously in such policy fields as housing, immigration, national security and public order) clothed in an appropriate 'neutral' rhetoric (Lacey, 1989). In the end, the judicial review outcomes in relation to the protection of human rights remain uncertain and unimpressive, as the courts continue to pay homage to the two traditional 'chestnuts' of English constitutional and administrative theory: parliamentary sovereignty and the rule of law (Jowell, 1989; Bradley, 1989).

Unfortunately for the traditionalists, these 'chestnuts' of English constitutional and administrative theory are out of step with the realities of modern international human rights protection. The European Convention on Human Rights, which Britain signed and ratified nearly forty years ago, applies to laws and decisions of all public institutions of a member state, whether legislative, executive, bureaucratic or judicial (Bradley, 1983). Thus, a judgment of the House of Lords may have the effect of breaching the Convention, as occurred in the celebrated *Sunday Times* (1979) case, and the Home Secretary's Immigration Rules (perfectly valid under English law) may meet the same fate, as happened in the *Abdulaziz* (1985) case. However, from the domestic perspective, holding the state responsible for judicial acts may appear to be difficult to reconcile with the doctrine of judicial independence. In a recent Canadian case, a Supreme Court justice refused to accept the proposition that courts are part of the state apparatus for the purpose of section 32 of the Canadian Charter of Rights and Freedoms (Slattery, 1987b). If this opinion (which has been severely criticised) prevails, judicial decisions and orders (e.g. injunctions) would be exempt from the application of the Charter, except possibly when the issue in the litigation clearly involves a governmental action (Slattery, 1987a).

The three British cases discussed above demonstrate the difficulty of bringing administrative decisions before domestic judicial review, consistent with the prevailing notion that courts must not examine substantive policy issues even when individual rights are at stake. This situation is in clear contrast with that which obtains in most countries of continental Europe. There, a parallel (to the civil law) system of public law and administrative courts provides a full range of judicial remedies against discretionary decisions of public authorities, remedies which are not constrained by the notions of procedural legality and rigid separation between law and the substance of policy. In *Silver* and *Abdulaziz*, access to the courts was impossible and the discretionary decisions of public officials would have been final had the parties not chosen to take the road to Strasbourg. In *Malone*, the civil action for damages against the Metropolitan Police Commissioner was dismissed on the ground that the court had no jurisdiction. The judge in this case had some harsh words to say about the state of English administrative law in relation to telephone tapping by the police:

> Certainly in law any 'adequate and effective safeguards against abuse' are wanting. In this respect, English law compares most unfavourably with West German law: this is not a subject on which it is possible to feel any pride in English law. I therefore find it impossible to see how English law could be said to satisfy the requirements of the [European] Convention [on Human Rights]. (*Malone*, pp.24–5)

These three cases demonstrate further that the European Convention does in fact provide access to a court even when the domestic law does not. This has two important implications: first, it transforms the administrative process into a judicial process whether the government likes it or not; and second, it subjects the administrative decision in question to a test of validity not available domestically, that is, the test of conformity with 'internationally entrenched' human rights. Paradoxically, then, national courts are kept out because British judges must not meddle in policy and administrative decisions while 'foreign' judges of the European Court of Human Rights are free to do exactly that. The distinction between 'substance' and 'procedure' (still viewed by the judiciary as fundamental) is easy to state but often difficult to follow in practice. Not infrequently, this distinction dissolves into thin air when a case is taken to Strasbourg. In *Abdulaziz*, leave to appeal to the Immigration Appeal Tribunal was refused because no illegality was committed by the British immigration officials who acted within the discretionary authority granted to them by the Immigration Rules. Before the European Court, on the other hand, the issue was no longer procedural. The same immigration officials were held to have denied the applicants their right to 'family life' when they prohibited the husbands from joining their wives permanently in Britain. Referring with disapproval to sexual discrimination, the European Court added that 'the advancement of the equality of the sexes is today a major goal in the member-states of the Council of Europe', a substantive policy preference that no British court would dare to rely upon in the course of judicial review (*Abdulaziz*, p.501).

The main difference between British and Canadian courts in relation to human rights enforcement is that the latter are compelled by the Canadian Charter of Rights and Freedoms to perform a role similar to that followed by the European Court of Human Rights in Strasbourg. Issues of law and issues of policy and administration are increasingly treated as related and interdependent, and are often examined contextually. This is especially evident in the interpretation and application of section 1 of the Canadian Charter. This section performs very much the same function as the provisions which are set out in several articles of the Convention permitting governments to limit certain rights on grounds of public policy provided that such limits 'are prescribed by law and are necessary in a democratic society'. The burden of justifying 'reasonable limits' rests on public authorities. The Canadian Court developed a test, known as the Oakes test, which requires an analysis of the policy objectives that the government wishes to pursue and the determination of their relative importance, to be followed by an analysis of the relationship and the proportionality between the policy objectives sought and the means to be employed (*R. v. Oakes*, 1986). This test, which is in part similar to the 'proportionality analysis' applied by the European Court in *Abdulaziz*, has been frequently used in subsequent decisions, albeit with differing degrees of intellectual rigour.

Although it is still seen as inappropriate for the Canadian courts to 'second guess' public officials explicitly on matters of policy or administration, many Canadian judges recognise that in the field of constitutional or administrative litigation, and especially in the field of human rights, 'policy content' is unavoidable. 'If what we are being asked to do is to decide whether any particular act of the executive violates the rights of citizens, then it is not only appropriate that we answer the question; it is our obligation under the Charter to do so' (Justice Wilson in *Operation Dismantle* v. *R.*, 1985). Three judgments of the Canadian Supreme Court are particularly relevant for our discussion of judicial review in relation to human rights protection. In *Operation Dismantle*, the Court dealt with the decision of the federal Cabinet to permit the United States government to test the Cruise missile over Canadian territory. The plaintiffs claimed that such tests would increase the risk of nuclear conflict and pose a threat to the lives and security of Canadians, and thus would violate section 7 of the Charter which protects everyone's 'life, liberty and security of the person'. The Government replied that its decision to permit testing was a matter of national security and foreign policy and not reviewable by the courts because (a) it was a Cabinet decision taken under prerogative authority and not 'within the authority of Parliament' and (b) the issues involved were inherently non-justiciable and political, which a court is incompetent to decide. The Court dismissed the plaintiffs' claim largely on narrow procedural grounds. It ruled that the plaintiffs' allegations were in the realm of conjecture not fact, that they could not be proved, and that no causal link could be established between them and the hypothetical result, that is violation of section 7 of the Charter. Justice Wilson in a separate opinion strongly disagreed with this part of the Court's decision. However, the Court was united in rejecting the Government's contention based on royal prerogative and stated, unequivocally, that Cabinet decisions are reviewable under the Charter, and that the executive bears a general duty to act in conformity with its provisions. Although this judgment failed to stop the testing of the Cruise missile, it did extend the scope of Charter review wider than had been expected.

In *Singh*, the Supreme Court had to examine a discretionary decision of the Minister of Employment and Immigration, acting on the advice of the Refugee Status Advisory Committee, which rejected the plaintiff's claim to refugee status. The Immigration Appeal Board turned down the plaintiff's appeal, stating that there were 'no reasonable grounds to believe that the claim could be established'. The Minister acted pursuant to the Canadian Immigration Act, which set out the procedure for the determination of refugee status. The procedure did not require a hearing and permitted the Minister to 'take into account policy considerations and information about world affairs to which the refugee claimant had no opportunity to respond' (*Singh*, 1985). Madam Justice Wilson, speaking for three judges, held that this procedure did not conform to the principles of fundamental justice, and thus there was a breach of section 7 of the Charter ('right to security of the person'). Turning to the question of 'reasonable limits' under section 1, Wilson condemned the 'utilitarian consideration' which the Government used as justification, and added that 'the guarantees of the Charter would be illusory if they could be ignored because it was administratively convenient to do so' (*Singh*, 1985). This decision resembles the judgment of the European Court in *Abdulaziz*.

Finally, the most recent Supreme Court decision in *Andrews* addressed the equality provisions of the Charter in section 15. Andrews, a British subject with permanent residence status in Canada, complied with all the requirements for admission to the Law Society of British Columbia except that of Canadian citizenship. The requirement of Canadian citizenship was written into the Barristers and Solicitors Act of British Columbia; consequently, the discretion involved pertained to legislative discretion (or jurisdiction) to enact the specific conditions for membership in the Law Society. Andrews claimed that he was a victim of discrimination based on national origin, contrary to section 15 of the Charter. The Court agreed with his contention and ruled that the citizenship requirement was unreasonable and not sustainable under section 1.

> The proportionality test was not met. The requirement of citizenship is not carefully tailored to achieve the objective that lawyers be familiar with Canadian institutions and customs and may not even be rationally connected to it ... Citizenship neither ensures the objectives of familiarity with Canadian institutions or of commitment to Canadian society ... Less drastic methods for achieving the desired objectives are available. (*Andrews*, 1989)

These three cases illustrate that all three types of governmental discretion are subject to the Charter review: the legislative discretion (or jurisdiction) which produces statute laws and regulations, the executive discretion which formulates policy decisions, and the administrative discretion which applies policy to concrete and specific situations. The Charter review inevitably draws Canadian courts into the examination of substantive policy issues and into the making of trade-offs between state interests and individual rights, between specific policy objectives and the human values and interests entrenched in the Constitution. The reasoning and contextual analyses employed by the Canadian judges are strikingly similar to those used so effectively by the Strasbourg court (*Merrills*, 1988). However, it must be recognised that courts perform only a 'second-order function' by reviewing the acts of others (i.e. public officials) for conformity with the protected individual rights, and they do so only when asked. The 'first-order function' belongs to the public officials routinely engaged in the decision-making processes which are likely to infringe human rights. It is they who should take rights seriously. From this perspective, both the Canadian Charter and the European Convention require 'equal responsibilities of the various branches of government to carry out the [human rights] mandate, and ... the reciprocal nature of their roles' (Slattery, 1987a).

PUBLIC SERVICE AND THE DUTY OF TAKING RIGHTS SERIOUSLY

The constitutional entrenchment of human rights should be seen as a necessary correction of majoritarian democratic politics. Its purpose is to limit the legitimate power of the majority (which tends to support the interests of the established power-holders) in order to protect those who are either economically disadvantaged, politically weak and unrepresented, or socially unorthodox. It represents a shield against intolerance and discrimination, and may at times afford a measure of justice against the existing and continuing inequalities in the distribution of scarce and valuable goods in society. The objections from the right and from the left to a written, constitutional protection of human rights have been admirably answered by Nicola Lacey in a recent article published in *The Political Quarterly*. She concludes as follows:

> In a society in which collective and co-operative values appear to be espoused only by a minority even at the level of ideals, it is dangerous to deny this measure of protection to citizens who may need it ... we must give serious consideration to any reform strategy which promises material improvements in the lives of those who may find themselves on the receiving end of abuses of state and corporate power. (Lacey, 1989, pp.440, 437–8)

Lacey's argument becomes especially compelling when we consider that the emergence of minority 'underclasses' appears to be a permanent feature of the global market place, which is likely to dominate for some time the economic life in Western and North American societies. The European Convention on Human Rights represents a form of international 'entrenchment' of individual rights. Even without its incorporation into domestic law in Britain, it conveys a powerful message to all those who govern. The cutting edge of this message can be found in the doctrine of 'margin of appreciation', a judge-made device which imposes a dialogue and a dialectic between the interests of the state and the interests (called 'rights') of the individual. Under the 'margin of appreciation' doctrine, the Court of Human Rights allows national authorities a band of discretion within which the rights enumerated in the Convention may be limited, without specifying a fixed and objective standard. *Prima facie*, the doctrine favours the state, but the final outcome emerges only after a thorough weighing of contradictions. Even if the individual loses the judicial battle in Strasbourg, he/she may gain a measure of satisfaction as the doctrine shifts the responsibility for human rights protection from international adjudicators to domestic public servants. This process appears to be

remarkably close to the description of the Canadian Charter review offered by
James MacPherson, Dean of Osgoode Hall Law School, Toronto:

> In reality a decision of the ... Court ... is only one statement in a continuous
> conversation among citizens, governments, and the Court. Citizens speak,
> governments respond, and the Court evaluates. But the Court's evaluation is
> not the final word. It invites a further response, either approval or condemna-
> tion, from citizens or governments. And if that further response is condemna-
> tion, there are tools available for altering the Court's position. (Quoted in
> Slattery, 1987a, p.709)

Slattery calls it a 'coordinate model' of human rights protection under which
'the proper functioning of the Canadian Charter [and of the European Convention]
depends less on the activities of those responsible for the policing of others [the
courts] than on the activities of those bound in the first-order way [ministers and
public servants] by its provisions' (Slattery, 1987a, p.709).

Case law cited by Lester suggests that the European Convention does not legally
bind ministers and public servants because it is not part of the domestic law in
Britain (Lester, 1989, p.355). This has been recently confirmed by the House of
Lords (*Brind* v. *Secretary of State for the Home Department*, 1991). Although this
decision appears to ignore the reality that international treaty obligations of a state
can only be concretely acted upon by its agents, that is, public officials, it does not
exempt the public service from an ethical and professional obligation to take into
account the impact that discretionary decisions are likely to have on the individual
rights of citizens and residents. If the modern meaning of the rule of law is
fundamentally moral rather than legal – 'a principle of institutional morality', to
use Jeffrey Jowell's phrase – then a primary duty to take rights seriously rests with
the public service, whose members are routinely faced with the endemic conflict
between state interests and individual rights. This principle, in Jowell's words,
'applies largely to the process of implementation. It seeks to constrain, though not
necessarily to deny, the discretion of the agents of enforcement and implementation
(including ministers, local authorities, commissions, the police, etc.) (Jowell, 1989,
p.19).

Concretely, the obligation of taking rights seriously requires that each administrative decision (which is likely to have an adverse impact on a specific human
right protected in the European Convention) must include an examination of the
two competing interests: the state's and the individual's. Thus, when prison
authorities intend to control, censor and prohibit private correspondence between
inmates and outsiders, they must first answer the following questions: Are the
objectives of promoting good order and discipline and preventing crime in the
prison realistic, and are they likely to be attained by the use of the proposed
measures? Are these measures proportionate to the magnitude of the problem, or
are they too sweeping? Can they be employed in such a way as to cause the least
impairment of prisoners' rights? The prison authorities involved should also
address the broader question: are these measures and the consequent infringement
of human rights necessary and appropriate in a democratic society? The final
trade-off between administrative objectives and individual interests (rights) must

be influenced by the answers to these questions, and the decision modified accordingly or withdrawn. A complete record of these deliberations should be kept and made openly available in the event of an appeal or review. Obviously, the length and scope of these deliberations presuppose normal routine administrative conditions and would be out of place in emergencies.

Similarly, when immigration officials consider accepting wives but rejecting husbands for permanent resident status in order to protect the domestic labour market in times of unemployment, they should first examine the following issues: Is this policy objective sound and will it be achieved by the proposed measure? Is the discriminatory effect of the measure justified, or will the intended impact on the labour market be negligible and disproportionate to the harm inflicted on the individuals? Are the proposed discriminatory measures acceptable in a free and democratic society, and if adopted will they have a negative effect on the goal of sexual equality pursued by the member states of the Council of Europe, which include Britain?

In conclusion, it is a moral and professional responsibility of the public service to engage in exactly the kind of legal and policy analysis that the text of the European Convention and the relevant case law require in order to determine whether a specific violation of human rights is justifiable. Clearly, one would not expect the scope and sophistication of the analysis to be undertaken by the national administrative officials to match the work done by the Strasbourg institutions. It should, however, give the officials an understanding of the main issues which will be raised if the contemplated decision contravenes the Convention. It should, also, provide them with an answer to the basic question: Is the decision justifiable, not under domestic law and domestic policy preferences, but pursuant to the rules of the European Convention? It is the recognition and acceptance of this responsibility by the public service that is most important. In this connection, the various professional associations of British civil servants should consider and eventually adopt in their respective codes of ethics an undertaking to respect the European Convention on Human Rights and not to breach its provisions in the exercise of official functions.

ACKNOWLEDGEMENT

The author wishes to express special thanks to Ian Leigh of the Faculty of Law, University of Newcastle upon Tyne, for his care in reading earlier versions of this chapter and pointing out my errors and omissions.

Abdulaziz, Cabales and Balkandali v. *United Kingdom* (1985) 5 E. H. R. R. 347.
Andrews v. *Law Society of British Columbia* (1989) 1 S. C. R. 143.
Bradley, Anthony W. (1983), 'The European Convention on Human Rights and Administrative Law: first impressions', Public Law Workshop, Toronto: Osgoode Hall Law School of York University.
Bradley, Anthony W. (1989), 'The Sovereignty of Parliament – in Perpetuity?', in Jeffrey Jowell and Dawn Oliver (eds), *The Changing Constitution*, 2nd edn, Oxford: Clarendon Press.

Brind v. *Secretary of State for the Home Department* (1991) 1 All E. R. 720.

Council of Civil Service Unions v. *Minister for the Civil Service* (1985) A. C. 374.

Drzemczewski, Andrew Z. (1985), *European Human Rights Convention in Domestic Law*, Oxford: Clarendon Press.

Dworkin, R. M. (1978), *Taking Rights Seriously*, rev. edn, London: Duckworth.

European Commission of Human Rights (1984), *Stock-Taking on the European Convention on Human Rights: The first thirty years, 1954–1984*, Strasbourg: Council of Europe.

Harden, I. and Lewis, N. (1986), *The Nobel Lie: The rule of law and the British constitution*, London: Hutchinson.

Hutchinson, Allan C. and Monahan, Patrick (eds), (1987), *The Rule of Law – Ideal or Ideology*, Toronto: Carsewell.

Jowell, Jeffrey (1989), 'The Rule of Law Today', in Jeffrey Jowell and Dawn Oliver (eds), *The Changing Constitution*, 2nd edn, Oxford: Clarendon.

Jowell, J. and Lester, A. (1987), 'Beyond Wednesbury: Substantive principles of judicial review', *Public Law*, pp.368–82.

Lacey, Nicola (1989), 'Are rights best left unwritten?', *The Political Quarterly*, 60, pp.433–41.

Leander v. *Sweden*, (1987), 9 E. H. R. R. 433.

Leigh, Ian (1986), 'A Tappers' Charter', *Public Law*, pp.8–18.

Lester, Anthony (1989), 'The constitution: decline and renewal', in Jeffrey Jowell and Dawn Oliver (eds), *The Changing Constitution*, 2nd edn, Oxford: Clarendon.

Malone v. *United Kingdom*, (1984), E. H. R. R. 14.

Merrills, J. G. (1988), *The Development of International Law by the European Court of Human Rights*, Manchester: Manchester University Press.

Operation Dismantle v. *R.* (1985), 1 S. C. R., 441.

Proceedings of the Second Seminar on International Law and European Law (1986), *La Fusion de la Commission et de la Cour Européennes des Droits de l'Homme*, Université de Neuchâtel.

R. v. *Deputy Governor of Parkhurst Prison* (1988) 1 A.C. 533.

R. v. *Oakes* (1986) 1 S.C.R. 103.

R. v. *Secretary of State for Home Affairs ex parte Ruddock* (1987) 2 All E.R. 518.

Silver v. *United Kingdom* (1983) 5 E.H.R.R. 347.

Singh v. *Minister of Employment and Immigration* (1985) 1 S.C.R. 177.

Slattery, Brian (1987a), 'A theory of the Charter', *Osgoode Hall Law Journal*, 25, pp.701–47.

Slattery, Brian (1987 b), 'The Charter's relevance to private litigation: Does *Dolphin* deliver?' *McGill Law Journal*, 32, p.905.

Soering v. *United Kingdom* (1989) 11, E.H.R.R. 439.

'The *Sunday Times* Case' (1979), Y. B. Eur. Conv. 402 (Eur. Ct.).

Seven

Freedom of Information and the Swedish Bureaucrat

*A popular government without popular information
or the means of acquiring it, is but a Prologue to a
farce or a tragedy; or perhaps to both.*
(James Madison)

BACKGROUND

A prerequisite for the proper functioning of political democracy is that the citizens have knowledge about the structure and contents of the public sector's activities. In modern society, the public administration – the bureaucracy – accounts for an important part of these activities. Information given to citizens about what the bureaucracy does therefore becomes an important democratic matter.

How does the citizen get information about the bureaucracy? Either the bureaucracy supplies it or the citizen procures it himself. In the post-war period, it has become increasingly common for the bureaucracy to inform the public. Since the 1960s, special posts of Information Officer have been created, and a range of diverse practices has developed. The bureaucracy produces informative material, which is sent directly to the citizens, holds press conferences, sends out press releases, etc. The advantage of this information is that citizens are instilled with an increased consciousness of their duties and rights. The disadvantage can be that they only receive that information which the bureaucracy finds appropriate to disseminate. This is particularly serious for democracy if the bureaucracy has the aim of obtaining increased control over the society (Abrahamsson, 1972).

How can the citizen inform himself about the public sector's activities? In the Swedish legal tradition, the manner of gathering information is much older than political democracy. Availability of information, often connected with freedom of the press, has a long tradition in Swedish political life. One expression of this tradition is that government documents are public. Discussion on this matter was lively during the latter part of the eighteenth century; and as early as the Freedom of the Press Act 1766, directives were issued that documents which pertained to public administration or the administration of justice should be available for all and could be freely printed.

During the reign of Gustaf III, public access to official documents was restricted, but it was reinstated in the Instrument of Government of 1809. The Freedom of the Press Act 1812 was constructed in roughly the same way as that of 1766. Access has never been total. Certain groups of documents have been exempt to protect, for example, important interests of a foreign policy, military, or economic nature (Strömberg, 1984).

After the Instrument of Government of 1809, the principle of public access to official documents has been valid without interruption. Since then, this principle has been governed by the Freedom of the Press Act, which is a constitutional law; this in itself indicates how much importance the issue is allocated in Swedish political life (SOU 1983/70, p.70).

The question of what to classify as secret is a problem related to power, which applies to control over an important part of the information flow in society. Information gives knowledge about what is happening, and without this knowledge the exercise of power is rendered more difficult (Bok, 1986, p.19). Even in the discussions preceding the Freedom of the Press Act 1766, it is evident that the actors saw differences in access to information as a problem of power (Lagerroth, 1915, p.590).

Public access to documents kept by the authorities is justified in different ways. From the citizen's point of view, it is important that he can procure information regardless of whether or not he is involved in the matter and regardless of what the bureaucracy does. To the bureaucracy, knowledge of the public nature of documents is an incentive for thoroughness and carefulness in dealing with a matter, which can be expected to result in greater adherence to the rule of law. Even effectiveness is perceived as positively influenced because public discussion can now be based directly on the documents. This has engendered well informed discussion about activities, especially those which lack unambiguous and distinct criteria for evaluation (SOU 1966/60, p.72).

The legislation on freedom of information thus continues to fulfil important functions in the modern Swedish welfare and interventionist state. This fact seems to be well known internationally. For example Shonfield, in his major work on modern capitalism, characterises the Swedish public sector with the expression 'the principle of the goldfish bowl' (Shonfield, 1965, p.399).

How does the principle of public access to official documents relate to freedom of speech and freedom of information? Both these freedoms are included among the constitutional freedoms and rights which, according to the Instrument of Government of 1974, are guaranteed to every Swedish citizen. Freedom of speech means 'the freedom to communicate information and express ideas, opinions and feelings, either orally, in writing, in pictorial representations, or in any other way'.

In order to benefit fully from freedom of speech, one must have information about what is happening in society. Freedom of information means 'the freedom to obtain and receive information and otherwise to acquaint oneself with the statements of others' (Instrument of Government).

The idea behind the Swedish freedom of the press is that 'in order to ensure free interchange of opinions and enlightenment of the public', each Swedish citizen shall 'have the right in print to express his thoughts and opinions, to publish official documents and to make statements and communicate information on any subject whatsoever'. The principle that official documents are made public can be considered a part of freedom of information (Freedom of the Press Act).

Some central concepts from the Freedom of the Press Act are briefly presented below. The concepts apply to the principle of public access to 'official documents'. 'Official documents' refers to all documents which are kept by the authorities, regardless of whether they were sent there or created there. All other methods of storing information, such as tape recordings, pictures and computer diskettes are considered equivalent to documents.

Most official documents are public. Anyone can request to see them, without having to give a reason. The authorities are under an obligation to help, as much as possible, any person who wishes to see a document. For a fixed fee, it is also possible to receive a copy of the document. Classified documents may not be released. If a document includes both public and classified information, then the citizen has the right to see the public sections. If an authority refuses to release a document, then the citizen can have the courts review the decision.

Those documents which the bureaucrats create during their preparation of a decision, such as memoranda, rough drafts, etc., are official documents only if they are filed with the decision. The justification for citizens not having immediate access to these documents is that this enables the authorities to carry out their work in peace and quiet.

THE PROBLEM

The average citizen probably receives a rather small part of his information about the public sector's activities by visiting the bureaucracy and reading documents or by reading information sent by the authorities. For the most part, he receives information through the mass media (Sjölin, 1985, p.7). The question then is how the mass media receives its information. Obviously, one expects the relationship between the bureaucracy and mass media to be of decisive importance for freedom of information.

In what way does the mass media receive information about the public sector's activities? The answer is that all possible channels are used. For the purpose of illustration, relations at a local level are used because most communication between bureaucracy and citizen occurs there.

The relations between local government and mass media involve a considerable amount of routine. In larger municipalities with extensive bureaucracies, the authority's initiative plays a major role. The mass media receives agendas from all municipal committees before their meetings. The larger committees also enclose the more important documents which support their decision. After the meetings, they hold press conferences or the chairperson calls the mass media and notifies them of the decisions. All large administrative units have special information secretaries who attend to contacts with the mass media (Sjölin, 1985, p.12).

In smaller municipalities, a more manageable amount of affairs makes it possible for the mass media to use the principle of public access to official documents in practice. Journalists visit almost daily the more important administrations, where they read incoming and outgoing mail. They also visit civil servants and politicians in order to get their commentaries on what is happening (Sjölin, 1985, p.72).

The following analysis will direct attention to the way the mass media gathers information through contacts with individual bureaucrats. The focus is on those institutional arrangements which can be expected to play a role in freedom of information. From the perspective of democracy, information from individual bureaucrats is important for several reasons:

1. The bureaucrat is so familiar with activities in his organisation that he can point out implications in public documents which are not immediately obvious to journalists.

2. The bureaucrat has knowledge about conditions gathered from, for example, preparation work, evaluations and inspections, but which is not written down in any document.

3. The bureaucrat has access to classified documents and can consequently inform the mass media about the contents.

Certain legal and ethical problems are accentuated when the individual bureaucrat gives information to the mass media for publication. To be able to understand the bureaucrat's point of view, it is necessary to bear in mind that he is imprisoned in a system of loyalties. Among these loyalties, the following should be given prominence: obedience to the law, loyalty to superiors (politicians, who pass laws, and superior bureaucrats) and consideration of citizens (which includes clients, and other interests). Loyalty to peers and consideration of subordinate bureaucrats also deserve to be specifically mentioned (Figure 7.1).

Figure 7.1   **The Bureaucrat's Ethical Relations**

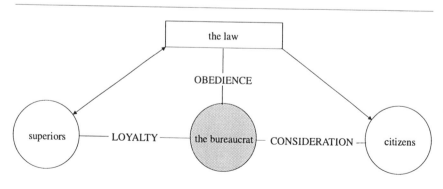

The bureaucrat's ethical standpoint is directed by several systems of ethics. He has to observe the ethics which all bureaucrats have in common (general bureaucratic ethics). He must also take into account his professional conceptions of what the right measures are (professional ethics). Finally, as an individual, he has to decide whether he considers the activity as good or evil and hence which measures he will take in a specific case (personal ethics). It is not certain that these three systems of ethics place the same demands on him in specific cases (Lundquist, 1988, p.172).

One quickly realises that all these ethical demands can come into conflict with each other and with other types of demands (efficiency, rule of law, etc.) which are placed on activities in the public sector. This discussion will focus on those cases where the bureaucrat's application of the rules on freedom of speech and freedom of information – in relation to citizens – comes into conflict with loyalty to superiors and, possibly, also with obedience to the law.

A dilemma immediately becomes apparent. According to traditional conceptions, the bureaucrat's professional secrecy is part of his duty of allegiance to superiors. This viewpoint can result in restrictions on disclosure of information. Legislation about official documents is, on the other hand, intended to minimise professional secrecy in favour of citizens' need for information (SOU 1975/102, p.152). On the whole, the debate about openness and secrecy includes a number of different strata of laws, traditions, professional convictions, ethical rules, prejudices, etc., which sometimes supply different messages. The problem in this paper can be summarised in the question:

> To what extent and under which circumstances may the individual bureaucrat inform the citizens through the mass media about what is going on within the bureaucracy?

The presentation of this problem is divided into four sections. The tools of analysis are introduced first, followed by two sections which deal with how the bureaucrat informs in, respectively, the cases *voice* and *obstruction*. A section containing reflections about the conditions for freedom of information in Sweden concludes the chapter.

TOOLS OF ANALYSIS

The problem under discussion can be related to the more general question 'How should the ethically responsible bureaucrat react if he judges the public sector's activities to be evil or unjust?' To be able to answer this question, we need analytical tools which are capable of capturing the existing alternatives of action. It immediately comes to mind to try to apply Hirschman's well-known categories: *loyalty*, *voice* and *exit*. Accordingly, the bureaucrat has three means of reacting to the superiors' activities, namely to be loyal (*loyalty*), to state his deviating point of view (*voice*), or to leave the organisation (*exit*) (Hirschman, 1970).

Because in Hirschman's version '*voice*' means an *open* protest, his three alternatives of action are not sufficient to describe all the possibilities of reaction which the bureaucrat has. A category is also required for those measures which the bureaucrat takes without directly notifying his superiors, and which they may not even be conscious of before those measures begin to result in annoying effects. This category can be called *obstruction*.

The bureaucrat has an important arsenal of actions which can be called obstruction: from small indications such as a slower work pace to pure sabotage (Rohr, 1980, p.207). A common method of showing displeasure is to rigidly follow all rules which are more or less necessary until the whole activity gradually falls apart. An effective means of obstruction is to change priorities by shifting personnel and by reorganisation, which delays the execution of the programme considerably. Inactivity, which is expressed by the bureaucrat doing nothing, has been designated the most formidable weapon in his arsenal (Warwick, 1981, p.107). In connection with freedom of information, leaks (i.e. the bureaucrat anonymously giving out information) are an important type of obstruction.

Figure 7.2   The Bureaucrat's Reactions to the Activities of his Organisation

| | | The bureaucrat looks upon activities as | |
		ethical	unethical
The bureaucrat's reactions	loyalty	1	2
	voice		4
	obstruction		6
	exit		8

By combining *obstruction* with Hirschman's categories of *exit, voice* and *loyalty*, four main types of bureaucratic reaction to activities of his organisation are obtained (cf. Thompson, 1985, who works with the same categories). We combine these types with the bureaucrat's perception of whether the activity is ethical or unethical, and thereby obtain eight cases, of which five can be labelled 'logical'. The basis of the argument below (where the numbers refer to Figure 7.2) is that the bureaucrat is morally obliged to react against what he considers unethical activities.

Loyalty (2) in this case means that the bureaucrat follows and executes instructions which are contrary to his moral conviction. He can do this for different reasons. One reason is that he judges that loyalty to superiors is more important than other current considerations; he consequently solves a moral dilemma by choosing to obey. Another reason for obeying is that he anticipates trouble or is afraid of coming into conflict with his superiors. In the last two cases, his attitude is unethical.

Voice (4) means that the bureaucrat openly expresses dissatisfaction about an activity which he finds evil or unjust. Voice can cause problems for him even when he complains *within* his own hierarchy. When the bureaucrat protests to actors *outside* that hierarchy, what one usually calls whistle-blowing, he runs the risk of coming into violent conflict not only with his superiors but also with his peers. The question is, what choices has he from an ethical point of view? If he has the evidence required to sound the alarm, it is unethical for him to choose 'loyalty' instead of voice.

Obstruction (6) is that case where the bureaucrat protests anonymously. These measures can be considered unethical because they involve a violation of loyalty, without informing superior officials. Therefore, this case is sometimes hard to justify in western democracies, with their demands for openness and debate. Obstruction can, however, be defended on moral grounds if it is directed against superiors' flagrant overstepping of the boundaries, with no opportunity for correction through voice; or in cases where the sanctions against open protests are so forceful that one can hardly require a person to subject himself to such unpleasantness.

Exit (8) is in most cases a very arduous solution to an ethical problem, because the bureaucrat is normally dependent on income from his job and therefore cannot leave it without further notice. If exit is to have any additional effects, it must be combined with voice. Sometimes, the bureaucrat can better serve a good cause by remaining employed and trying to work against evil and injustice through obstruction. For the bureaucrat to continue as before – to evade taking a stand – is not an ethically commendable alternative.

These types of reaction can be related to the question about the individual bureaucrat's freedom of speech and freedom of information. Two cases are discussed below: when the bureaucrat discloses information about unsatisfactory conditions to the mass media for publication *openly* (*voice*) and *anonymously* (*obstruction*).

VOICE

What does the bureaucrat do when he informs openly (*voice*)? In Max Weber's ideal type of bureaucracy, only one possibility exists: the bureaucrat conveys his critical viewpoints to his superiors. Whether this course of action really has the intended effects depends on the situation. Normally, bureaucrats have institutional arrangements for voice, but these are not always effective. Superiors often perceive voice negatively, and the person who protests risks being subjected to reprisals.

What does the bureaucrat do if he conveys criticism to his superiors, but they do not react in the way he wishes? How should he then express voice? The alternative which remains for him is usually discussed in terms of *whistle-blowing*. The bureaucrat then informs the surroundings about the unsatisfactory conditions in his organisation. Because whistle-blowing occurs openly, the bureaucrat who protests is immediately identified by his superiors.

What moral status does whistle-blowing have? Peter French specifies those situations in which such measures are morally justifiable and in which loyalty to superiors and the organisation must come second. In the first place, all established channels must have been tried already. Second, the bureaucrat must have carefully weighed which moral or legal rules are broken by the activity he reacts against. Third, the activity must have directly harmful effects on the country or citizens. Fourth, the bureaucrat must bring up specific events rather than general complaints. Fifth, the accusations must be supported by unambiguous evidence (French, 1983, p.135; Bok, 1981, p.213).

One problem for a whistle-blower is to determine exactly when he may react with signals directed outwards. Most questions are, of course, of such a nature that reasonable people can have different opinions about what should be done. Differing opinions consequently belong to the normal course of things and should not automatically result in voice. In order to be morally justified when disclosing information about problems, the bureaucrat must convince himself that he is acting correctly (e.g. in agreement with French's five points). Unfair treatment still occurs, however, and therefore every bureaucrat must be mentally and emotionally prepared to meet and respond to it (Stahl, 1983, p.22).

Whistle-blowing has a very important effect on the bureaucratic organisation: it is inconsistent with the subordinate's general duty to be loyal towards superiors. This moral dilemma can be avoided if the bureaucrat considers demands for loyalty as illegitimate if they conflict with higher ideals (e.g. honesty or rule by the people) (French, 1983, p.136; Graham, 1974, p.92).

Whistle-blowing can lead to significant problems for the individual bureaucrat. If he runs into trouble with his superiors for conveying complaints directly to them, it is not difficult to understand that they react even more strongly in a case of whistle-blowing, which makes the bureaucracy's internal problems public. Several factors endow the situation with a special degree of urgency and bitterness: the bureaucrat accuses specific persons for whom he works, or with whom he co-operates, of error or crime; he deviates from his organisation's general policy and ethos; and he violates his loyalty to the organisation. All this causes strong reactions from superiors and peers (Bok, 1981, p.206; Williams, 1985, p.14).

The accumulated experience of what happens to a whistle-blower is unambiguous. Numerous examples from many different countries illustrate that even in those cases where it was highly justified to blow the whistle, the person doing so has afterwards had a very difficult career. He has been given very disagreeable tasks, the worst office, the most incompetent secretary, etc. (Williams, 1985, p.14). He has lost his good personal contacts with his co-workers, been left out, had rumours spread about being untrustworthy (Bok, 1981, p.204) and been characterised as a trouble-maker. Sometimes, the situation at the workplace has become so unbearable that he has been forced to leave his job. His prospects of getting a new job have not always been bright (Boling and Dempsey, 1981, p.15).

Because the reactions in his own organisation result in such serious effects for the person blowing the whistle, one can assume that alarms are sounded in only a small proportion of the cases where they would be objectively justified (Boling and Dempsey, 1981, p.15). Merely examining the criteria which people should consider before blowing the whistle for it to be justifiable clearly shows that whistle-blowing is generally considered an extreme measure, even in western democracies (Williams, 1985, p.15).

There are, however, reasons for carefully scrutinising each case of whistle-blowing. In practice, the basis for such measures is not always good intentions, and the results are not exclusively positive. Bok enumerates a number of problematic points. Groundless accusations from 'the disappointed, the incompetent, the malicious, and the paranoid' occur, and lead to situations 'of work and reputations unjustly lost for those falsely accused, of privacy invaded and trust undermined'. An organisation which continuously has its activities exposed by whistle-blowing can face difficulties in functioning properly. 'There comes a level of internal prying and mutual suspicions at which no institution can function' (Bok, 1986, p.213).

Do the bureaucrats in the Swedish system have special opportunities to sound the alarm to the public through the mass media? To a certain extent, this is the case. The bureaucracy may not introduce restrictions on information which could be considered a limitation to freedom of speech – that is, managers cannot forbid their personnel from disclosing information which is not classified by law. Everyone has the right to freedom of expression. Even if the management chooses an employee to take care of contacts with the mass media, this does not mean that the rest of the personnel must remain silent (Norström and Sverne, 1981, p.8; JO 1985/86:340).

The bureaucrat's right to inform is part of the general freedom of speech. The main guideline is that he can freely disclose what he has learned in his job. This also means that he can actively seek out the mass media to disclose information. However, he does not have any duty to inform (JO 1975/76:324).

Because secrecy stands in opposition to the western democracies' demand for openness, the following question arises: 'Can secrecy be defended ethically?' Bok's starting-point for a justification of secrecy is that the moral basis for each case must be open to public discussion (Bok, 1986, p.112). She then states (pp.175–6) three arguments which speak in favour of secrecy within the bureaucracy, which may be summarised as follows:

1. Complete openness reduces the possibilities for discussion and optimal decision-making in the bureaucracy. A policy is seldom ready from the beginning; the process requires that different arguments are weighed against each other. If this were to occur completely openly, a risk exists that the bureaucrats would always choose the most uncontroversial and safest alternatives instead of the tentative and creative ones.

2. Elements of surprise can be important in administrative affairs in order to prevent wrongful opposition from different special interests and not to give unjust advantages to certain groups. Investigations of crime which were

conducted completely openly would hardly help imprison any crooks, and public deliberations before a decision to devalue the currency would give undesired effects.

3. There are often reasons to avoid harming individuals by disclosing information about their private lives, which they voluntarily gave to the bureaucracy.

What does Swedish legislation say about disclosure of information? The basic principle is clear: openness is the rule, and exceptions may only be granted after special consideration and must be openly accounted for in law. The reasons for secrecy are discussed in more detail in the preparation of legislation. It is emphasised that secrecy may not become a matter of routine. When someone requests to look at a document which is classified, the assessment of secrecy of that document should always occur in relation to the law. The authority cannot refuse to hand it out by just referring to a 'classified' stamp on the document.

What documents are classified? The Freedom of the Press Act divides secrecy into seven main categories:

1. The security of the Realm or its relations to a foreign state or to an international organisation.
2. The central financial policy, the monetary policy, or the foreign exchange policy of the Realm.
3. The activities of a public authority for the purpose of inspection, control, or other supervision.
4. The interest of prevention or prosecution of crime.
5. The economic interest of the State or the communities.
6. The protection of the personal integrity or the economic conditions of individuals.
7. The interest of preserving animal or plant species.

The Secrecy Act states the specific rules for professional secrecy and for prohibition upon handing out classified documents. The writing of such regulations into law, which is instituted by the parliament (*Riksdagen*), is justified by arguing that openness is so important that only parliamentary decisions may impinge upon it. The authorities may not classify a document as secret if the law does not specifically give them the right (JO 1985/86:346).

Secrecy, then, pertains to the administrative body which classified the document and that administration's employees, and also applies to its relations with other administrative bodies. Secrecy is normally set for a specific time, which varies according to the length of time during which revelation of the document's contents could hurt the interest protected by the secrecy. For example, events related to the nation's security are classified as secret for a maximum of forty years; the nation's central finance policy for a maximum of ten years; and individual's condition of health or other personal circumstances for a maximum of seventy years.

What determines the structure of classification of secrecy in Swedish legislation? The basic idea is the least possible secrecy in order to protect the public interest. Information may only be classified as secret when disclosure would hinder or make an activity substantially more difficult. Secrecy to protect the interests of individual citizens extends considerably further (Corell *et al.*, 1980, p.39). It is noteworthy that in some cases, the classification of documents is much more extensive than the bureaucrat's professional secrecy. These cases will be discussed below in the section on obstruction.

When a bureaucrat discloses official information for publication, the Freedom of the Press Act thus supports his actions. His superiors may not prevent him from disclosing information. Neither can his revelations lead to any form of reprisal such as disciplinary punishment, criticism, or warnings; nor may his actions reduce his possibilities of promotion; nor may references from the old employer to potential employers mention that he disclosed official information. Superiors may not meddle at all in the bureaucrat's disclosure nor even judge whether his action is appropriate or not. On the other hand, the authority has the right to respond to information in the mass media which it considers erroneous (JO 1975/76:317; JO 1985/86:340; cf. Norström and Sverne, 1981, p.9) .

Does this mean that a Swedish whistle-blower is not afflicted by those social sanctions which normally occur in other countries in corresponding situations? Hardly. The Swedish experience shows that even informers with unambiguous support from the law can run into problems. The expulsion mechanism functions in the same manner in Sweden as in other countries (Granholm, 1986).

OBSTRUCTION

Obstruction is probably more common than the extreme forms of voice. The bureaucrat who engages in obstruction is not always discovered by superiors, which means he remains anonymous, and can thereby circumvent the unpleasantness which normally afflicts a whistle-blower. The bureaucrat, however, takes a risk which should not be belittled. In all probability, he will be subjected to the same type of sanctions which normally accompany voice if he is discovered. His superiors and peers will, at any rate, not consider his clandestine activities as extenuating circumstances that might make their judgment of him more mild.

Anonymous information given to outsiders about what happens in the bureaucracy, the so-called 'leaks', is used rather systematically in certain countries. Leaks can take different forms, such as anonymous telephone calls and messages or personal contacts between bureaucrat and journalist. Not even the journalist always knows who has disclosed the information. Leaks can also be used by those in power for tactical reasons – for example, to get an idea of opinions on a specific question. As with whistle-blowing, the information given in leaks is not always true (Bok, 1981, p.216).

To all appearances, leaks play a relatively minor role in Swedish politics, which may reflect the fact that public access to official documents is so extensive. Leaks from the bureaucracy do, however, occur, and the question is how the Freedom of the Press Act judges them. Are there any special circumstances allowed in the Swedish legal system for obstruction, meaning that the bureaucrat anonymously discloses information for publication?

Leaks presume that the bureaucrat remains anonymous. Consequently, the issue about right of anonymity for the person who discloses information is of central importance. Swedish legislation is very explicit on this point. Special rules exist to guarantee anonymity. The right of anonymity for informers has for a long time been considered one of the most important elements in the Freedom of the Press Act (Bet. 1912, p.60). The need to protect anonymity has been asserted very strongly in, among other things, a famous committee report from 1912:

> The ongoing self-examination, which society needs, cannot – least of all in a society of our limited dimensions and with a people of our character – do without an effective protection of anonymity. Consideration of the social surroundings – family, superiors, friends, business relations, etc. – and fear of intellectual or economic discomfort from them exercise an overwhelming pressure on the individual's freedom of speech ... False *'esprit de corps'* and false 'feeling of solidarity' remain factors which are injurious to society and must be taken into account. The protection of anonymity is the safety-valve which releases this pressure, and in many cases, it alone makes it possible for a word to be said which should be said, facts brought forward which should be brought forward. (Bet. 1912, p.63)

That the bureaucrat may disclose official information is a result of the principle of public access to official documents. What happens when he discloses classified information? In fact, freedom to inform also applies in many such cases. The bureaucrat can be held responsible only if the disclosure makes him guilty of the following:

1. High treason, espionage, grave espionage, grave unauthorised dealing with secret information, sedition, treason, treachery, or attempts aiming at such crime, or preparation for or instigation to such crime;
2. Wrongful delivery of an official document which is not available to the public, or making such a document available in contravention of a restriction imposed by a public authority when delivering the document, where such act is committed deliberately; or
3. Deliberate disregard of duty to observe secrecy in cases which shall be specified in a special act of law. (Freedom of the Press Act)

The bureaucrat has the right, within rather wide boundaries, to disclose classified information without risking unpleasant consequences. How should this be interpreted? Where exactly is the boundary determining what he can allow himself to do? The first two points in the above list are relatively unproblematic. In the first, the bureaucrat may not commit certain serious crimes and in the second he may not, independent of the nature of the secret, hand out a classified document nor dictate long passages from it. In both of these cases, professional secrecy precedes freedom to inform. No protection of the informer's anonymity exists.

Classified information can still be disclosed without the informer being punished, however. Why does this construction exist? Of course it appears strange first to classify information as secret and then allow it to be disclosed for publication. The rules about freedom to inform are based on the ambition of achieving the greatest possible openness. If the mass media are to be capable of giving complete, comprehensive and correct information, they sometimes require access to classified information. The regulations about secrecy express general guidelines which prioritise between the demands of openness and of secrecy. It is impossible to foresee the effects of the application of regulations in all specific cases. Sometimes, it can be reasonable to allow the desire for openness to weigh heavier than the demand for secrecy (Corell *et al.*, 1980, p.36; SOU 1983/70:131).

In certain situations, classification of secrecy to protect an interest can prevent desirable insights into the bureaucracy's manner of handling its affairs. This particularly applies to the exercise of public authority. If the classification of secrecy will protect instead, for example, business secrets or the personal lives of individuals, then the situation is different. In such cases, freedom to inform is normally judged to be less important than professional secrecy (ibid.)

It is not obvious that all classified information which the mass media learns about is published. The journalist can be aware that publication would be inappropriate. Knowledge about secrets can, however, be of great use to the journalist when he tries to explain what has happened (ibid.)

As to classified information which is not covered by the three points in the Freedom of the Press Act, the bureaucrat decides himself – without risking reprisals – whether to inform the mass media or not. His anonymity is protected in different ways. The authorities may not try to find out who the informer is, and the person who has received the information may not reveal the informer's identity. A person who even so much as makes enquiries to identify the informer, that is tries to convince a journalist to give the name or arranges an investigation with that administration's employees, can be fined or sentenced to prison for a maximum of one year. The informer is protected to the very last. When there exists reasonable suspicion that the informer has committed a crime, then the person who received the information has to answer, in response to a direct question, if it was really the suspect who disclosed information.

The basis for the legislation's emphasis on freedom to inform also lies in a confidence in the mass media's capability to handle classified information judiciously. The press has self regulation, with ethical rules and a special organisation which oversees their observation. In addition to this, the rules of responsibility in the law also apply (SOU 1983/70:131; Strömberg, 1984, p.248). Therefore, the informer cannot normally be held responsible. But somebody is always liable for information which is published. A chain of liability is defined in detail. In the case of crime by periodicals which violate the freedom of the press the publisher is responsible. If no such person exists, then the owner of the newspaper is responsible. If an owner cannot be found, then the printer is responsible.

Only one case has occurred where the Attorney-General (*justitiekanslern*), who has the overriding responsibility to see that legislation concerning freedom of the press is observed, has tried to persuade a journalist to testify against an informer. The reaction of the press to the Attorney-General's action was severe. A leading journalist asserted, for example, that being prosecuted for violating the Freedom of the Press Act was less serious for a newspaper than breaking a promise of anonymity to an informer. Newspapers are, of course, dependent on protection of sources for their continued existence (Nycander, 1988).

A lack of complete clarity was apparent in the debate which arose around this case. Part of the explanation can be found in the fact that different actors argued from different points of view. A lawyer asserted, contrary to the journalists in particular, that the case pertained to more than the ethics of the press. Freedom of the press comes before many statutory laws, of course, but not before all. This means that a newspaper which publishes information forbidden by law acts irresponsibly if it 'does not take into account that the source can be discovered and punished' (Axberger, 1988). This particular case later came to nothing, partly because the informer revealed himself (when he believed the statute of limitations had expired), partly because in court the Attorney-General refrained from doing anything more than asking the journalist to confirm the identity of the informer.

The rules on freedom to inform mean that the bureaucrat, when he judges that the bureaucracy's activities are evil or unjust, has extensive possibilities for disclosing even classified information for publication. We thus have a situation where the bureaucrat takes society's members into consideration and obeys the law while, at the same time, he is not loyal to his superiors. The law supports the bureaucrat in this type of moral dilemma. It is no exaggeration to say that the law directly encourages obstruction in the form of leaks. Freedom of information and of speech are judged to be so important that other loyalty relationships come second.

There is, of course, no conclusive information about the extent of leaks from the bureaucracy. As one example of an estimation of its frequency, we can examine a report from a prominent peace association about information on Swedish weapons exports, which is under the especially severe classification of secrecy in foreign affairs and defence. When the association saw this as a problem, they decided to send a letter to about one hundred and fifty civil servants in the ministries and directly encouraged them to 'use their right to leak classified information if they perceived that it should be known'. The justification given was that such information could contribute to a better discussion about Swedish national security policies and weapons exports. The letter ended with the following exhortation:

> Be loyal to the truth and an honest debate based on relevant information. Even if the employer expects silent and loyal subordinates.
> If you have access to classified information which you believe should be made public, then you should know that the constitution is on your side if you decide to disclose information for publication. (Jederlund *et al.*, 1989)

The reaction from the authorities came rather quickly. Three persons who are heads of legal departments (the highest judicial expert in a ministry) asserted in an article in *Dagens Nyheter* (an influential newspaper) that in this letter the peace association had encouraged civil servants to commit a crime. The article reviewed those rules which regulate the freedom to inform (Hirschfeldt, 1989).

In its reply, the association stated that it was conscious of the rules about secrecy, but that the classified information referred to in the letter to civil servants in the ministries would not result in the civil servants themselves having to bear the responsibility for leaking, because it was protected under the Freedom of the Press Act. In addition, it announced that the letter had had effects: the association had received classified information from bureaucrats in the ministries (Jederlund *et al.*, 1989). This exchange of opinions illustrates how people can agree about what the law says and yet have different opinions about the degree to which those rules are applicable in a particular case.

SOME REFLECTIONS

There are no empirical investigations about how the rules of freedom of speech and of information are implemented in Swedish society. A preliminary assessment could be based on an estimation of those conditions which speak in favour of these freedoms and against them. The starting-point is that the law, in a significant way, favours freedom of information.

There are numerous factors which indicate that the Swedish legislation on freedom of information works well in practice. An important circumstance is its long tradition. During two hundred years, the principle of public access to official documents has applied to the Swedish bureaucracy and is still highly valid today. The fact that this access is regulated in the constitution indicates its importance.

Another positive factor is the interest from different quarters in the issue of the freedom of the press and openness. Administrative bodies of review with high status devote much attention to problems of freedom of information. In the Attorney-General's duties, it is explicitly stated that he must ensure that the boundaries of the freedom of the press are kept, and his concrete intervention sometimes leads, naturally enough, to strong reactions in the mass media. In their yearly report to parliament, the parliamentary Ombudsmen (*justitieombudsmännen*) discuss problematic cases of public access to official documents under a special heading. As soon as a case involving principles important for freedom of information is brought up it is discussed in the mass media. Because the mass media are, in their activities, heavily dependent on access to official documents and other information about the activities of the public sector, they react forcefully to all attempts to impose limits.

There are also factors which counteract whistle-blowing and leaks. Despite the very strong emphasis on openness and despite all attempts to protect the informer, persons who appear openly or who are revealed as the persons who leaked information are subjected to the same type of reprisals which usually occur in other countries in similar situations. The bureaucrat can be frightened into silence by this, even in cases where informing the mass media would be clearly justified. An especially sensitive question is the protection of anonymity, because leaks can be more attractive than whistle-blowing to the bureaucrat.

Legislation can never be so exact that it foresees all cases which can occur, and events can be interpreted in light of the law in such a way that the authorities take much harsher measures than justifiable. Potential conflicts between the parties obviously exist. The mass media tend to see the area covered by freedom to inform as more extensive than the authorities do. Representatives for the Swedish mass media foster a certain distrust of the authorities' good will, which they express by questioning whether the protection of anonymity for informers is sufficiently strong. When the whole institution of laws, etc. built up around freedom of information presumes trust between authorities and mass media, dissonance can lead to problems (SOU 1983/70:13, 178).

We can only speculate as to why the bureaucracy has this power to persuade dissatisfied employees to remain quiet. The discourse about 'the modern organisation' includes argumentation which could possibly help explain this. All activities will, according to this discourse, be subordinate to the organisation's good. 'A manager may behave like Attila the Hun, but if he or she contributes substantially to organisational effectiveness, all is forgiven' (Scott and Hart, 1989, p.37).

This means that organisational values are placed before those of the individual, who finds it natural to adjust himself to the organisation's wishes. The effect is that

> individual morality becomes synonymous with organisationally useful attitudes and behaviors. Individuals are rewarded for 'adjusting' their personal attitudes and behaviors to bring them in congruence with the organisational imperative. The result is the substitution of obedience for individualism, so the organisation will be better served. (Scott and Hart, 1989, p.52)

With such a conformist view of morals, it is hardly surprising that people in the modern organisational culture receive powerful negative reactions against behaviour such as whistle-blowing or leaks. The question is whether those factors which work in favour of openness constitute a counteracting force of sufficient strength.

ACKNOWLEDGEMENT

The author wishes to thank Michael Hunt, Sheffield City Polytechnic, for his comments on an earlier draft of this chapter.

Abrahamson, K. (1972), *Samhällskommunikation: Om kontakten mellan myndigheter och medborgare*, Lund: Studentlitteratur.

Axberger, H.G. (1988), 'DN:s okunnighet förvånar', *Dagens Nyheter, 7 December.*

Bet. (1912), *Betänkande med förslag till tryckfrihetsförordning*, Afgifvet den 20 December 1912 af Särskilda kommitterade inom Justitiedepartmentet, Stockholm: 1912.

Bok, S. (1981), 'Blowing the Whistle', in J.L. Fleishman, L. Liebman and M.H. Moore (eds), *Public Duties: The moral obligations of government officials*, Cambridge, MA: Harvard University Press.

Bok, S. (1986), *Secrets: On the ethics of concealment and revelation*, Oxford: OUP.

Boling, T. E. and Dempsey, J. (1981), 'Ethical dilemmas in government: Designing an organisational response', *Public Personnel Management Journal*, 10, pp.11–19.

Corell, H. *et al.* (1980), *Sekretesslagen, 1980 års lagstiftning med kommentarer*, Stockholm: Norstedt.

French, P.A. (1983), *Ethics in Government*, Englewood Cliffs, NJ: Prentice-Hall.

Graham, G.A. (1974), 'Ethical Guidelines for Public Administrators: observations on rules of the game', *Public Administration Review*, 34, pp.90–2.

Granholm, A. (1986), *Uppror i byråkratin, Om dålig arbetsmiljö i den offentliga sektorn under 200 år*, Stockholm: Prisma.

Hirschfeld, J. (1989), 'Meddelarfriheten har gränser', *Dagens Nyheter*, 2 May.

Hirschman, A.O. (1970), *Exit, Voice, and Loyalty*, Cambridge MA: Harvard University Press.

Jederlund, L. (1989), 'Glädjande läcktor från Rosenbad', *Dagens Nyheter*, 7 May.

Jederlund, L. *et al.* (1989), 'Läck hemlig information', *Dagens Nyheter*, 18 April.

JO (1975–6, 1985–6), *Justitieämbetsmännens ämbetsberättelse.*

Lagerroth, F. (1915), *Frihetstidens författning*, Stockholm: Bonniers.

Lundquist, L. (1988), *Byråkratisk etik*, Lund: Studentlitteratur.

Norström, C. and Sverne, T. (1981), *Offentlighet och sekretess i socialtjänsten*, Stockholm: Skeab.

Nycander, S. (1988), 'Vad tycker journalister om påtryckningar på vittnen', *Dagens Nyheter*, 12 November.

Rohr, J.A. (1980) 'Ethics for the senior executive service', *Administration and Society*, 12, pp.203–16.

Scott, W.G. and Hart, D.K. (1989), *Organisational Values in America*, London: Transaction Publishers.

Shonfield, A. (1965), *Modern Capitalism. The changing balance of public and private power*, London: OUP.

Sjölin, M. (1985), *Kommunalpolitiken i massmediernas spegel*, Lund: Dialogos.

SOU (1966/60), *Offentlighet och sekretess. Offentlighetskommitténs betänkande Lagförslag med motiv*, Stockholm 1966.

SOU (1975/102), *Tystnadsplikt och yttrandefrihet. Betänkande av tystnadspliktskommittén*, Stockholm 1975.

SOU (1983/70), *Värna Yttrandefriheten. Förslag av yttrandefrihetsutredningen*, Stockholm, 1983.

Stahl, O.G. (1983), 'Public service ethics in the United States', in K. Kernaghan and O.P. Dwivedi (eds), *Ethics in the Public Service: Comparative perspectives*, Brussels: International Institute of Administrative Sciences.

Strömberg, H. (1984), 'Press law in Sweden', in P. Lahav (ed.), *Press Law in Modern Democracies*, New York: Longman.

Thompson, D.F. (1985), 'The possibility of administrative ethics', *Public Administration Review*, 46, pp.555–61.

Warwick, D.P. (1981), 'The ethics of administrative discretion', in J.L. Fleishman, L. Liebman and M.H. Moore (eds), *Public Duties: The moral obligations of government officials*, Cambridge MA: Harvard University Press.

Williams, B. (1985), 'Whistle-blowing in the public service', in B. Williams *et al.*, *Politics, Ethics and Public Service*, London: Royal Institute of Public Administration.

Eight

Reasons of State and the Public Interest: A British Variation of the Problem of Dirty Hands

RICHARD A. CHAPMAN

INTRODUCTION

The problem of 'dirty hands' in political action was the subject of an article by Michael Walzer published in *Philosophy and Public Affairs* nearly twenty years ago (Walzer,1973). It discussed the circumstances in which a particular act of government which may be right in utilitarian terms may leave the man who does it guilty of a moral wrong. R.M. Hare had previously explained how it was that when the precepts and principles of an ordinary man, the products of his moral education, come into conflict with injunctions developed at a higher level of moral discourse the conflict is, or ought to be, resolved at a higher level; there was no real dilemma (Hare, 1972). Walzer's concern was about the conflict which arises when an individual gets his hands dirty while doing what he feels he ought to do. It was about the individual who feels moral guilt when he is doing his duty. It was about the individual who knows he has done something wrong even if what he has done was the best thing to do on the whole in the circumstances – or, at least, he feels that way. In essence, it was about conflict in morality, where official obligation is inconsistent with personal standards or duty.

This dilemma of 'dirty hands' is not uncommon. It is experienced by everyone who has principles or standards of conduct when faced with dual loyalties and a choice has to be made. In general, people who resolve such conflicts to their own satisfaction are people who make a decision, consciously acceptable to themselves, about what is the higher principle or higher morality. Some do this by referring the problem higher in the line of authority. Some do it by compromise, though the compromise may not be as simple for them personally as it appears to others. Others cope with the dilemma by various tactics, including some outlined later in this chapter.

This chapter is, however, concerned with only a limited sphere of the problem of 'dirty hands' to which Walzer drew our attention. It is limited to considering the relationship between the two concepts reasons of state and public interest. In the context of British experience these concepts are closely related. Indeed, in the minds of many actors in government they are often presumed to be synonymous. Moreover, there is no generally agreed and authoritative definition of the terms – and, just to add some spice to the debate, when conflict occurs in British central government, involving reasons of state and the public interest, it is adorned with the cloak of official secrecy.

REASONS OF STATE: BACKGROUND TO THIS DISCUSSION

'Reasons of State' is a term which used to appear in the confidential memorandum known as *Questions of Procedure for Ministers*. In recent years, according to the version printed in the *New Statesman* (21 February 1986, p.13), the term has been replaced by 'the public interest'. It is, of course, not possible, without the co-operation of a minister or official, to be certain when and why the change was made, and it is difficult to justify dirtying the hands of others if they believe pursuit of this sort of knowledge has no more important purpose than academic discussion. *Questions of Procedure* was first drawn up in 1945 as a sort of practical guide for ministers, but extracts have been published since the trial in 1985 of Clive Ponting. This present discussion, however, begins with the extract from the 1950s version of *Questions of Procedure*, quoted in recently released files in the Public Record Office (PRO) as saying:

> *Reasons of State* may require, in appropriate cases, the confidential communication of some information to a responsible Editor, Lobby correspondent, etc. for purposes of guidance; but such communication is only justified where it can be ensured that the confidence and terms on which it is made are respected. (PRO/T233/1430, emphasis added)

According to S.C. Leslie, the Chief Information Officer at the Treasury in 1957, this had been the standard doctrine for at least eight years (PRO/T233/1430). In the most recently published extract, however, the wording is slightly different. It reads:

> In appropriate cases it may be *in the public interest* to communicate certain information in confidence to a responsible editor, Lobby correspondent etc., for purposes of guidance; but this is permissible only when it is known that such confidence will be respected. (*New Statesman*, 21 February 1986, p.13, emphasis added)

The circumstances leading to the quotation from the 1957 issue of *Questions of Procedure* are, briefly, as follows. In 1957 there were allegations that there had been improper disclosure of information about a proposal to raise the Bank Rate to the then very high level of seven per cent. Subsequently there was a Tribunal of Inquiry which investigated all aspects of the allegations and found that there had been no prior disclosure (Parker Report, 1958). The Tribunal's published proceedings made available an unprecedented amount of information about the raising of the Bank Rate, information which subsequently became the basis for a number of research projects (Parker Proceedings, 1957). Recently, as a result of the Public Records Act 1967, official files relating to that period have become available in the PRO and this has made even more material available.

As far as the 1957 events are concerned, the currently relevant details relate to the briefings given to selected individuals by the Chancellor of the Exchequer before the announcement of the Bank Rate increase. What happened was this. On the day before the announcement the Chancellor saw a number of journalists from a selection of influential newspapers. The other details from 1957 are not relevant to this present discussion, but the setting up of a Tribunal of Inquiry, an awe-inspiring inquisition, meant that officials inside the Treasury had to review even the most minute details of the events, be absolutely clear where responsibility lay for each detail, and also be absolutely clear what was the basis for each element of authority and how it related to all the relevant precedents within the ambit of Treasury responsibility.

As part of the Treasury's internal preparations for the Inquiry, Leslie wrote a paper which amounted to an official justification for briefing selected journalists. The journalists were given prior information, not about the Bank Rate increase, but about the package of other measures that were associated with the change in the Bank Rate. Indeed, to ensure that everything went according to plan, the Treasury laid on a rehearsal, with Treasury officials role-playing as journalists, so that the Chancellor of the Exchequer would be as fully prepared as possible for questions likely to be put to him during his briefing interviews. The Chancellor was not to discuss the Bank Rate nor was he to allow it to be discussed. The plan was for the Chancellor to hold a series of meetings with journalists during the afternoon of Wednesday 18 September; this would be followed by a Lobby Conference the next day, after the Bank Rate announcement had been made, and that Conference would also be followed by a meeting with a group of US correspondents.

Two questions of policy arose from this procedure. One concerned the giving of advance information to journalists, and the other concerned the method of doing so – whether or not it should be done on a selective or discriminatory basis. The first question, concerning the policy of giving advance guidance to newspapers, together with the information needed to give it meaning, in fact related to a well-established procedure. It was in this connection that Leslie quoted, in justification, from *Questions of Procedure*, with its reference '*Reasons of State* may require ...'.

Peter Hennessy has recently explained that, although classified as confidential (meaning that its release would be prejudicial to the interests of the nation), *Questions of Procedure* 'is the nearest thing we have to a written constitution for British Cabinet Government' (Hennessy, 1986, p.7; 1989, p.549). *Questions of Procedure* may be confidential for thirty years from the date of a particular issue, but it is quite evident that, even if it is not generally available to the public, it is a document of fundamental importance in the British system of government. Furthermore, it is a document that contains key concepts that have no generally agreed and authoritative meanings. For example, not only may 'reasons of state' give rise to debate, so may even a term like 'the State'. These, and closely related terms, occur very rarely in British legal or official documents. Constitutionally, there is no such legal concept; instead, in Britain there is the Crown.

The most significant appearance of 'interests of state' is in the Official Secrets Act(s) 1911 and 1920 where, in section 2 of the 1911 Act reference was made to a person being guilty of an offence if that person communicates with any person other than 'a person to whom it is in the interest of the State his duty to communicate ...'. Section 2 has, however, been repealed by the Official Secrets Act 1989, and with its repeal the test is no longer relevant. Indeed, when the legislation was going through Parliament the Government repeatedly rejected calls for a 'public interest' defence which would be equivalent. The only other significant reference is in the Prevention of Terrorism Act 1989, where emergency power is given to a police officer (of at least the rank of superintendent) if he has reasonable grounds for believing that immediate action is necessary 'in the interests of the State'.

Clearly, the terms 'reasons of state', 'interest of the state' and 'public interest' are very similar. In general they may be expected to refer, in the British context, to policies properly formulated in accordance with accepted constitutional practice – the details of which may vary from time to time because of changing circumstances and the flexibility of the constitution. In essence, they refer to what the Government, or even the Prime Minister, whose authority primarily rests on the results of the previous General Election, decides the interest of the State is. This is made abundantly clear in Hennessy's quotation from the 1952 version of *Questions of Procedure* which, in the context of a paragraph on secrecy, says 'the essential need is ... an attitude of mind which puts first the interests of the Government as a whole and subordinates everything to that end' (Hennessy, 1986, p.13). This is further clarified by Sir Robert Armstrong in his memorandum to civil servants *The Duties and Responsibilities of Civil Servants in relation to Ministers* (Armstrong, 1985). In that memorandum he made clear the constitutional and practical implications for civil servants: 'Civil servants are servants of the Crown. For all practical purposes the Crown, in this context, means and is represented by the Government of the day.'

This interpretation is well illustrated by the procedures associated with the Bank Rate rise in 1957. In 1957 the main reasons for ministerial discussions with journalists and others were to guard against damaging first reactions to the rise in Bank Rate and to encourage helpful reactions. As Leslie put it:

> The pound was under almost intolerable pressure, some of it deriving from uncertainty about the Government's short term intentions regarding the exchange rate, some from doubt of its will and ability to defeat inflation in the long term. The Government had been operating a credit squeeze for some 2½ years and there had been quite a long succession of measures to intensify or extend it. Neither these nor the Chancellor's warning, late in July, that there would be more to come if needed, had carried conviction with the doubters. Indeed, in a sense they had made confidence harder to regain, by devaluing official promises and expressions of intent. It was the immediate purpose of

the measures announced on 19th September to stop the rot by carrying the fullest possible conviction of the firmness of the government's intentions. It is obvious that the nature of the measures themselves, and the government's follow-up action during the ensuing weeks, would be the main determinants of confidence. But something – perhaps a good deal – would turn on Ministers' success in conveying the full measure of their resolve at the outset. (PRO/T233/1430)

The briefing of journalists and others in 1957 involved risk, but the risk was weighed and set aside. Subsequent events proved that judgment to have been correct: the risks were avoided and the advantages achieved – the guidance was given without arousing suspicions about the Bank Rate. However, as Leslie also put it, a more important question was:

would it have been justifiable to let the measures arrive in Fleet Street, with only such explanation as could be given after the event? The risk here was that some influential newspapers, left to themselves, would have taken them *prima facie* as just one more in the long series of inconclusive turns of the credit screw, coupled with a panic-stricken last-minute move on the bank rate. After the event it is very easy to assume that this could not have happened. In fact, in some important instances, it very well might. (PRO/T233/1430)

Individuals and groups, journalists and others as well, are often given briefings in this way by ministers. This applies equally in connection with foreign policies and home policies. Leslie went on to argue:

The supreme criterion of what is right and proper in these circumstances is at all times the public interest – what the official doctrine calls 'reasons of state' ...

Public policy in its more important sense – the 'reason of state' – may in some circumstances require discrimination. When advance information or guidance of a particularly delicate kind is to be given, it may be improper to give it to a number of newspapers which are not in a position to further the public purposes involved. It might well be wrong and blameworthy to make a confidential statement to all newspapers because it is being made to some, and because there might be some tactical risk in making distinctions. Equally it would be blameworthy to refrain entirely from giving guidance which would benefit the national interest on the grounds that it could not properly be given to everyone, and that it was awkward or might (if known) be unpopular to discriminate. In some instances the proper course will be to give confidences, with all due precautions that they shall be respected, to all those and only to those whose receipt of them is likely to benefit the public interest. (PRO/T233/1430)

The Chancellor in 1957 sought to carry conviction to the editors of all those publications whose official attitude to the measures would carry weight with financial opinion at home and abroad. The essence of the problem at that time, the 'reason of state', seems to have been the desire of the Government in the public interest to secure understanding of a point of view, and to have the point of view presented in a way that best secured that objective. In these circumstances of widespread support, official duty and personal standards would seem not be have been in conflict. The political interests of the Government and 'reasons of state' were in harmony.

REASONS OF STATE: WIDER ISSUES

The reasoning so far has been uncomplicated and largely common-sense. In Britain the Government consists of a number of ministers, appointed by the Queen but chosen by the Prime Minister, who have the support of a majority in the House of Commons. The House of Commons consists of Members of Parliament who are elected not less frequently than once every five years. This provides the democratic link with the people and is the basis for arguing that it is the government (who else?) which decides what the public interest is in given circumstances. To complete the picture, civil servants hold office as servants of the Crown but, for all practical purposes for a civil service that is non-partisan, the Crown means the Government of the day. This is apparently straightforward and really rather elementary. The facts of experience are not always so uncomplicated.

In general, it is believed that actions of government should be carried out honourably. That is, they should be done honestly, as far as possible openly, in accordance with generally accepted patterns of behaviour, and always in the best interests of the people. But any thinking person will know that, as in private life, situations arise when, for perfectly justifiable reasons of prudence and best intentions, the order of the day requires less than complete openness and truthfulness. Sometimes circumstances suggest that public silence is the best course of action, sometimes it is considered best to be 'economical with the truth' (Armstrong, 1986); sometimes it may be best to mislead or to lie – as with public relations and propaganda in wartime. In any case, as already indicated, there might be considerable debate about what the interests of the people are, and how they might be ascertained. The example outlined above, about raising the Bank Rate, illustrates this well. If the intention is to protect a currency, and protection requires confidence from interested parties, it may be necessary to make confident statements about the strength of a currency and about determined intentions to safeguard it, even though the currency may be less than strong and intentions may be less than firm. These are acceptable tactics in public affairs, the intention to protect a currency generally does not give rise to differences of opinion (though the tactics to achieve that objective might), and it may be argued that when the policy objective is not achieved then honourable politicians resign – as James Callaghan, the Labour Chancellor of the Exchequer, did when sterling was devalued in 1967 (Callaghan, 1987, p.221). In such circumstances politicians and others may have regrets, they may even be criticised for errors of judgment, but they do not incur personal disgrace or shame. Everyone understands that this is the way the system works. Following resignation in such circumstances politicians may, after an appropriate interval of time, even be appointed again to high office. Indeed, immediately after his resignation as Chancellor, Callaghan was appointed Home Secretary.

Troubles result and hands can become dirty when events are less than straightforward. Numerous examples could be given to illustrate this but three will suffice. The first relates to unacceptable lying. The second relates to unacceptable reasons of state. The third relates to more extreme tactics, only very recently revealed in public as apparently part of governmental activities, and increasingly referred to as disinformation.

The example of lying which was later thought to be unacceptable concerns misleading statements in Parliament by Michael Heseltine and statements containing errors of fact by other ministers between 1982 and 1984, and the subsequent trial and acquittal of Clive Ponting (Ponting, 1985). The case arose because government ministers had lied to Parliament. The Argentine ship *Belgrano* had been sunk by the British submarine *Conqueror* during the Falklands War. However, when it was sunk the ship had been sailing away from the Falklands for eleven hours. Questions were later asked about when and in what circumstances the decision was made to sink it, whether the *Belgrano* was still a threat at that time, and whether sinking it was justifiable in terms of self-defence under the United Nations Charter. Even after the end of the Falklands War, Heseltine and other ministers told the House of Commons that it would not be in the public interest to give information about the *Belgrano*. Later it was announced that the log book of the *Conqueror* was lost and therefore details important in the political controversy could not be checked.

When further information was not forthcoming, Ponting, a fairly senior official in the Ministry of Defence, wrote an anonymous letter to Mr Tam Dalyell, the Labour MP who had persistently but unsuccessfully asked questions about the Belgrano affair (Ponting, 1985, ch.5). Later, he sent two classified papers to Dalyell (who gave them to the Chairman of the House of Commons Select Committee on Foreign Affairs). Ponting did this because he believed he should place his loyalty to Parliament and to what he believed to be the public interest above his obligation to the interests of the government of the day (Norton-Taylor, 1985, p.48).

At Ponting's trial, Mr Justice McCowan drew attention to the question of whether Dalyell was a person to whom it was 'in the interest of the State' (and therefore legitimate in the context of the Official Secrets Act 1911) Ponting's duty to communicate such information (Birkinshaw, 1988). The judge also directed the jury that the words 'in the interest of the State' meant the policies of the State. He added: 'The policies of the State mean the policies laid down for it by its recognised organs of government and authority' and 'The policies of the State ... were the policies of the government then in power' (Norton-Taylor, 1985, p.103).

Two questions for further consideration arise from this case. The first question arises from the judge's direction. In rather simplistic terms of constitutional propriety there is no person or group of persons higher than the Government and its ministers (especially when it is remembered that in Britain ministers speaking individually are expected to speak for the Government and to be supported by collective responsibility). Therefore it was argued that the legitimate body authorised to express the interest of the state was the government of the day. It also follows that where issues of national security are involved, it is only the Government that can determine what it is permissible to reveal: no other institution, individual, or group of individuals is more in command of the facts. This is made clear in the classic test expressed by Lord Parker in *The Zamora*: 'Those who are responsible for national security must be the sole judges of what the national security requires' (*The Zamora*, [1916] 2AC 77, p.107). But governments are made up of human beings whose views of the State's interests and their own responsibilities are intertwined with and influenced by other factors including ideological commitment and personal ambition. Without a written constitution and constitutional review of legislation much must depend on integrity and trust.

Furthermore, this question involves an appreciation of the purpose of government in modern societies. For example, it may be argued that the basic purpose of government is to secure stability in society, to ensure that there is a sufficient degree of safety and security so that individuals can pursue their own interests, experience self-development and live satisfying lives. Reasons of State may then be regarded as necessary reasons to protect these conditions. As Heseltine was told in 1984, there had undoubtedly been a breach of trust by Ponting, but the leak of information could not be held to be seriously damaging to national security, though the revelation of the leak would be embarrassing to the Government (Norton-Taylor, 1985, p.50).

The second question relates to the role of the official who feels he has dirty hands in this context. When such an official becomes aware, from his position of privilege, of perceived improprieties on the part of his political superiors, has he a responsibility to do something about it and, if so, what? The Ponting case illustrates unacceptable lying (by a minister) as well as the personal dilemma of an official with an ethical problem because, although Ponting's behaviour may be regarded as reprehensible, at the end of his trial he was acquitted by the jury. Ponting may have behaved less than prudently, but he was not found guilty even though the facts quite clearly showed that he was technically guilty of an offence according to the provisions of the Official Secrets Acts; furthermore, he had signed a confession and tendered his resignation. It has been suggested that the Ponting case is similar to the Tisdall case (where a junior clerk leaked information to the press because she did not agree with government policy). However, the cases differ in two respects: Tisdall pleaded guilty; and the Government was not accused of acting improperly. Ponting's problem was a problem of dirty hands because he took all legitimate measures to remove himself from his difficult predicament, but failed, and was faced with a conflict between his obligation as an official to support his ministers and his standards of personal integrity which required accepted practice to be followed and statements made in accordance with expected standards of public conduct.

The second example, an example of unacceptable reasons of state, is the Government Communications Headquarters (GCHQ) affair. On 25 January 1984 the Foreign Secretary, Sir Geoffrey Howe, announced in the House of Commons that all civil servants working at GCHQ were to cease to have the right of access to industrial tribunals or to belong to independent trade unions: this affected about seven thousand officials. The decision to change the conditions of service for these officials was made under prerogative power and there was no prior consultation with the civil service unions (Employment Committee, 1984, evidence by Sir

Geoffrey Howe and Appendix 1). The decision was debated in the House of Commons on 27 February 1984. Later the matter was considered by the High Court and the Court of Appeal. On 6 August the Appeal Court ruled that the courts could not interfere with the ban because it was imposed in the interests of national security. The Court of Appeal decision was later upheld in the House of Lords, on 8 October 1984 (O'Toole, 1989).

The decision to ban trade unions at GCHQ led to a Trades Union Congress campaign on behalf of GCHQ trade union members, and legal action via the International Labour Organisation and the European Court of Human Rights, as well as through the British courts. It also stimulated industrial action by British trade-unionists in support of their fellows. In the High Court on 16 July 1984 Mr Justice Glidewell argued that since staff had the right, and indeed had been encouraged, to belong to trade unions before the imposition of the ban on membership, then fairness and the rules of natural justice demanded consultation before the right was taken away (O'Toole, 1989). The Government accepted that there had been no recent industrial disruption at GCHQ, though there had been industrial action between 1979 and 1981, as part of a national campaign over pay and conditions of service generally – industrial action which union officials claimed was not a threat to operational capability at GCHQ (see evidence to Employment Committee, 1984). The Government claimed that its ban was for reasons of national interest, which could not be explained in public because of security implications. The House of Lords later accepted that only the Government could decide what national security required and upheld the Court of Appeal's reversal of Glidewell's judgment.

The case is used as an example because it illustrates the extraordinarily wide and sometimes unquestionable powers available to government in Britain. It is possible that full details of the reasoning behind this decision will never be made public, yet the decision affects what many people and organisations, including the International Labour Organisation, would regard as a matter of right in employment conditions. If doubts arise about the propriety of government decision-making relating to a time of war (as in the Ponting case) it is not surprising that comparable questions are raised about motivation and standards of conduct when government is exercising prerogative power in peacetime conditions. Questions may be raised about the role of the advisers to the Foreign Secretary and about the role of the Directorate of the GCHQ which had to implement the decision. These people may at the time have had to square their consciences with the requirements of their relationship to the Government about a decision which in retrospect may seem to have been, and was adjudged to have been by a High Court Judge and by respected legal authorities, an arbitrary decision. It may also have been a decision for which there was no pressing 'reason of state' since, in this case, the judge of whether national security required the ban was the Government, which decided for security reasons not to give further details. If debate surrounded the damage to national security by Ponting's leak, even more questions of doubt could be raised about the circumstances of the GCHQ ban.

The third example relates to what is increasingly becoming known as disinformation. Some anxieties were expressed about this form of activity by security agencies in connection with the publication of Peter Wright's *Spycatcher* (Wright, 1987). Further anxieties have recently (1990) been stimulated about British government behaviour in the 1970s, especially as a result of allegations by Colin Wallace, the former Army press officer in Northern Ireland. Wallace claims to have knowledge of illegal operations, particularly Operation Clockwork Orange, which smeared leading politicians in the 1970s. The existence of Clockwork Orange was not confirmed in the House of Commons until January 1990 – but that information did not confirm that the project did what Wallace and the press alleged it did. However, Wallace's allegations seem to confirm what was said in *Spycatcher* about disinformation from official security sources concerning Harold Wilson, Edward Heath and Jeremy Thorpe (*The Independent*, 3 February 1990; *The Observer*, 4 February 1990). The substance of the allegations was also confirmed by David Leigh in his book *The Wilson Plot* (Leigh, 1988). Again, this is a subject associated with national security so there is continuing rumour, with apparent snippets of confirmation from various sources, but no possibility of either reliable and conclusive information or denial of the allegations. This is because there can be no public discussion where national security is involved, and again the judge of the involvement of national security is the government, or parts of it, whose conduct is the subject of complaint. However, Mr David Calcutt QC, who in 1990 conducted an inquiry into whether injustice was done to Colin Wallace when he was dismissed from the civil service in 1975, found impropriety in civil service procedures and as a result Wallace was awarded £30,000 compensation from the Ministry of Defence. As Wallace has therefore been proved right about his dismissal it seems at least possible that he is right in his other allegations (Foot, 1989), but further details may never be clarified as a result of the new Official Secrets Act 1989, which prevents any past or present members of the security and intelligence services from disclosing details obtained in their official capacity – regardless of public interest or the guilt of others. Nevertheless, the practice of spreading disinformation is likely to have been known about and approved by senior officials and perhaps ministers, and it is to be wondered whether they suffered doubts about the tactics they were authorising. Did they have dirty hands or is it a requirement that the security services should be staffed by persons specially selected because they are lacking in principles or standards of conduct?

Important questions arise from these examples in connection with the terms which give broad discretionary power to governments to act for reasons of state or in the public interest. People may doubt whether reasons of state are the same as the public interest and whether the unquestionable judge of the public interest should be the government of the day. Indeed, the interests of the government of the day may be primarily to remain in power, to enable it to pursue commitment to a particular ideology and/or vision of the future; and enthusiastic pursuit of this goal may lead to judgments that, if known about, would not lead to widespread public support. Much depends on the aim(s) of any particular government and its efficiency in achieving its aim(s). It is, of course, difficult to resolve questions such as these because there is no higher temporal authority than the Government, and no other individual or group sufficiently well informed to effectively question its judgment. Sometimes, as with Ponting, an individual may observe or be involved with matters that are wrong (or, if not wrong, then clearly not quite right). To say that in such circumstances of conflict between obligation and duty the only avenue open to an official is to resign may not be satisfactory for two reasons. One reason is that resignation would not necessarily resolve the issue, especially if the conflict is deep and profound – to some people resignation may look like weakness, to others it may have overtones of cowardliness for walking away from a difficult situation. The other reason is that resignation may focus attention on what might simply be a variation of the master–servant relationship where the master is always conceived as right and has to be obeyed even when wrong. Servants who are not guilty of criminal offences may, according to this reasoning, be justifiably sacked for breach of trust if in the eyes of their masters they are thought to have been disloyal. This, however, may imply that they should have an almost dog-like loyalty to their masters whatever their masters might decide to do. This master–servant analogy may have been acceptable in the past, but it may be regarded as irrelevant and unacceptable in modern times. If, however, this predicament involving dirty hands is more widely recognised as one that actually and understandably occurs from time to time in any country, but especially in a country with a peculiarly 'unwritten' constitution, and if resignation is not considered acceptable or the only alternative, a re-examination of the source of the conflict and its prospects for resolution may be not only overdue but unavoidable.

CONFLICT AND RESOLUTION

The focus for the discussion in this chapter is the area of conflict where an individual finds that an aspect of official work conflicts with the personal standards he or she regards as the norm for such behaviour. In particular, it relates to the practical implications of reasons of state and public interest. An important aspect of this problem is the meanings of these two related terms: this aspect has been illustrated but not yet resolved. Nevertheless, the argument is moving in the direction of concluding that reasons of state may be more helpfully reserved for decisions where the safety or security of the system of government is in jeopardy; where, because of the importance to all citizens of maintaining certain conditions of life, widespread public support may reasonably be expected (even if it is not possible to reveal all details of reasons of state decision-making); and where the intentions are essentially non-partisan. This would be consistent with such other definitions as that of Lord Harris of Greenwich on subversion: 'activities ... which threaten the safety or wellbeing of the State, and are intended to undermine or overthrow Parliamentary democracy by political, industrial or violent means (357 H.L. Deb., 6s., Col.947, 26 February 1975). In contrast, the public interest may be reserved for decisions where partisan policies may be involved, where the government exercises judgment based not only upon its own beliefs but also upon the degree of support it has, or believes it has, in the community. The public interest may still be regarded as above the narrower and more partisan interest of the government of the day – because it must be acknowledged that the Government is a group of individuals who may also be concerned about their own future in government. The problem of dirty hands is, however, further complicated, especially in Britain, by the moral standards of officials in relation to their work.

Some, but by no means all, of these official standards or expectations are laid down in official rules. Unlike most other countries in the world, Britain has no fundamental and comprehensive legal document to which officials can refer; there is no Civil Service Act which serves as the overriding legislation that controls official behaviour. This is, of course, consistent with the British constitution: there is no single document which can be regarded as the fundamental law, determining how government should proceed and how its various agencies interrelate. What may be correct or acceptable at one time may change according to different circumstances at another time.

Constitutionally, the position of civil servants is, however, clear. Civil servants are servants of the Crown and for day-to-day purposes loyalty and duty to the Crown means loyalty and duty to the Queen's ministers who act in her name and are accountable to the Queen's Parliament. One of the reasons why this arrangement has worked so well in the past is that people to whom this line of authority was unacceptable were unlikely to be attracted to work in the civil service. Furthermore, in Britain, civil servants are permanent, which means that they are non-partisan servants of ministers and do not change with changes in government.

There are numerous rules that are, in fact, written down, though they are not usually available in one comprehensive source. They include the 1977 Croham Directive on the Disclosure of Official Information; the 1980 Memorandum of Guidance for Government Officials appearing before Parliamentary Select Committees; the 1985 statement (revised in 1987) by Sir Robert Armstrong on *The Duties and Responsibilities of Civil Servants in relation to Ministers*; and the *Pay and Conditions of Service Code* (formerly known as *Estacode*) and its companion the *Establishment Officers' Guide*. These and other statements and guidance may sound a formidable collection of authoritative pronouncements when considered together, but from time to time circumstances arise which are beyond the formal guidance of these formal rules. In any case, it should be stressed that these formal rules are by no means comprehensive. Indeed, the *Establishment Officers' Guide* says:

> It has never been thought necessary to lay down a precise code of conduct because civil servants jealously maintain their professional standards. In practice the distinctive character of the British civil service depends largely on the existence and maintenance of a general code of conduct which, although to some extent intangible and unwritten, is of very real influence. (*FDA News*, December 1984)

Often, it seems, when difficulties arise, their source is not so much officials who break the rules but ministers who have failed to act in accordance with accepted constitutional practice. This, of course, may involve ministers dirtying their hands in the course of public service. In particular, problems may result from decisions about the public interest where ministerial decisions appear contrary to normal practice, and where there is no opportunity for appeal. Indeed, the practical difference between reasons of state and public interest may generally be that reasons of state are not matters for public discussion, whereas the public interest is more amorphous, more open, more debatable, and doubts about it may be resolved by democratic procedures. In such circumstances, and in order to reconcile differences, individuals in public service cannot avoid making judgments and the quality of the administrative system may therefore be seen in the overall pattern produced by many public servants making individual judgments. It would not be acceptable for officials unthinkingly (and therefore irresponsibly) to carry out official instructions: senior officials are appointed and promoted because they have certain desired qualities which include intellectual abilities and an absence of strong partisan allegiance. They are appointed for their capacity to make judgments in the context of a particular political environment.

In British central government the quality of individual judgments is affected at least as much – perhaps more – by family and educational background and the post-entry socialisation of officials as it is by reference to rule-books and guidelines. This socialisation is important for developing in individuals the values and beliefs that contribute to the patterns and guidelines for behaviour that are so important in the administrative culture of the civil service. It is therefore not surprising that when Sir William Armstrong, as Head of the Civil Service, was questioned on television about his personal attitude to the considerable power he had, he explained that for him being accountable to oneself was the greatest taskmaster. He added: 'I am accountable to my own ideal of a civil servant' (Armstrong, 1969). Sir Edward Bridges offered similar reflections. From his wide practical experience he found that there was

> in every Department a store of knowledge and experience in the subjects handled, something which eventually takes shape as a practical philosophy, or may merit the title of a departmental point of view ... in most cases the departmental philosophy is no more than the slow accretion and accumulation of experience over the years ... Every civil servant ... finds himself entrusted with this kind of inheritance. (Bridges, 1950)

Sometimes important cases reach the headlines in such a way that they contribute to the officials' learning process and have a significant impact on the administrative culture. One such case occurred in 1928 and is known as the Francs case. The often-quoted statement from the Report of the Inquiry chaired by Sir Warren Fisher concluded: 'The public expects from Civil Servants a standard of integrity and conduct not only inflexible but fastidious' (Fisher *et al.*, 1928, para.59).

As far as official attitudes and standards are concerned, the position is this. There are few detailed and fundamental rules and no code of behaviour against which all questions of conflict and controversy can be measured with confidence of resolution. Nor, indeed, is there any widespread or popular demand for such an authoritative statement, though some aspects of this problem have been considered by the First Division Association (O'Toole, 1990). Decisions and judgments cannot be avoided. There are, of course, certain constraints imposed by rules and codes, and there is increasing scope for judicial review, which means that judicial review is developing into a body of administrative law. Ultimately, however, in the British system of government there are two safeguards to misuse of power. One is the political system and in particular the provisions for regular elections from a wide popular franchise and the acceptance of parliamentary sovereignty. The other is the integrity of the public service (encompassing both politicians and officials) and the trust it inspires. Difficulties arise when it seems these safeguards are inadequate. Difficulties arise when the well-established traditions are set aside as part of policies intended to cut the cost of government and to change the administrative culture in the direction of making government more business-like (Chapman, 1988b). These difficulties lead to demands to review current practice and to questions about possible reform measures.

PROPOSALS AND CONCLUSIONS

It would be unreasonable to expect that without fundamental constitutional and administrative reform there will be a time when British government will never involve issues of conscience arising from conflict between official responsibilities and personal standards in official life. If staff are recruited with qualities appropriate for the work to be done, if processes of training and socialisation further contribute to the development of these qualities in appointed staff, and if there are institutional procedures to act as safeguards in particular circumstances, issues of conflict should be rare. However, some of these features of public service may be due for review, especially in the context of issues raised in this chapter.

First, there are matters of definition. 'Reasons of state' is a concept that seems overdue for analysis and debate. At first encounter it seemed a term best suited to the environment of 1945. It was not surprising to discover that its early use in *Questions of Procedure* had been replaced with alternative wording. It may simply be a term left over from the highly developed atmosphere of wartime security: reasons of state in that context may have meant reasons that could not be publicly revealed but that related to government policies in pursuit of a well-established and widely accepted national objective. The courts have helped in interpreting interests of state to the extent that it has been authoritatively stated that interests of state, as the term appears in the Official Secrets Acts, refers to the interests of the Government. This might have been sufficient had not the new Prevention of Terrorism Act (1989) given a police officer emergency powers if he believes he has reasonable grounds for believing that in the interests of the State authority should be given by the issue of a search warrant. Perhaps it refers only to circumstances where the system of government is under threat. If so, the position is probably covered in police training and, for clarification, it might be useful to know how the term is there defined. Meanwhile other public servants might benefit from having the term drawn to their attention in discussion. Indeed, where it is possible without breaching state security, benefits may even result from public discussion.

This matter has not entirely escaped the attention of the Treasury and Civil

Service Committee of the House of Commons. In 1986 it wrestled with a related problem. The previous report from the Committee, on 'Ministers and Civil Servants', referred to accountability for the 'actions' of civil servants. The Government, in a reply to the Defence Committee's report, had referred to 'actions or conduct of individual civil servants' and said that 'civil servants giving evidence to select committees ... should not answer questions ... directed to the conduct of themselves or of other named civil servants'. The Treasury and Civil Service Committee therefore recommended that actions and conduct should be defined separately, to distinguish two different concepts. It defined 'actions' of civil servants as 'those activities which are carried out on the instructions of, or are consistent with the policies of the Minister concerned' and 'conduct' as 'activities which fall outside that definition and may indeed amount to "misconduct"' (Treasury and Civil Service Committee, 1986, para.15). The Government accepted the Committee's recommendation (Cm 78). It would have been easy to extrapolate and make ministers alone accountable for 'reasons (or interests) of state' decisions, but that may be too easy to be accepted in practice.

Secondly, apart from delay while awaiting an authoritative court case on this question, there is also the problem of openness – or, rather, the lack of it. 'Reasons of state' cannot, apparently, be divulged, at least for long periods of years. The whole question of doubt, or possible conflict, involving reasons of state is therefore bound up with the innate secrecy characteristic of the administrative culture in Britain.

Thirdly, administrative culture may be changed, over time, if different criteria are used when appointing and training staff, but at least in the meantime there may be a case for instituting a new office of Ombudsman for civil servants. Clearly, opportunities for staff to transfer, and the seeking of advice from superior officials up to Permanent Secretary (or even the Head of the Civil Service), can prove inadequate – as they did in Ponting's case. Either they should be reinforced (would it be so impractical to authorise direct approaches, in confidence, to the Head of the Civil Service – the number of cases is unlikely to be large?) or an Ombudsman for the Civil Service should be appointed. A Civil Service Ombudsman could act as a disinterested point of appeal, outside all departments, perhaps reporting directly to the Head of the Civil Service, and be ultimately accountable to the Minister for the Civil Service. There is a useful precedent in the creation, in 1987, of a Staff Counsellor for the security and intelligence services, who reports not less frequently than once a year to the Prime Minister (121 H.C. Deb., 6s., Col.508, 2 November 1987). Perhaps it is time for a public statement on the experience gained from this innovation, to see whether lessons from it may be relevant to the proposal for a Civil Service Ombudsman?

This chapter began by taking a theme from an article by Walzer, written at a time when American scholars were re-examining questions of ethics in political action at the time of the Vietnam War. That theme, of dirty hands, has been used to examine a variety of related issues in the context of a different political and administrative system. Some of the issues relevant to the discussion twenty years ago are relevant in the different context of another political system in a different decade. It may be recognised, for example, that some actions may be dirty even where it is accepted at the time that they are right – such as the tasks of an executioner. Moreover, there may be repercussions after an event where a morally repellant act does not achieve the intended result – as, for example, with city bombing in wartime. From other perspectives, however, new questions arise, questions that will neither go away with the passing of time nor will be resolved by applying solutions accepted in another environment.

In the British civil service there have been numerous checks and balances that have aided the resolution of conflict between official obligations and feelings of moral duty. They have included the posting of staff, recruitment on the basis of open competitions with objective assessment of applicants, and socialisation to stimulate and encourage the highest standards of integrity and public service. It should, however, be noted that they have not included a Civil Service Act or a formally agreed and officially promulgated code of conduct.

The British civil service has a long and unbroken history with its own traditions and standards. It works within and is daily conditioned by a distinctive but changing political environment. It seeks to be efficient, effective and economical, however these terms happen to be defined, and to work for the 'common good' not in a Utilitarian sense but in the 'Idealist' sense that its actions are determined by enhancing the well-being of society. These pursuits, however, as Barry O'Toole has argued, are quite different from a public interest that has become nothing more than the sum of the interests of the public (expressed specifically as the interests of the duly elected government) (O'Toole, 1990). Consequently, whilst in most respects civil servants are, indeed, servants of ministers, they sometimes have a quite different role. It is not merely a role resulting from their permanence. Their permanence is, however, still a distinctive feature when compared with the ex- perience of other countries – despite a few recent widely publicised exceptions and a clearly recognisable trend towards less permanence and more opportunities for recruitment to senior positions from other environments. Another distinctive fea- ture of the British civil service is its constitutional role. Graham Wallas put this well when he wrote: 'The real "Second Chamber", the real "constitutional check" in England, is provided, not by the House of Lords and the Monarchy, but by the existence of a permanent Civil Service appointed on a system independent of the opinion or desires of any politician and holding office during good behaviour' (Wallas, 1908). From time to time civil servants offer advice on constitutional practice, interpret constitutional conventions and sometimes write them down for the guidance of others (Chapman, 1988a, ch.7). Part of the problem of dirty hands in the British context is therefore that in the past civil servants have been regarded as keepers of the public interest, but this is no longer generally accepted.

The constitutional position therefore enhances and complicates the problem of civil servants who feel they have dirty hands. Of course the line previously taken by Hare may still be relevant in some circumstances. Hare argues that if armies were to say to soldiers 'on the battlefield, always do what is most conducive to the general good of mankind', or even 'of your countrymen', nearly all soldiers would easily convince themselves (battles being what they are) that the course most conducive to these desirable ends was headlong flight. Instead they say, 'Leave those calculations to your superiors; they are probably in some bunker somewhere out of immediate personal danger, and therefore can consider more rationally and dispassionately, and with better information than you have, the question of whether to withdraw. Your job is to get on with the fighting' (Hare, 1972). When applied to the British civil service this is the line of argument officially adopted. It runs as follows. If a conflict should arise between an official's understanding of the standards to be applied in official work, and the standards evident in, or instructed to be applied in, particular circumstances, then the conflict should be resolved by reference to superior officials right up the line of authority. Ultimately the buck stops, as the saying goes, at the desk of the minister. It is, however, impractical to suggest that officials can survive by the tactics of Nelson when he put his telescope to his blind eye. Nor is the position helped by an adaptation of that other well-known saying, if an official doesn't like the heat he should get out of the kitchen.

This formal approach cannot resolve all difficulties. The administrative culture has changed from conditions where that approach could have been applied, partly by reforms (by conscious intent as a result of ministerial decisions), partly by evolution (by increasing complexity, without conscious awareness of the end result). The political and constitutional culture has also changed, incorporating effects from the European Community. There is now an expectation that officials should be personally accountable – at least for their conduct even if ministers are answerable for their actions. It is thought acceptable that officials should demonstrate initiative and commitment ('Is he one of us?', 'Is he a can-do person?' are questions sometimes heard). The attitude expressed by Richard Wilding, a few years ago, certainly does not seem to be acceptable today. Wilding's attitude was as follows:

> It is absolutely necessary to pursue today's policy with energy; it is almost equally necessary, in order to-survive, to withhold from it the last ounce of commitment ... and to invest that commitment in our particular institution, the Civil Service itself, with all its manifest imperfections. (Wilding, quoted by Norton-Taylor, 1985, p.115)

At the end of the day, in the British context, the question of dirty hands may amount to a re-examination of one of the traditional safeguards: the trust and integrity of public servants (both politicians and officials). If such integrity is no longer evident, or where evident if it is no longer highly regarded, or if new approaches are adopted in public service management which undermine the traditional administrative culture, then new procedures, new rules, new relationships between ministers and their officials, may have to be introduced. It is in this context that recent experience of changing standards and demands must be fully understood. It is only after the best possible understanding of past experience and present pressures that new approaches can be considered to enable individuals to develop frameworks to resolve moral dilemmas in official work.

ACKNOWLEDGEMENT

The author wishes to thank John Rohr, Virginia Polytechnic Institute and State University, for comments on an earlier draft of this chapter.

Armstrong, Sir Robert (1985), Note by the Head of the Home Civil Service, *The Duties and Responsibilities of Civil Servants in Relation to Ministers*, London: Cabinet Office.

Armstrong, Sir Robert (1986), quoted in Richard V. Hall, *A Spy's Revenge*, Sydney: Penguin, 1987.

Armstrong, Sir William (1969), quoted in Richard A. Chapman, *The Higher Civil Service in Britain*, London: Constable.

Birkinshaw, P. (1988), *Freedom of Information: The law, the practice and the ideal*, London: Weidenfeld & Nicholson.

Bridges, Sir Edward (1950), *Portrait of a Profession: The civil service tradition*, Cambridge: CUP.

Callaghan, James (1987), *Time and Chance*, London: Collins.

Chapman, Richard A. (1988a), *Ethics in the British Civil Service*, London: Routledge.

Chapman, Richard A. (1988b), *The Art of Darkness*, Durham: University of Durham.

Employment Committee (1984), *First Report from the Employment Committee, Session 1983–4, Trade Union Legislation – Unions in the Government Communications Headquarters: together with Proceedings of the Committee, Minutes of Evidence taken before the Committee on 1 and 8 February 1984 and Appendices*, HC238, London: HMSO.

Fisher, Sir Warren *et al.* (1928), *Report of the Board of Enquiry appointed by the Prime Minister to Investigate Certain Statements Affecting Civil Servants* (Cmd 3037), London: HMSO.

Foot, Paul (1989), *Who Framed Colin Wallace?*, London: Macmillan.

Hare, R.M. (1972), 'Rules of war and moral reasoning', *Philosophy and Public Affairs*, 1, pp.166–81.

Hennessy, Peter (1986), *Cabinet*, Oxford: Basil Blackwell.

Hennessy, Peter (1989), *Whitehall*, London: Secker & Warburg.

Leigh, David (1988), *The Wilson Plot*, London: Heinemann.

Norton-Taylor, Richard (1985), *The Ponting Affair*, London: Cecil Woolf.

O'Toole, Barry J. (1989), 'The FDA and the GCHQ affair: a prediction made manifest', *Public Policy and Administration*, 1, 3, pp.22–31.

O'Toole, Barry J. (1990), 'T.H. Green and ethics of senior officials in British central government', *Public Administration*, 68, pp.337–52.

Parker Proceedings (1957), *Proceedings of the Tribunal Appointed to Inquire into Allegations that Information about the Raising of the Bank Rate was Improperly Disclosed, with Minutes of Evidence taken before the Tribunal*, London: HMSO.

Parker Report (1958), *Report of the Tribunal to Inquire into Allegations of Improper Disclosures relating to the Raising of the Bank Rate* (Cmnd 350), London: HMSO.

Ponting, Clive (1985), *The Right to Know: The inside story of the Belgrano Affair*, London and Sydney: Sphere.

Treasury and Civil Service Committee (1986), *First Report from the Treasury and Civil Service Committee, Session 1986–7, Ministers and Civil Servants: Together with the Proceedings of the Committee*, HC62, London: HMSO.

Wallas, Graham (1908), *Human Nature in Politics*, London: Constable.

Walzer, Richard (1973), 'Political action: the problem of dirty hands', *Philosophy and Public Affairs*, 2, pp.160–80.

Wright, Peter (1987), *Spycatcher*, New York: Viking.

Nine

Public Service and Democratic Accountability

COLIN CAMPBELL SJ

This chapter examines public servants' democratic accountability. Its analyses and findings consider how systems might foster ethical behaviour among civil servants. It recognises from the outset that officials experience serious conflicts between adherence to the internal discipline of bureaucratic organisations and the requirements of public service in a democratic society. In this regard, two schools of thought have emerged. One – that of the hierarchs – seeks to channel accountability so that it flows directly and exclusively up through superiors, then to ministers and, eventually, to legislators. The other – that of the pluralists – asserts that life is not that simple. Officials often press their views within the policy arena as persuasively, though more discreetly, as politicians. Furthermore, not all situations they meet fit neatly into hierarchical modes of resolving conflicts of conscience. This chapter makes a special effort to assess the viability of changes in accountability prescribed by public-choice and managerial theories of bureaucracy.

HIERARCHICAL AND DEMOCRATIC ACCOUNTABILITY

As a Jesuit, I have little difficulty understanding the reasoning behind hierarchical accountability within complex organisations. One follows explicit orders. One consults with superiors over what should be done. One does not want to be pestering those in charge – and they do not always make themselves available for immediate consultation. In many instances, one makes judgments and uses discretion. When doing so, however, one always tries to keep within the parameters of the superior's 'mind'.

If one considers the bureaucratic culture in United States, United Kingdom, Canada and Australia, one finds that in all four systems – though more in the United

Kingdom than anywhere else – officials have frequently expressed their relation-ships with civil service superiors and/or their political masters in terms very similar to those used in religious orders. Take, for instance, this rendering of accountability by a member of Canada's Finance Department:

> I'm most accountable to my minister. I must assist him in the discharge of his mandate. I work, of course, most closely with [the assistant deputy minister of my department] ... In my view, however, even if the minister knows only 2 per cent of all that is going on in the department, he still is responsible and accountable for the whole 100 per cent. I must hold up my per cent of the whole by giving the best possible advice, from a professional point of view. (Campbell and Szablowski, 1979, p.193)

One can detect in the above statement a dynamic similar to that which rests behind obedience within the religious order:

> All should keep their resolution firm to observe obedience and to distinguish themselves in it, not only in the matters of obligation but also in the others, even though nothing else is perceived except the indication of the superior's will without an expressed command. (Ignatius of Loyola, 1559, No.547)

Thus, neither hierarchically accountable public servants nor obedient members of a religious order construe their obligations to their superiors as being confined to explicit orders. Their commitment to serve extends to the anticipation of superiors' wishes and the duty to apprise them of matters which they might otherwise have overlooked.

Democratic accountability in public service, however, constitutes a different subject from hierarchical accountability. Democratic accountability takes us out-side the framework of obligations within a specific organisational structure. Even hierarchically-oriented officials keep a weather eye open beyond their immediate superiors to the political leadership of their department. The latter derive their legitimacy through their claim to embody the will of the people as defined in periodic elections.

Democratically-oriented officials take the notion of political legitimacy a step further. They know that the popular support of their political masters ebbs and flows. Close to election time, for instance, they will attempt to divine whether the government will receive a renewed mandate or whether an opposition party will obtain power. In the former case, they will be trying to ascertain the likely strength of the government after the election and the types of priorities which it will be pursuing. If it looks as if the 'outs' will probably become the, 'ins', democratical-ly-oriented officials will begin preparations which they hope will anticipate the type of mandate received by the new government and will assess which planks in its platform will rise to the top of its agenda.

Apart from by assessing the standing of the current government or administration, officials develop other ways of deciphering the public will than simply ascertaining what their political masters want. For example, they take an independent sounding of the public mood – especially as found among their client groups. Or, they might try simply to read what would be the 'mind' of average citizens if they became aware of one or another problem. As an Australian official put it:

...if we are dealing with a ticklish problem, I always ask myself, 'If the public knew what I was doing, how would my actions look?' I keep that in mind very consciously. (Confidential Interview, December 1988)

Research has indicated that systems vary considerably in the degree to which officials weigh the general interests of the public along with other factors in their view of accountability. Virtually every official interviewed in US, UK and Canadian central co-ordinating agencies in the late 1970s reported at least some element of hierarchical thinking in their rendering of their accountability. On the other hand, only forty-two, twenty-four and thirty-five per cent of, respectively, US, UK and Canadian respondents cited accountability to the general public as an important factor when they dealt with conflicts over their responsibilities (Campbell, 1983, p.304).

Interestingly, US political appointees interviewed in 1979 during the Carter administration proved slightly less likely than career civil servants to consider accountability to the general public as important (forty per cent compared with forty-five per cent). Data from a series of interviews conducted in 1983 under Reagan yielded a dramatically lower figure for appointees, seven per cent (Campbell, 1986, p.233). This finding would seem to staunch any inclination for scholars to assume that politicisation rests at the root of officials' openness to democratic accountability.

In the formulation of accountability rendered by the Australian official cited above, the role of a notional John Q. Public peering over one's shoulder parallels that played by an omniscient God in the minds of the obedient religious:

> They should keep in view God our Creator and Lord, for whom such obedience
> is practised ... all of us should exert ourselves not to miss any point of perfection
> which we can with God's grace attain ... (Ignatius of Loyola, 1559, No.547)

However, a sense of democratic accountability differs from the feeling that one holds a special responsibility to adhere to the dictates of one's conscience.

In some respects, conscience – whether based on religious belief or secular-humanistic conviction – overarches the various issues associated with conflicting obligations of a hierarchical or democratic nature. When officials consider the dictates of their consciences, they engage in the process of prioritising various obligations. For instance, officials could conceivably construe their loyalty to their superiors and/or responsiveness to the public as moral obligations on the basis that they have committed themselves to serve one or the other or both.

Many officials might believe that more fundamental moral values might – in extreme cases – override loyalty and responsiveness as criteria upon which to base their decisions and actions. Such officials might fudge answers to enquiries from the press about a scandal in order to prevent disproportionate damage to their superiors' reputations, the national security or the public interest. However, they probably would not go so far as to lie under oath about the facts surrounding the scandal.

The parallel between the mind-set of the obedient religious and the democrati-cally-orientated civil servant might prompt us to conclude that the latter constitutes simply a secular instance of the former. Indeed, Benjamin Jowett – the Oxford don who advised Sir Stafford Northcote and Sir Charles Trevelyan on reform of the

British civil service – implied as much when he argued that students not choosing Holy Orders might well find a similar outlet in becoming government officials:

> [The new opportunities] would provide us what we always wanted, a stimulus reaching far beyond the Fellowship, for those not intending to take Orders ... The inducement thus offered to us would open a new field of knowledge: it would give us another root striking into a new soil of society. (Jowett, quoted in Chapman and Greenaway, 1980, pp.40–1)

However, religious obedience assumes only one ultimate divine master while democratic accountability affirms the responsibility of the public servant to the will of the people.

Hierarchical accountability works well for the religious because it focuses on divine will as discerned by superiors. Also, it holds very great sway in the secular state if the system imparts to superiors a special aura of legitimacy. In Whitehall, for example, officials act in the name of the Crown and on behalf of ministers who base their credibility on the confidence of the House of Commons. Max Weber noted the overlap between appeals for loyalty based on religion or secular authority:

> ... status groups that are attempting to rule over large territories or large organizations – the Venetian aristocratic counsellors, the Spartans, the Jesuits in Paraguay, or a modern officer corps with a prince at its head – can maintain their alertness and their superiority over their subjects only by means of very strict discipline ... Military leadership uses emotional means of all sorts – just as the most sophisticated techniques of religious discipline, the *exercitia spiritualia* of Ignatius Loyola, do in their way. (Weber, 1921a, pp.253–4)

In some senses, the discipline of bureaucracy poses very clear threats to political accountability. Weber drew attention to this in his renowned characterisation of the actual relationship between politicians and bureaucrats:

> The 'political master' finds himself in the position of the 'dilettante' who stands opposite the 'expert', facing the trained official who stands within the management of administration. (Weber, 1921b, pp.232–3)

Weber did not exempt democracies from this analysis. In fact, he asserted that his assessment holds even when bureaucracy

> serves a 'people', equipped with the weapons of 'legislative initiative', the 'referendum' and the right to remove officials ... Every bureaucracy seeks to increase the superiority of the professionally informed by keeping their knowledge and intentions secret.

In such civil service cultures, an admission by any official that he conducted himself as if John Q. Public were observing his every move would strike horror into the hearts of his colleagues.

Some scholars have argued that the United States has limited the role of its merit-based, permanent public service precisely because it values democratic more than hierarchical accountability. The framers of the American constitution laid the groundwork for this with the system of checks and balances which constrained discretion of executive authority. This formed the basis for the pluralistic character of American government.

Within this context, the state and its authority became fragmented – with pressures from the president and his appointees, Congress and outside groups all bearing down on the career civil servant in almost equal proportions. Many observers have even gone so far as to assert that the US executive lacks almost totally a unifying dimension and, by extension, internal coherence:

> To whom ... would the permanent legion of bureaucrats be accountable? The answer is to no single source of authority ... The quandary is how to induce harmony in the executive branch ... the response is to politicize ... Despite occasional victories, the myth of civil service neutrality, essential for the legitimization of the bureaucracy ... failed to take hold among the American political elite. (Rockman, 1984, p.48)

The US situation contrasts sharply with that in systems which derive from the Westminster tradition. Yet the latter have changed very substantially in the past two decades. Even in Whitehall, officials feel much more comfortable dealing directly with client groups than they had previously. The creation in 1979 of House of Commons select committees which shadow specific departments greatly enhanced the exposure of civil servants to parliamentary inquiries.

Furthermore, the long duration of Margaret Thatcher's government enabled her to leave her mark on the upper echelons of the permanent civil service – perhaps more than any prime minister in this century. In this regard, a distinguished Royal Institute of Public Administration Working Group which looked into Mrs Thatcher's influence on the upper reaches of the public service characterised this as 'personalisation' rather than 'politicisation'.

> To some extent the appointment process has become more personalized in the sense that at the top level 'catching the eye' of the Prime Minister ... may now be more important than in the past. Evidence to our group suggests that personal contacts and impressions play a role in promotion decisions. Downing Street communicates more opinions about the performance of civil servants, even down to quite junior levels, based on impressions made at meetings with the Prime Minister (RIPA Working Group 1987, p.43)

One wonders about this benign interpretation. My own interviews with over 130 present and recently resigned Whitehall officials since 1986 suggest that personalisation has, in many cases, altered respondents' views of themselves as agents. Significant numbers have begun to consider themselves quasi-independent operators with considerable scope for functioning outside the usual parameters of Whitehall hierarchical control. The following remarks of an official involved in a major initiative put the matter bluntly (I have edited the passage so as to protect the identity of the respondent and his Department):

> I think what was interesting while I was doing it ... I did it for four years ... was that it became clear that it would not be possible for me to revert to a traditional position in the department. I was unusual in having a rather personalized position. I'm not sure it would have done me any good in the long tern. But, within the short term, it was very useful. I had a good relationship with my minister ... I really constructed the series of speeches he delivered on [the initiative] ... I did all that, really as originator as well as author. He was very receptive about having words put in his mouth ... I don't want to make it sound too grand, but it meant that I was running the political side in terms of presenting the arguments as well as the implementation in terms of delivering [the policy] ... It wasn't altogether easy to see where I would find anything as satisfying to do after that. (Confidential Interview 1987)

It becomes clear that we must reassess the compatibility of hierarchical and democratic accountability in Westminster systems as well as in the United States.

POLITICAL AUTHORITIES, BUREAUCRATS AND ACCOUNTABILITY

No matter what the system, we find jagged edges in the boundary between elected political authorities and their appointees, on the one hand, and the permanent bureaucracy, on the other. Normally we view the United States as the extreme case. Career officials often seem as eager to keep in the good graces of key senators and congressmen as in those of appointees. Each president, of course, hopes that the latter will turn their departments and agencies around to his priorities and policies.

In response to the tendency for permanent officials to play legislators and appointees off against each other, successive presidents – especially Republican ones – have tried in the past two decades to impose greater discipline on civil servants. Their main devices have included: strict screening of appointees to ensure that their commitment to the administration has reached a depth which will allow them to withstand pressures from their host department to 'go native'; deeper penetration of the various levels of department hierarchies – political appointments now encompass three levels below secretaries and have spread to around half of the fourth level; and exclusion of career officials from policy deliberations – both by keeping them out of meetings and assigning them developmental work for pieces of policies while denying access to the comprehensive plans through which the parts will fit into the whole (Nathan, 1975; Nathan, 1983; Newland, 1983, p.2; Campbell, 1986, pp.69–75, 183–8, 217; Hansen and Levine, 1988, pp.264–6).

Politicisation American-style has really amounted to open warfare against the career civil servant. The Reagan and Bush administrations in particular have abandoned the hope of establishing creative working relationships with permanent officials. They have chosen instead to drive a wedge between appointees and their officials. As a result, officials lose on two counts. They must adhere rigidly to the orders that they have received from political masters. However, they take these instructions from on high and gain little exposure to the processes from which these evolved.

One Reagan appointee who occupied a senior position in the Office of Personnel Management presented the strategy in stark terms:

> Control over the process ... must be retained by the political executive and his immediate political staff. Very little information will be put in writing. Career staff will supply information, but they should never become involved in the formation of agenda-related objectives. Similarly, once controversial policy goals are formulated, they should not be released in total to the career staff. Thus, the political executive and his political staff become 'jigsaw puzzle' managers. (Sanera, 1984, pp.514–5, quoted in Hansen and Levine, 1988, p.264)

In my research interviews several budget examiners in the Office of Management and Budget portrayed in vivid terms the extent to which the Reagan administration had closed them out of the policy process. In the words of one respondent:

They didn't want analysis. They pretty much knew what they wanted to do. So, an analytic piece which either said 'Yes, you're right, go ahead' or 'No, you're wrong, this is going to create havoc' wasn't the kind of thing they needed. They didn't want to hear if it was wrong. And, if it was right, it was a waste of time to do the analysis. (Campbell, 1986, p.185)

An irony presents itself here. In the United States, presidents have opted for the strategy of keeping permanent officials where they will be seen but not heard. In Westminster systems, officials have been moving toward greater symbiosis with their political masters. At least, the developments in the United Kingdom under Mrs Thatcher discussed above suggest this.

In Canada, officials have since 1940 attended and participated relatively freely in Cabinet committees (Heeney, 1949; Granatstein, 1982) – still a rare occurrence in either Britain or Australia. Notwithstanding periodic attempts on the part of Canadian prime ministers to curtail this practice (Van Loon, 1985, p.311; Campbell, 1988a, pp.321–2), it has persisted right up to the current government (Campbell, 1985, pp.323–4; Campbell, 1988a, pp.329–30). Gordon Robertson, while cabinet secretary – Canada's top mandarin – defended the Canadian practice as follows:

The relationships between ministers and officials are seen in interesting and sensitive focus at cabinet committee meetings. Ministers in general carry the discussion, but officials participate actively, especially on factual and operational aspects ... Both normally participate in active discussion. It is a blend of roles that requires mutual confidence ... The exposure of senior officials to the thinking and policy concerns of ministers helps them to explain to their departments the logic of decisions that might otherwise seem wrong, incomprehensible or 'petty politics'. (Robertson, 1971)

In Australia, the most obvious symbiosis between politicians and officials has occurred in the relationship between recent prime ministers and their Department of the Prime Minister and Cabinet (PM&C). Gough Whitlam (1972–5) and Malcolm Fraser (1975–83) expected PM&C to go beyond simply processing cabinet business to actively advancing the progress of their top priorities through the governmental apparatus – even though PM&C organisation consists of career civil servants (Weller, 1985, pp.138–9).

Weller has also observed that PM&C has learned to adapt to the 'demands and style' of individual prime ministers (p.13). This fact takes on special significance when we reflect upon the appointment process for the permanent heads of departments in Australia. In recent years, prime ministers have revealed a marked preference for PM&C deputy secretaries when selecting new departmental secretaries (Weller, 1985, pp.95–9; Kelleher, 1989, pp.9–11). Bob Hawke's PM&C proved less interventionist in specific issues than did Whitlam's or Fraser's. However, some officials in PM&C, the Treasury and the Finance Department struck a very strong alliance with the 'economic rationalists' in the Hawke cabinet who pressed for budget stringency and deregulation. One committee – the pivotal Expenditure Review Committee – increasingly allowed extensive participation by officials in its deliberations.

The two strategies for dealing with permanent officials – the recent US approach of taking them out of the policy loop and the Westminster one of seeking officials with whom a government can establish symbiosis – constitute different responses to the same difficulty. At the beginning of this century, reformists had sought to strengthen the integrity of government by sharpening the distinction between policy-making and administration. They saw their age as an era in which detached managerialism would supplant the inefficiency and ineffectiveness of patronage.

Woodrow Wilson became the most prominent advocate of this perspective (Wilson, 1941). It soon began to dominate thinking about the relative roles of politicians and bureaucrats. The fact that the policy/administration dichotomy gained such currency in public administration serves as testimony of the influence of the reformist view. General Charles G. Dawes – who became the first director of the Bureau of the Budget in 1921 – reflected the spirit of his time in this description of the role of his new agency:

> No Cabinet officer on the bridge with the President advising as to what direction the ship of state should sail ... will properly serve the captain of the ship or its passengers, the public, if he resents the call of the director of the budget from the stoke-hole, put there by the captain to see that coal is not wasted. (Price, 1951, p.169, quoted in Berman, 1975, p.6)

Inevitably, a reaction to this formulation of the relationship between politicians and bureaucrats emerged. Along the lines of Weber, observers began to note that officials – through astute use of their knowledge of the 'stoke-hole' – could establish the parameters within which the politicians determined the course of the ship of state (Galloway, 1946, p.150). In 1952, Norton C. Long went so far as to assert that civil servants' relative independence within the policy process posed a significant menace to the system of checks and balances as prescribed in the Constitution (1952, p.810).

Students of public administration still have not resolved the issues raised by the critics of bureaucracy. Essentially two schools have developed. One – that of the hierarchs – advocates measures which would place permanent officials under clearer political control. The other – that of the pluralists – does not believe that career civil servants' ability to effect the contours of policies necessarily jeopardises democratic accountability. They conceive of the policy process as a multidimensional arena in which permanent officials win and lose some just as in any other sector.

HIERARCHS

The previous section drew attention to the similarities between hierarchical accountability in the religious order and that found in traditional public services. In both cases, individuals obey superiors because society ascribes to them special charisma. However, in both contexts individuals exercise considerable discretion – even though the norms of their organisations prescribe that they do so with constant attention to the likely preferences of their ultimate superiors.

I noted that – in democratic regimes – the insertion of the will of the people as the ultimate object of accountability makes it much more difficult to achieve discipline in bureaucratic organisations. Religious and/or aristocratic reflexes do not undergird discipline in modern public-service organisations. Therefore, their leaders do not enjoy the qualitative edge in claiming legitimacy that their predecessors did in traditional regimes.

Relatively closed organisations in which hierarchical accountability holds sway rely in no small part on the symbiosis that develops between superiors and the individuals under them. The former frequently find it unnecessary to give explicit orders to the latter if the 'minds' of the two correspond on most matters. The Constitutions of the Society of Jesus acknowledge this fact. The early Society operated with numerous members in far-off missions. These often found regular communication with Rome difficult if not impossible.

In this regard, the Constitutions state that, in principle, members should receive as explicit instructions as possible before going on a mission:

> No matter where the superior sends anyone, he will give him complete instructions, *ordinarily* in writing, about the manner of proceeding, and the means which he desires to be used for the end sought. (Ignatius of Loyola, 1559, No.629, emphasis added.)

However, the assumption of a certain amount of symbiosis enters the equation in this important qualification:

> All this should be done with a care proportionately greater according to the nature of the work, whether important or difficult, and of the character of the persons sent, and insofar as they do or do not need advice and instruction ... *The word 'ordinarily' is used because sometimes the person sent is so instructed and sagacious that this writing is not necessary. But in a word, whenever these instructions are necessary they should be given.* (Ibid., Nos. 629–30)

I am arguing here that democratic processes operate on such a broad canvass and with such a cacophony of voices that some observers – those I have termed hierarchs – have despaired of maintaining bureaucratic accountability without clear and binding constraints.

We find hierarchs on either side of the political fence in the United States. In the liberal camp, the perspective gained currency among those frustrated during the 1960s with the difficulty with which social and civil rights legislation gained the approval of Congress. In some respects, James MacGregor Burns provided the liberal hierarchs' manifesto in his *The Deadlock of Democracy: Four party politics in America* (1963). This work attributed the intractability and non-responsiveness of the American system to the separation of powers. The sharp dichotomy between Congress and the executive had led to four-party government – with presidential Democrats and Republicans and congressional Democrats and Republicans. Burns advocated several structural changes which would reduce the relative autonomy of the congressional branch of both parties (pp.327–30).

Even in our current era in which the social and civil rights agendas have taken a back seat to sustaining economic growth, liberal hierarchs have continued to promote the view that greater party discipline would improve the coherence of American governance – even if reducing the deficit and raising taxes have supplanted social and racial justice on the political agenda. For instance, James L.

Sundquist – who characterises the current American system as 'divided government' – describes Anglo-parliamentary systems in almost idyllic terms:

> Those who have been frustrated with the stalemates of the American system ... have looked longingly across the Atlantic and northward toward Canada and admired the streamlined unity of other democratic governments. In the parliamentary democracy, the legislative majority is sovereign, and a committee of that majority – the cabinet – both leads the legislature and directs the executive branch. Power is unified. Responsibility is clearly fixed. Strong party discipline assures prime ministers and their cabinets that they can act quickly and decisively without fear, normally, of being repudiated by their legislatures. (1986, p.14; see also Sundquist, 1988–9)

Obviously, those of us who hail from either Britain or Canada might not readily recognise our systems in Sundquist's glowing description. However, we probably all would find just a kernel of truth in his rendering of coherence in London and Ottawa. This, in turn, might tempt us to conclude that making bureaucrats more sensitive to the priorities of politicians did not rate as a major concern during the expansive phase of governance in parliamentary systems.

In fact, from the late 1960s through to the mid 1970s both conservative and liberal governments sought ways to improve their ability to respond coherently to public demands through the enhancement of the central staffs available to the Prime Minister and/or Cabinet. Thus, we saw the creation of the Central Policy Review Staff in the UK Cabinet Office under Edward Heath, the emergence of the first Policy Unit in No.10 under Harold Wilson, the ascendancy of both the Prime Minister's Office and the Privy Council Office under Pierre Trudeau, and politicisation of the Department of the Prime Minister and Cabinet under Whitlam. Richard J. Van Loon – a Canadian political scientist who has occupied several top government positions in Ottawa – has maintained that Trudeau expanded the central co-ordinative and control capacity in the public service as part of a conscious strategy to set up a counter-bureaucracy to that which he believed had thwarted his agenda for change:

> Trudeau and his advisors appear to have hypothesized that the most effective counter for one bureaucratic institution is another with parallel responsibilities. The political advisory power of the mandarins was to be attenuated through the increase of size and influence of PMO and PCO and their planning functions were to be faced with competition from a revamped PCO using a more systematic approach to the divination and implementation of political priorities. (Van Loon, 1981)

Conservatives came relatively lately to the view that imposition of discipline might advance their agendas. Public choice theorists – among whom William Niskanen has achieved the greatest prominence – have spearheaded the hierarch movement in the conservative camp. Essentially, they have sought greatly to constrict the discretion of permanent officials.

From the standpoint of comparative study, we should keep in mind the fact that Niskanen chose bureaus as the unit of his analysis. He distinguishes these organisations from others according to two criteria: (1) the owners and employees of bureaus do not derive personal income from the profits of the organisation; (2) at least part of the revenues of bureaus accrues from appropriations or grants rather than simply sales (1971, pp.15–6).

Many organisations might satisfy the criteria that Niskanen employs. However, he centres his attention on governmental institutions (1971, pp.21–2). Significantly, he includes among bureaucrats both those who have dedicated themselves to a permanent career in the civil service and those who received their appointments from the elected executive. The identification of the latter with the former reflects the degree to which writers of the time assumed that appointees rarely failed to succumb to the pressures on them to 'go native'.

Niskanen wrote in a period of governmental expansion. Thus, the tendency in that epoch for bureaucracies to seek and, usually, gain enhanced budgets absorbs Niskanen's attention. He asserts that bureaucrats demonstrate a deep-seated inclination toward 'budget maximization' (1971, p.38). This phenomenon owes its strength to the link between individual officials' personal utility and the benefits that a robust budget can advance. These include an adequate salary, perquisites, public reputation, power, patronage and the output of the bureaucrats' organisation.

In prescribing a method for restraining budget maximising Niskanen departed from the conventional wisdom of the day. This held that those seeking to control bureaucrats would advance their cause by acquiring more detailed information on the actual operation of policy programmes (Niskanen 1973a, pp.6–8; author cites Wildavsky, 1961 in support of his position). To Niskanen, those trying to control budgets should set aside instrumental objectives such as comprehensiveness, detail, procedural rationality and control. Instead, they should adopt budgetary processes according to whether these achieve the desired outcome – control of deficits.

To this end, Niskanen proposed a number of structural changes in the budgetary process which would focus both Congress and the executive branch on the task of limiting budgets. Many of these would rely upon automatic rather than *ad hoc* mechanisms. For instance, a committee of congressional budget leaders would agree to 'target' outlays which would then be approved by both houses and the President, Congress would have to offset spending beyond that recommended in the agreed budget with dollar-for-dollar increases in personal income taxes, and the Executive Office of the President would assume an active role in providing express guidance to the Office of Management and Budget on budget priorities – making 'the proposed budget a more effective instrument of the political interests of the President' (1973a, pp.17–19, 55–7).

Subsequently, Niskanen recommended steps to break down the seniority system which allowed senators and congressmen to develop specialties and to become captives of their bureaucratic clients. These measures would involve the randomisation of the assignment of committee positions (1973b, p.59).

The public choice perspective, as articulated by Niskanen and others, has gained a wide readership outside the United States. In fact, Niskanen wrote a monograph – published in the United Kingdom for a British audience – which professed to offer an American view of the task of controlling bureaucracy (1973b). The work did little to fine-tune the advice it offered to the circumstances of the British system.

Niskanen urged that cabinet secretaries receive their initial portfolios independent of their personal and regional backgrounds and that prime ministers periodically shuffle their cabinets on a random basis (p.60). Such recommendations would doubtlessly strike any knowledgeable observer of parliamentary systems as extremely naïve.

Notwithstanding the lack of detailed and salient content, Niskanen's book – allegedly – so influenced Margaret Thatcher that she urged all the members of her first cabinet to read it. Moreover an examination of how Mrs Thatcher's government handled the deficit suggests that it took a leaf from the public-choice approach by making budgeting less *ad hoc* and more automatic (Campbell, 1983, pp.186–9; Wildavsky, 1983, p.164).

Mrs Thatcher extended the imposition of cash limits – specific cash ceilings on departments' expenditure first introduced by Callaghan – to many sectors of government which previously had been exempted. She was not the first prime minister to rely upon a Star Chamber system whereby a group of senior ministers impose spending constraints in cases where the Treasury has failed to win compliance from departments. However, her use of this device exceeded that of her predecessor both in terms of its regularity and effectiveness. Further, she let fall into disuse Policy Analysis and Review – a technique introduced under Heath whereby interdepartmental Whitehall groups assessed in depth the effectiveness of programmes which had come under question. Much as with the Reagan administration in the United States, the Thatcher government had taken the view that the key to getting bureaucracy under control was to tilt the playing field in favour of macro-economic criteria.

The automation of budgeting has never taken root in Canada – notwithstanding several failed attempts under Mulroney (Campbell, 1988a). However, it has served as the guiding principle behind the operation of the Expenditure Review Committee in Australia and the group of economic rationalist ministers upon which its effectiveness relies (Keating and Dixon, 1988).

At the same time that public-choice assaults on the discretion and latitude for independent advocacy have become the order of the day in the United States and several other parliamentary systems, the political leadership of many of the same countries has also sought ways of making officials more creative in managerial terms. Using the private sector as a model, this approach has tried to make government agencies function more like business corporations. The movement has operated from the premise that – as they become more aware of their objectives and running costs – individual public-service managers will make more imaginative decisions about the types of projects they embrace and will get more value for money out of their resources.

Interestingly, US advocates of managerialism have found that the fragmented nature of their governmental system has made the dissemination of this approach very difficult. The fact that Ronald Reagan's principal advisers on management – Joseph R. Wright (the deputy director of OMB through much of the administration) and J. Peter Grace (an industrialist) – both launched grandiose plans (Campbell,

1986, pp.192–3) meant that the administration took on much more change than it could possibly accomplish in eight years. In addition, the administration did little to counter the traditional OMB instinct to promote change through 'tightly focused internal control systems and initiatives' (Hansen and Levine, 1988, pp.267-8). On the other hand, the UK, Canadian, Australian and New Zealand governments have all introduced managerialist programmes which – whatever their actual effectiveness – have made their presence felt throughout the bureaucratic apparatus (Aucoin, 1988; Boston, 1987; Considine, 1988; Fry, 1988; Fry *et al.* 1988; Keating, 1988).

In a recent article, Peter Aucoin has argued that the public choice and managerialist paradigms derive from different – in some respects inconsistent – premises (1990, pp.125–6). Public choice styles the problem of bureaucracy as one of control and seeks measures through which elected politicians might 'tame' the public service by putting it under tighter political direction. Managerialists, on the other hand, believe that the difficulty goes beyond bureaucracy *per se* to its tendency to operate overly hierarchically.

Notwithstanding the intuitive appeal of Aucoin's observations, neither the public-choice nor the managerialist literature seems to recognise the potential incompatibility of the two paradigms. Niskanen, for instance, expressly advocated managerialist strategies. He called for more competitive and less specialised bureaucracies whose survival would depend upon their ability to market their services to the political authorities:

> Bureaucrats ... would be permitted to offer a wide range of public services ...
> There would be no 'strong' departments or 'strong' secretaries. The choice of
> which bureau or combination of bureaus to supply a specific service would be
> forced to the level of the executive review. (1973b, p.61)

Similarly, Graham Scott and Peter Gorringe – two members of the New Zealand Treasury who have offered the most theoretically elaborate expression of managerialism provided by practitioners to date – fashion their approach as working in tandem with public choice (1988, p.2). Scott and Gorringe base their analysis on the concept of agency as developed by A. A. Alchain (they cite, for instance, Alchain and Woodward, 1987). Here bureaucrats serve as the agents of politicians who, in turn, function as the agents of the populace. In this regard, the authors distinguish between strategies for improving 'performance' and those for enhancing 'accountability' (Scott and Gorringe, 1988, p.6). The former concern whether officials 'produce the outputs of services agreed to, and whether they do so efficiently'; the latter focus on whether 'politicians ... buy the right services to achieve social goals like wealth, justice and the relief of suffering.' Politicians need not purchase all of the services which advance social goals from the bureaucracy.

Over the past few years, I have been conducting a study, with Donald Naulls and John Halligan, of the implementation of managerial reforms in two countries – the United Kingdom and Australia. We have found that, in each system, officials in line departments give very mixed reviews of efforts to improve their delegated authority over running costs. These expenses – which take in personnel and management – normally constitute a relatively small proportion of departments' budgets.

By way of example, one top UK official in a department which has distinguished itself by the seriousness with which it has pursued Britain's Financial Management Initiative believed that the Treasury still had not devolved the most significant central controls of running costs:

> I said to Treasury, and so did many others, 'This is a fine doctrine, but unless you believe it and are prepared to implement it and accept what goes with it, it won't work.' Because you can't say to someone, 'You're responsible for your budget and you won't get any more money, and you can carry your own account', if at the same time you are saying, 'I will determine your staff, what they will be paid, how much you will pay for accommodation ...' And, this is exactly how it worked out. The amount of delegation of eventual control was at most five per cent. (Confidential Interview, July 1988)

Several Australian respondents pursued a similar line in reference to the Finance Department. In the words of one:

> I really don't see ... this enormous extra flexibility. Year by year when you're in a situation of 'OK, here's another 2.5 per cent, here's another 4 per cent or here's your target of 200 million that you've got to save ...' Yes, you have some flexibility in terms of attempting to identify how you save those couple of hundred million dollars. But, that's not totally new. We've always tended to have that sort of flexibility anyway. The sort of flexibility that I heard touted was more a question of 'Here you are with a certain size bucket and we'll be flexible about how you rearrange your priorities within it'. When they were talking about flexibility, they weren't talking about the bucket getting smaller and smaller all the time. (Confidential Interview, January 1989)

RE-EXAMINING PLURALISM IN THE AGE OF GOVERNMENTAL MINIMALISM

Aucoin's argument about the potential incompatibility of public-choice theory and managerialism brings us to the issue of whether we can expect any players or institutions within the policy arena to espouse and adhere to monotonic motives and goals. For instance, the assertion found in Scott and Gorringe to the effect that we should evaluate bureaucrats on the basis of efficient delivery of outputs and politicians on accountability for outcomes obfuscates a great deal of overlap between both – including the orientations of the two types of players and what they actually achieve.

In recent analyses of orientations toward budget maximisation among senior government officials in the United States, United Kingdom and Canada, Donald Naulls and I argue that overly zealous pursuit of public-choice strategies can unjustifiably ascribe self-serving motives to public servants and underrate institutional factors which serve as checks on bureaucratic expansionism (1991; 1992). With respect to its portability from the US to parliamentary systems, we cautioned that differences in both the structure of bureaucratic careers and the nature of power relationships – between the political executive, the bureaucracy, the legislature and interest groups – make it unlikely that the conditions which lead to a high degree of budget maximisation in the United States will prevail elsewhere.

Both political appointees and career civil servants in the United States – especially the latter – tend to focus their careers much more narrowly than their opposite numbers in the United Kingdom and Canada (Heclo, 1977, pp.116–20; 1985, pp.18–20). For US career officials, movement from one specialised section of a department to another occurs rarely. Much less would we expect transfers from department to department. Thus, permanent officials in the United States develop blinkered perspectives early on and become much more territorial than their counterparts in parliamentary systems. In addition, parliamentary systems all lack truly transformative legislatures. That is, legislators in Britain and Canada do not usually enjoy the capacity to mould and reshape laws and budgets independent of the guidance provided by the political executive as embodied in the leadership of the government party (Polsby, 1975, p.277).

The absence of long and reasonably secure tenure in specialised fields and transformative legislatures greatly retards the development of strong client–patron relationships in parliamentary systems. In the United States, the currency that such terms as 'sub-government', 'iron triangles' and 'atomization' have attained suggests the extent to which officials can play both the political executive and Congress against each other to get their own way (see, for instance, Olson, 1982, pp.50–2; Aberbach and Rockman, 1981, pp.94–100).

To date, Naulls' and my analysis has focused on officials working in central co-ordinating departments. We looked at five groups – political appointees and career officials interviewed during the Carter administration (1979), political appointees under the Reagan administration (1983), career officials in the United Kingdom at the end of the Callaghan government (1978) and career officials in Canada in 1976 under Trudeau. Broadly, we found that officials who credited their careers as dedicated to public service as a vocation and/or a relatively specialised field scored the highest as budget maximisers.

Interestingly, in all five groups those who focused their careers on budget examination throughout the bureaucratic system proved strongly inclined toward maximisation when it came to the needs of their own unit. Niskanen himself worked in the Office of Management and Budget at the time of *Bureaucracy and Representative Government*'s publication and – notwithstanding his advocacy of stringency for everyone else – made a strong plea for the enhancement of the resources of OMB (1971, pp.221–2). Is it possible that budget examiners heap burdens upon others which they are not prepared to bear themselves?

Most strikingly – with respect to the central assertion of the public-choice perspective – officials who viewed their careers from the standpoint of personal utility came out as budget minimisers not maximisers. We coded officials as orientated towards personal utility if they cited, when asked what they would miss if they left government service, personal opportunities such as the experience of managing a large number of people, the facilities and materials available for conducting research or carrying out one's responsibilities, lifestyle issues (including an adequate living or job security), advancement denied in other sectors (for example, for women or members of minorities) and/or an outlet for a professional skill not highly prized in the private sector.

Among the US groups, Reagan appointees cited personal utility as something they would miss if they left government much more than did career officials or appointees interviewed during the Carter administration (57 per cent compared with 17 and 8 per cent respectively). Indeed, the Reagan appointees who stressed this factor also yielded exceedingly low scores on maximisation. Generally, the results of this research suggest a proactive/passive dichotomy among officials. Those motivated toward the positive task of governance tend to be maximisers while those happy with imbibing the sense of 'being there' lean toward minimisation.

This observation should call back to mind Scott and Gorringe's assertion, as noted above, that officials provide services while politicians pursue goals. The orientations of the Reagan respondents might well suggest to us that officials working under a minimalist view of government have placed themselves on the passive side of the proactive/passive dichotomy. On the other hand, many officials still wrestle with the desire to pursue specific goals which fit, they believe, within the framework of the public interest. Discerning the public interest and advising politicians about the wisest course of action add the element of moral agency to being a civil servant.

While neo-liberal governments have busied themselves over the past few years reinventing the policy/administration dichotomy scholars have almost uniformly abandoned it as an empirically valid concept (Campbell and Peters, 1988; Campbell, 1988b). Even students of Whitehall have for years now asserted that the dichotomy bears little or no resemblance to reality (Chapman, 1959, p.275; Puttnam 1973, pp.227, 257–8; Heclo and Wildavsky, 1974, p.3; Christoph, 1975, p.32–6; Chapman and Greenaway, 1980, pp.53, 62).

Aberbach, Putnam and Rockman have identified four 'images' which have informed enquiry into the relationships between politicians and bureaucrats (1981). The first holds that politicians make policy and bureaucrats administer it. The second allows that officials involve themselves in policy but confine their interventions to assembling and communicating the relevant facts and knowledge. The third accepts that public servants engage in political calculation and manipulation. However, they do so in response to a narrower band of concerns and with less passion or ideological commitment than do politicians. The fourth asserts that bureaucrats do develop and employ a full range of behind-the-scenes political skills and passionately commit themselves to attaining specific policy goals.

Aberbach, Putnam and Rockman consider the fourth image as applying only at the highest level of bureaucracy and in the most strategically located units. Campbell and Peters have argued, on the other hand, that 'Image IV' might prove more common than scholars might conclude at first blush (Campbell and Peters, 1988; Campbell, 1988b).

First, officials need not pursue new initiatives to develop intense views. They can hold as tenaciously to stances which preserve the status quo. Second, systemic norms which require officials to maintain an external image of detachment and operate privately should not lull us into thinking that they do not respond passionately to winning and losing. Third, the sheer size of some bureaucratic milieux preordains that officials will have to develop high-order skills at integrating policy views in a highly charged environment. Quite apart from frequent and direct exposure to political masters, the sheer size of some policy sectors and their high stakes force participants – even if the system styles them as administrators or experts – to develop political skills.

Johan P. Olsen has made the persuasive point that the styles that bureaucrats assume vary greatly according to changes in the overarching expectations of political masters (1988). He notes, for instance, that the Norwegian civil service went through a painful period of adapting its style from the 'corporate-pluralist' to the 'institutional' state with the advent of a conservative-centre government. Under the latter format, Olsen argues, the political leadership tried to increase the distance between the state and the various spheres of societal activity.

I would maintain that, despite the fact that that boundary shifts between a tight and loose fit, neo-liberals will never achieve the point where officials view themselves as 'in' but not 'of' society. The neo-liberal approach has appeared to be most successful at narrowing the band of society to which the bureaucracy believes it must, at the bidding of its political masters, attend. Further, it appears to have staunched any progress towards the view that officials who find themselves in crises of conscience ultimately owe a greater responsibility to the public interest than to the political survival of their masters.

All of the Anglo-American democracies discussed in this chapter operate within the framework of pluralism. Indeed, the US system has fragmented considerably more in the past twenty years and the parliamentary systems – through very gradual reform – have increased the opportunities for legislators to function more independently of their parties' leadership. Governments in the United States, United Kingdom, Canada and Australia have all adopted strategies seeking to constrain the substantive input of officials at the very time when others in policy arenas have found new ways to assert themselves. While the desire to restrain government spending has motivated political executives, their actions bear the cost of making public service something to which no able person would dedicate his or her life.

Accountability runs on information. Cabinet secretaries – in order to keep officials reasonably accountable – must make every effort to apprise themselves of what their department is doing. By the same token, we might expect legislatures which take their work seriously to devise structures through which they can extract information about the executive and employ this to the fullest possible extent. In both the American and the parliamentary systems, career civil servants normally believe that their accountability runs through the political leadership of their departments to the legislature – although permanent officials in parliamentary systems have followed this convention much more rigidly than have those in the United States.

Problems arise when officials – whether lower-level appointees in the United States or career civil servants in any of the systems – have acted in an unethical way at the request of their superiors or have become aware of improper behaviour on the part of their political masters. In all four systems, the cultural tendency has to some significant degree supported officials in gritting their teeth and protecting their political masters.

Thus, Rear Admiral John Poindexter – the White House national security adviser to Ronald Reagan during the Iran–Contra Affair stoically rendered an account of his actions which absolved the president of any knowledge of the diversion of funds to the Contras:

> So, although I was convinced that we could properly do it, and that the president would approve, if asked, I made a very deliberate decision not to ask the president so that I could insulate him from the decision and provide some future deniability for the president if it ever leaked out. (Poindexter, 1987)

Of course, Poindexter rescinded this testimony when defending himself during his trial on criminal charges. In a less serious case – a matter of omission rather than commission – Sir Robert Armstrong, then Secretary of the Cabinet and Head of the Home Civil Service, had to correct his own testimony in an Australian court examining the British government's case against the publication of Peter Wright's book *Spycatcher*. In this instance, Sir Robert admitted to being 'economical with the truth'.

Governments themselves might react quite differently in situations where officials leak information deemed to be confidential. In 1984, the British government came down with a vengeance on Clive Ponting for sharing information which contradicted Mrs Thatcher's public statements about location of the Argentinian cruiser *General Belgrano* at the time the Royal Navy sunk it. Following suit, the judge who presided over the case instructed the jury to ignore Ponting's defence that he leaked the information in the interest of the state. The judge opined that the interests of the government of the day and those of the state are identical. He failed to sway the jury which acquitted Ponting.

In a 1986 case, the government took an entirely different view regarding officials involved in the release of excerpts from correspondence of the Solicitor-General to the Secretary of State for Defence. The letter identified certain inaccuracies in the latter's rendering of the facts concerning the future of Westland PLC in correspondence to the managing director of Lloyds Merchant Bank (House of Commons, 1986). Three officials in the Department of Trade and Industry – whose Secretary of State was locked in a bitter dispute with the Secretary of State for Defence over Westland – arranged the leak in consultation with two colleagues in No.10 Downing Street. They did so with the approval of their Secretary of State.

The leak consisted of selected passages from the letter which were made available anonymously to the Press Association. The Secretary of State for Trade and Industry resigned in the resulting furore. However, notwithstanding a formal inquiry headed by Sir Robert Armstrong, the government failed to charge or discipline the officials who had participated in the leak. Of these, only one – the head of information in the DTI – had even tried to seek advice from a permanent department head about the leak. She was not able to reach her permanent secretary. None of the officials, thus, followed the guidelines laid down by Sir Robert in a 1985 memorandum on the duties and responsibilities of civil servants when confronted with 'crisis of conscience' cases.

A July 1986 government response to a House of Commons Treasury and Civil Service Committee's report on the duties and responsibilities of civil servants and ministers dwelt at length upon Clive Ponting's behaviour in the light of the Armstrong memorandum. It did not seem to matter that the memorandum had been issued in response to Ponting's transgression:

> ... the fact is that Mr. Ponting did not follow those procedures and did not take his specific problem either to his Permanent Secretary or to the Head of the Home Civil Service. When questioned on this matter by the Committee, Mr. Ponting indicated that he had decided that there was no point in approaching his Permanent Secretary formally because, he assumed, the Permanent Secretary was already aware of his views through previous discussions. Mr. Ponting would have been better placed to reach a conclusion if he had approached his Permanent Secretary formally with his specific problem. Instead he chose to ventilate his grievances by means of anonymous letters while he continued to occupy a position of high trust. (Prime Minister and Minister for the Civil Service, 1986)

From this author's scholarly perch on the other side of the Atlantic, the government appears to have applied a double standard in continuing to condemn Ponting – long after a jury had exonerated him – while declining to seek any punishment whatever of the officials involved in the Westland leak. Richard Chapman and Peter Hennessy have registered – though less poignantly – a similar discomfort with the belief that it is the responsibility of officials to assist their political masters in misleading the public or sharing information in an improper way (Chapman, 1988, pp.295–7; Hennessy, 1989, pp.167, 664–7, 728).

CONCLUSION

This chapter began by drawing attention to the parallels between hierarchical accountability in a religious order and that in a bureaucratic institution. To be sure, subjects in both organisations attempt, as best they can, not only to follow explicit directions but also to take on the 'mind' of their superiors. An even stronger parallel with religious orders might have existed in monarchies and aristocratic systems. All three relied upon ascriptive criteria for maintaining their legitimacy. However, democracies replace a monocratic or oligarchic leadership with popular authority. Insofar as democracies adopt pluralistic methods of decision-making officials will be likely to find themselves exposed to and torn between multiple expressions of the public interest.

Even within religious orders hierarchical accountability operates with either a tight or loose fit. In the latter case, subjects have earned the implicit trust of superiors. Thus, they exercise considerable discretion. Similar relationships develop within bureaucracies. Indeed, a symbiosis might well emerge. This process quickens when political masters consciously seek out and advance officials whose sympathies correspond. In addition, public servants – sensing a change in the wind – might adapt their priorities and styles to the political leadership of the day.

Symbiosis seems to occur more readily in parliamentary systems than it does in the United States. Still the dynamics of pluralism make such a process considerably more complicated in the bureaucracy of a democratic system than in a religious order or the state apparatus of a monarchy or oligarchy. This fact has prompted some observers to conclude that the only way to control bureaucracy in a pluralistic system is to sharply curtail its discretion and latitude for advocacy.

Both the government-expansion and budget-stringency camps have produced 'hierarchs' who have attempted to make bureaucracy more responsive to their agendas by imposing greater top-down discipline. This chapter has dwelt on the latter more than the former. This emphasis is owed largely to the degree to which public choice and managerial approaches to governance have dominated the political landscape in the past decade. Even Labour governments in Australia and New Zealand have embraced these approaches.

The analysis draws attention to several difficulties with both perspectives. First, public choice makes assumptions about the budget-maximising instincts of officials which find – at best – mixed support in empirical analysis. Second, a very substantial proportion of officials who have worked at the receiving end of managerial reforms questions fundamentally whether these actually impart the discretion that their promoters promise. Third, both theories seem to derive from naïve formulations of the proper roles of politicians and bureaucrats which students of public service roles have abandoned long ago.

The chapter has, more than anything else, concerned itself with ascertaining how officials might maintain both their accountability and their moral agency. Neo-liberal regimes have, it appears, been prepared to compromise the latter in an effort to attain more fiscal restraint. But the intrusions upon moral agency have not stopped there. They have extended to the very heart of responsible government. Conservative regimes in the United States, the United Kingdom and Canada have rolled back the advances made in the previous decade by advocates of freedom of information and open government. Here the promoters of neo-liberal economics have entered a marriage of convenience with those who style themselves as the guardians of national security. This union has ushered in an era in which those who dream about what government might do and those who cannot silence their conscience have found public service very difficult indeed.

Aberbach, Joel D., Putnam, Robert A. and Rockman, Bert A. (1981), *Bureaucrats and Politicians in Western Democracies*, Cambridge MA: Harvard University Press.
Alchain, A.A. and Woodward, S. (1987), 'Reflections on the theory of the firm', *Journal of Institutional and Theoretical Economies*, 143, pp.110–36.
Aucoin, Peter (1988), 'Contraction, managerialism and decentralization in Canadian government', *Governance*, 1, pp.144–61.
Aucoin, Peter (1990), 'Administrative reform in public management: Paradigms, principles, paradoxes and pendulums', *Governance*, 3, pp.115–37.

Berman, Larry (1975), *The Office of Management and Budget*, Princeton NJ: Princeton University Press.

Boston, Jonathan (1987), 'Transforming New Zealand's public sector: Labour's quest for improved efficiency and accountability', *Public Administration*, 65, pp.423–42.

Burns, James McGregor (1963), *The Deadlock of Democracy: Four party politics in America*, Englewood Cliffs, NJ: Prentice-Hall.

Campbell, Colin (1983), *Governments Under Stress: Political executives and key bureaucrats in Washington, London and Ottawa*, Toronto: University of Toronto Press.

Campbell, Colin (1986), *Managing the Presidency: Carter, Reagan and the search for executive harmony*, Pittsburgh: University of Pittsburgh Press.

Campbell, Colin (1988a), 'Mulrony's broker politics: the ultimate in politicized incompetence?', in Andrew B. Gollner and Daniel Salee (eds), *Canada Under Mulrony: an end of term report*, Montreal: Vehicule.

Campbell, Colin (1988b), 'The political roles of senior government officials in advanced democracies', *British Journal of Political Science*, 18, pp.243–72.

Campbell, Colin and Szablowski, George J. (1979), *The Superbureaucrats: Structure and behaviour in central agencies*, Toronto: Macmillan.

Campbell, Colin and Peters, B. Guy (1988), 'The politics/administration dichotomy: death or merely change?', *Governance*, 1, pp.79–100.

Campbell, Colin and Naulls, Donald (1991), 'The limits of the budget maximizing theory: some evidence from official's views of their roles and career', in André Blais and Stephane Dion (eds), *The Budget Maximizing Bureaucrat: The empirical evidence*, Pittsburgh: University of Pittsburgh Press.

Campbell, Colin and Naulls, Donald (1992), 'The consequences of a minimalist paradigm for governance: A comparative analysis', in Donald F. Kettl and Patricia W. Ingraham (eds), *Agenda for Excellence: Public service in America*, Chatham, NJ: Chatham House.

Chapman, Brian (1959), *The Profession of Government*, London: Unwin.

Chapman, Richard A. (1988), *Ethics in the British Civil Service*, London: Routledge.

Chapman, Richard A. and Greenaway, John R. (1980) *The Dynamics of Administrative Reform*, London: Croom Helm.

Christoph, James B. (1975), 'Higher civil servants and the politics of consensualism in Great Britain', in Mattei Dogan (ed.) *The Mandarins of Western Europe: The political roles of top civil servants*, London: Routledge.

Considine, Mark (1988), 'The corporate management framework as administrative science: A critique', *Australian Journal of Public Administration*, 47, pp.4–17.

Fry, Geoffrey (1988), 'The Thatcher Government, the financial management initiative and the "New Civil Service"', *Public Administration*, 66, pp.1–20.

Fry, Geoffrey, Flynn, Andrew, Grey, Andrew, Jenkins, William, and Rutherford, Brian (1988), 'Symposium on improving management in government', *Public Administration*, 66, pp.429–45.

Galloway, George B. (1946), *Congress at the Crossroads*, New York: Crowell.

Granatstein, J.L. (1982), *The Ottawa Men*, Toronto: OUP.

Hansen, Michael G. and Levine, Charles H. (1988), 'The centralisation-decentralisation tug-of-war in the new executive branch', in Colin Campbell, S.J. and B. Guy Peters (eds), *Organizing Governance: Governing Organizations*, Pittsburgh: University of Pittsburgh Press.

Heclo, Hugh (1977), *A Government of Strangers: Executive politics in Washington*, Washington: Brookings.

Heclo, Hugh (1985), 'In search of a role: America's higher civil service', in Ezra L. Suleiman (ed.), *Bureaucrats and Policy Making: A Comparative Overview*, New York: Holmes & Meier.

Heclo, Hugh and Wildavsky, Aaron (1974), *The Private Government of Public Money: Community and Policy inside British Politics*, Berkeley: University of California Press.

Heeny, A.D.P. (1949), 'Cabinet government in Canada: some recent developments in the machinery of the central executive', *Canadian Journal of Economics and Political Science*, 12, pp.282–301.

Hennessy, Peter (1989), *Whitehall*, London: Secker & Warburg.

House of Commons (1986), *Westland PLC: The Governments Decision-Making*, Report and proceedings of the Defence Committee 4th report, London: HMSO.

Ignatius of Loyola (1559) (1970 edn), The Constitution of the Society of Jesus, Translation with commentary by George E. Ganss, St Louis: Institute of Jesuit Sources.

Keating, Michael (1988), 'Managing for results: the challenge for finance and agencies', *Canberra Bulletin of Public Administration*, 54, pp.73–80.

Keating, Michael and Dixon, Geoffrey (1988), 'Australian economic policy: problems and processes', a paper presented at the Canadian Institute for Research on Public Policy 1988 Workshop on Economic Policy-Making in the Asia-Pacific Region, Bangkok, Thailand.

Kelleher, S.R. [pseudonym] (1989), *Canberra Bulletin of Public Administration*, 58, pp.9–11.

Long, Norton C. (1952), 'Bureaucracy and constitutionalism', *American Political Science Review*, 46, pp.808–18.

Nathan, Richard P. (1975), *The Plot that Failed: Nixon and the Administrative Presidency*, New York: Wiley.

Nathan, Richard P. (1983), *The Administrative Presidency*, New York: Wiley.

Newland, Chester (1983), 'The Reagan presidency: limited government and political administration', *Public Administration*, 43, pp.1–21.

Niskanen, William A. (1971), *Bureaucracy and Representative Government*, New York: Aldine Atherton.

Niskanen, William A. (1973a) *Structural Reform of the Federal Budget Process*, Washington, DC: American Enterprise Institute.

Niskanen, William A. (1973b), *Bureaucracy: Servant or Master? Lessons From America*, London: Institute of Economic Affairs.

Olsen, Johan P. (1988), 'Administrative reform and theories of organization', in Colin Campbell and B. Guy Peters (eds), *Organizing Governance: Governing Organizations*, Pittsburgh: University of Pittsburgh Press.

Olson, Mancur (1982), *The Rise and Decline of Nations: Economic growth, stagflation and social rigidities*, New Haven: Yale.

Poindexter, John (1987), Testimony to the US Senate and House of Representatives hearings on the Iran-Contra affair.

Polsby, Nelson W. (1975), 'Legislatures', in *Governmental Institutions and Processes* Vol. 5 of Fred I. Greenstein and Colin Campbell (eds), *Handbook of Political Science*, Reading, MA: Addison-Wesley.

Price, Don (1951), 'General Dawes and executive staff work', *Public Administration Review*, 11, pp.167–72.

Prime Minister and Minister for the Civil Service (1986), *Civil Servants and Ministers: Duties and responsibilities*. Government response to the Seventh Report from the Treasury and Civil Service Committee, London: HMSO.

Putnam, Robert A. (1973), 'The political attitudes of senior civil servants in Western Europe: A preliminary report', *British Journal of Political Science*, 3, pp.257–90.

RIPA Working Group (1987), *Top Jobs in Whitehall: Appointments and promotions in the senior civil service*, London: Royal Institute of Public Administration.

Robinson, Gordon (1971), 'The changing role of the Privy Council Office', *Canadian Public Administration*, 14.

Rockman, Bert A. (1984), *The Leadership Question: The presidency and the American system*, New York: Præger.

Sanera, Michael (1984), 'Implementing the Mandate', in Stuart M. Butler, Michael Sanera, Colin Campbell and W. Bruce Weinrod (eds), *Mandate for Leadership II: Continuing the conservative revolution*, Washington: Heritage Foundation.

Scott, Graham and Gorringe, Peter (1988), 'Reform of the core public sector: The New Zealand experience'. A paper delivered to the Bicentennial Conference of the Royal Australian Institute of Public Administration.

Sundquist, James L. (1986), *Constitutional Reform and Effective Government*, Washington DC: Brookings.

Sundquist, James L. (1988), 'Needed: a political theory for the new era of coalition government in the United States', *Political Science Quarterly*, 103, pp.613–35.

Van Loon, Richard (1981), 'Kaleidoscope in grey: the policy process in Ottawa', in Michael Whittington and Glen Williams (eds), *Canadian Politics in the 1980s: Introductory readings,* Toronto: Methuen.

Van Loon, Richard (1985), 'A revisionist history of planning processes in Ottawa? An open letter to Colin Campbell, S.J.', *Canadian Public Administration*, 28, pp.307–18.

Weber, Max (1921a), 'The meaning of discipline', in H.H. Gerth and C. Wright Mills (eds), *From Max Weber: Essays in Sociology* (1948), London: Routledge & Kegan Paul.

Weller, Patrick (1985), *First Among Equals: Prime Ministers in Westminster systems*, London: Allan & Unwin.

Wildavsky, Aaron (1961), 'Political implications of budgetary reform', *Public Administration Review*, 21, pp.183–90.

Wildavsky, Aaron (1983), 'From chaos comes opportunity: the movement towards spending limits in American and Canadian budgeting', *Canadian Public Administration*, 26, pp.163–81.

Wilson, Woodrow (1941) (reprint), 'The study of administration', *Political Science Quarterly*, 16, pp.481–506.

Ten

The Law and Officials

PAUL FINN

Public or civil servants, no less than practitioners of other professions, cannot claim to be independent moral actors judging and expecting others to judge the propriety of their decisions and actions by reference to the imperatives of each official's individual moral code. The very role they have assumed – a public office – carries its own constraints, imposes its own discipline. Legal and constitutional norms, some spanning many centuries, colour and contrive the propriety or otherwise of many facets of official behaviour. These may not always be well adapted to modern conditions of government: the criminal law governing official misconduct is susceptible to this criticism (Finn, 1977). They may in some instances reflect pious aspirations not practical realities: the principle of individual ministerial responsibility is problematic on this score. But any consideration of ethics in public service which ignores a country's law and its constitution ignores a vital part of the context in which the 'ethical question' arises for resolution.

It is not the object of this chapter to canvass in any systematic way the legal and ethical constraints which can inhere in the holding of a public office. Rather it focuses from a lawyer's perspective upon some of the themes and assumptions which inform other chapters in this collection. Necessarily its treatment of subjects is eclectic. Two matters in particular will receive detailed treatment. They are, first, the two-dimensional nature of offices in the public or civil service – the one, that of trustee for the public, the other that of servant of the Crown – and secondly, the handling of information acquired by, or generated within, government. Before considering these, several more general comments should be made.

International consideration both of ethical concerns in public administration and of their resolution can be at once illuminating and hazardous. It is on the hazards that I wish to comment. In his *Spirit of Laws* Montesquieu observed that 'the political and civil laws of each nation ... should be adapted in such a manner to the people for whom they are made, as to render it very unlikely for those of one nation to be proper for another'. We need to remind ourselves of this particularly when we are minded to introduce into one country the institutional or procedural devices adopted by another to enhance public confidence in the integrity of its own governmental system or to protect its public from undue imposition. Interventions, no matter how well intentioned, into an administrative order require some sensitivity to the constitutional framework which actually informs it, to the culture, conventions, principles and practices which enliven it.

By way of illustration one can note that in some Westminster-derived systems of government maintenance of the principle of individual ministerial responsibility is often advanced as a significant impediment to proposed change which would make officialdom more directly accountable for its decisions and actions. But, as between countries, that principle is chameleon-like. If, as in Australia, (i) it is an attenuated one in practice exacting only personal responsibility from a minister for that minister's own neglects and misconduct, (ii) parliamentary question time provides a somewhat illusory vehicle for probing administrative action, (iii) important governmental functions are conducted through statutory authorities subject to diluted ministerial control and (iv) the overwhelming majority of public sector employees are not subject to Public Service legislation and are not located within ministerial departments, then the demands of that principle, even if they are to be respected and preserved, stand as no significant obstacle (a) to an Ombudsman system based on direct citizen complaint; (b) to freedom of information legislation; (c) to a merits based system of review of administrative decision; and (d) to an enlarged system of judicial review carrying with it a requirement for decision-makers to give reasons for decisions. Such innovations have in fact been introduced at the federal level in Australia in the last fifteen or so years and are being adopted, progressively, in the Australian States. But desirable though these developments may seem to critics in other Westminster-style polities, the question must be asked in each instance as to the effect (and the desirability thereof) their introduction would have on existing practices and principles. In the British case, for example, does ministerial responsibility have a different signification in the governmental system? Does it give a character to the structuring and conduct of public administration different from that found in Australia? Has it an importance in the parliamentary and executive systems which counterbalances the diminishing effects that the adoption of any of the Australian innovations would have on it? I will comment further on ministerial responsibility below. My immediate purpose here is not to presume to answer such questions. Rather it is to signal that what has been done in Australia is suited to its particular governmental order. But it may for just that reason be unsuited for export, at least in an unmodified form.

Similarly, there is a shared concern in many countries to protect fundamental rights of the citizen from undue invasion by governments and their officials. A judicially administered Charter or Bill of Rights has provided North America's response to this concern. But is this the only possible, or even appropriate, approach to be taken in other countries minded to take positive action in this manner? In Britain, for example, where a quiescent judiciary positively extols the sovereignty of Parliament, may not parliamentary devices (e.g. scrutiny of Bills and of legislative instruments committees) offer another way to rights protection and one which reflects more sensitively than a judicially administered Charter the relationships and balances which over time have been struck in the British constitutional system? Again I venture no answer. I simply mean to emphasise the burden of Montesquieu's observation adverted to above.

In Westminster systems the principle of individual ministerial responsibility has much claimed for it, much asked of it. Though its precise burden varies considerably between polities, discussion of it centres for the most part on its parliamentary and political dimensions and their consequences – on its impact on the minister–Parliament, minister–civil servant, and Parliament–civil service relationships. Consideration of these doubtless important matters has, however, tended to obscure understanding of the older, legal dimension of the principle. And it is that dimension which gives vitality to the rule of law's impact upon the operations of government. The political principle looks, essentially, to the Parliament and accentuates a minister's parliamentary accountability in and for administration in his or her portfolio, with departmental officials being shielded in consequence from a like accountability in respect of their participation in that administration. The legal principle, on the other hand, looks to the law and to the courts. It contracts the personal responsibility of ministers and it is by no means as benign to departmental officials. To oversimplify somewhat, if in the course of governmental administration a wrong is committed to a member of the public, the official who actually commits that wrong is, at law, personally responsible for it to that member of the public. It is no defence for that official to say that in acting as he did he was merely implementing official policy or the instructions of superiors: 'it is fundamental to our legal system that the executive has no power to authorize a breach of the law and that it is no excuse for an offender to say that he acted under the orders of a superior officer' (*A. v. Hayden*, 1984, p.84). Importantly, the official cannot assert even a concurrent liability and responsibility in his minister save where the official is acting with the authorisation or at the direction of the minister. The long-standing legal rule of ministerial responsibility is that, save in cases of authorisation or direction, ministers 'like all other public officers ... [are not] liable for any negligence or misconduct of the inferior officers in their several departments' (*Whitfield* v. *Lord Le Despencer*, 1778, p.766). What is true here of an official's civil liability is equally true of criminal liability.

The legal principle so briefly described was evolved in a constitutional climate in which the maxim 'the King can do no wrong' had real substance. The object of the principle was, consistently with that maxim, to bring every facet of executive administration under the control of the law. And this was achieved by making every public official personally responsible at law for the legality of his or her own actions. The maxim referred to has now lost much of its substance with the introduction of Crown proceedings legislation in Britain in 1947. But the legal regime the maxim spawned remains of abiding, if overlooked, significance. It precludes now, as it has always done, official participation in unlawful activity. An officer, in consequence, may be accountable to his or her minister, but that officer is equally accountable to the law. When the demands of the former conflict with the requirements of the latter, it is the latter which prevails. I emphasise this for three reasons. First, official participation in illegal activity is a muted theme in some chapters of this work. Secondly, it is necessary to be reminded that the principle of ministerial responsibility is multi-faceted and that it does not exact an unswerving loyalty to ministers. That loyalty is limited by the dictates of legality. Ministerial responsibility may go some distance in immunising officials from the scrutiny of the first arm of the State, the Parliament. It does not similarly immunise them from the scrutiny of the third, the courts. Thirdly, once one begins to acknowledge the relativity in official responsibility and accountability and the asymmetry between a minister's legal and political accountability, objections raised to 'administrative law' reform (and I use this in a large sense to include Freedom of Information, Ombudsmen, etc.) based on ministerial responsibility and civil service anonymity, become distinctly more problematic. To the extent that such reform draws its substance from the promotion of legality and the vindication of the rights of the citizen against the State it is compatible with notions of long established lineage in the British constitutional system and, in particular, with the legal doctrines of ministerial and official responsibility I have noted. Parliament, it needs to be emphasised, does not have the exclusive constitutional prerogative to call the executive government to account. Ministers, likewise, have no constitutional claim to the unswerving and unthinking loyalty of their departmental officers.

The final introductory comment which should be made is of a general character. Increasing interest is being shown in many countries in the use of 'codes of ethics' for public officials. These differ significantly in their emphases and particularity. The matter to be emphasised, however, is that the ethical behaviour enjoined by codes must itself be compatible with the behaviour that, as a matter of law, is expected of officials. If sight is lost of this, a code may itself encourage or authorise conduct which is unlawful. The Australian Commonwealth Government's *Guidelines on Official Conduct* is not beyond criticism on this score. Ethical and legal propriety obviously should harmonise. Though the demands of the law may in particular matters be themselves defective or inappropriate and thus be in need of reform, codes for their part manifestly must be sensitive to the law. They should complement and supplement it, not be in opposition to it. Otherwise a code itself can create an ethical dilemma.

PUBLIC OFFICES

One of the more curious by-products of Britain's nineteenth century civil service reform has been the almost virtual amnesia it induced about the constitutional nature of public office holding, about the legal constraints public office holding itself imposes on officials. For many centuries public officials even though occupying offices under the Crown, were conceived first and foremost as holders of offices of 'public trust and confidence'. In consequence they were accountable to the public (primarily, but by no means exclusively, through the processes of criminal law) for their conduct in office (Finn, 1987, ch.2). Blunt instrument though it may have been, the law none-the-less contrived and controlled the permissible freedom officials enjoyed in the manner of exercise of their offices. It ordained what they were obliged to do, were empowered to do, in their various offices. And for the protection of that 'trust and confidence' reposed by the public in its officers, it developed over six centuries a large and distinctive body of rules designed to exact a lawful, fair, full and impartial discharge of office. Extortion, bribery, conflict of interest, the misuse of public property, abuse of discretion, participation in illegal activity, acting on unlawful instructions, neglect of duty, oppression and more were addressed explicitly. Ineffective the law on its own may have been in securing compliance with those standards of conduct it demanded of officialdom. But it did – as it still does – address many of the issues which today we subsume under the rubric of 'integrity or ethics in government'.

For offices located in what was to become the modern civil service, the most profound practical effect of the reform movement was to accentuate an essentially employer-employee view of the Crown–civil servant relationship and this at the expense of the older public officer-public relationship. Hierarchy and subservience to superiors, not individual responsibility and accountability to the public, were to become the dominant features of the new order. A complete assimilation of civil servants into a purely employee status has, however, not been fully realised. Their lack of a contract of service is one reason. But more importantly, they remain public officers still: they discharge duties 'in the discharge of which the public are interested' (*R. v. Whitaker*, 1914, p.1,296). Despite the now overwhelming significance given to accountability up the bureaucratic chain to a responsible minister, the distant memory of this long-standing constitutional responsibility to the public still finds oblique reference in modern discussion of the obligation of a civil servant. That reference tends, however, to be diffuse and amorphous in character. On some occasions it connotes no more than a requirement to provide courteous and efficient service to a client public. On others, it is used as an informing idea in the formulation of policy or in the exercise of discretion. Yet again it is invoked to justify action in opposition to the formal requirements of official duty. If there is recognition in all of this of a distinctive and public character to engagement in the civil or public service, it is a confused recognition.

It is not altogether fashionable today to talk of government under law – at least when that is taken to signify that public officials, high and lowly, are systematically constrained by law in what they properly can do in office. Too readily now it is assumed that officials are the ciphers of their superiors; too readily it is assumed that individual conscience can be put in opposition to the demands of official position; too readily it is assumed that administrative requirement or executive expediency are the operative imperatives of, or constraints on, officials; too readily it is assumed that an official's loyalty is solely to the government he or she serves.

Modern civil servants occupy a somewhat ambiguous position in the governmental order. Quite obviously, as servants of the Crown employed in the executive arm of government, they are expected to serve faithfully the government of the day particularly as represented by their respective responsible minister. The nature of that service, the demands it makes, the privileges it accords, have considerable expression today in constitutional principle and convention, and in employment codes and disciplinary regimes. It is here, incidentally, that one finds the heartland of the principle of ministerial responsibility. But distinct from all of this, sometimes complementing it, sometimes in opposition to it, is the official's obligation as official to the law and to the constitution – in short, the obligation to the public whose interests an official serves. Unlike with the employee in the private sector, there are two roles, not one: servant of the government, and servant of the law and the constitution (the public). Of the two the former manifestly is of pervasive significance on a day-to-day basis. But it is the latter which provides the irreducible core of the role and the responsibility of the civil servant.

If this today seems a curious matter to emphasise there is, none-the-less, an important reason for so doing. Though we often fail to recognise that it is so, many issues which we now consider to be ones of predominantly ethical concern for officials are matters upon which the law has a direct and immediate bearing. We accept readily enough that the law proscribes certain forms of conduct that we would unhesitatingly characterise as unethical and improper: fraud, corruption and extortion are obvious examples. But in a larger range of issues which we see as raising primarily matters of individual conscience or ethical dilemma, we tend to overlook that the law often enough is there providing a principled resolution, or the guidelines to a principled resolution, to the matter in question. That resolution may not necessarily accord with the dictates of a particular individual's conscience. But there is every reason why, in the interests of the public, it should not do so in many cases. An official, for example, may without disclosure to superiors continue to act in a position of conflict of interest in a fashion which is fair, impartial and high minded. Or an official may, for the most meritorious reasons of sympathy and compassion, act to alleviate the plight of a member of the public by the provision of a benefit where the applicant in fact has no lawful entitlement to that benefit. In both instances the individual official may according to his or her own lights have acted ethically and with propriety. None-the-less, in both cases they have acted unlawfully and, importantly, in a way that puts at risk the very public interest their office binds them to serve. For reasons of public confidence in the institutions of government in the one case, and because of the outright danger to the public in allowing officials a 'dispensing power' in the other, their conduct cannot be countenanced. Important as an ethical issue may be to a particular official given his or her own value system, much more important in many cases is the maintenance of public confidence in the disinterested and lawful conduct of government itself. It is here that the law on public officials holds sway. It is here, for the purposes of our concern with ethics, that the public interest trumps individual conscience.

I do not wish to claim too much for the law. What I do wish to emphasise is that, in the same way as it provides on public interest grounds what is or is not permissible to private sector trustees and fiduciaries, the law likewise prescribes and proscribes for public officials. In so doing it aims to exact integrity and probity in government. But it proceeds upon the premise that an official enjoys a public trust which must be safeguarded. It does not allow to the official the luxury to act simply as an independent moral actor. Having assumed a particular role, an official as an official bears the burden of the obligations and limitations that entails. These, first and foremost, are legal and constitutional.

Given the reference I have made to the 'public trust' it is worthy of final note that under Canada's *Criminal Code* it is an offence for an 'official, in connection with the duties of his office, [to commit] a breach of trust' (*Criminal Code*, C.46, s.122)

INFORMATION IN THE HANDS OF GOVERNMENT

My purpose here is not to discuss the virtues and vices of official secrets legislation. Rather it is to highlight the complex issues of public interest that inhere in the acquisition, handling and dissemination of information by the officers and agencies of government. Who, within a government department is entitled to access to information in its hands? What use can be made of information obtained under coercive powers? What use can be made by government of information given by a member of the public to obtain a service? Are government employed professionals (e.g. doctors or lawyers) who provide a client service to the public in a materially different position in relation to professional secrecy from their private sector counterparts? Should information generated by government be accorded the same extensive protection from disclosure that is given to confidential information acquired in private and business relationships? The questions can be multiplied. But even the questions themselves suggest that no single inexorable rule can govern the permissible uses and disclosures that can be made of information in government's hands. And if we have here quite complex questions of law, we equally have, involved in these, very acute questions of ethical behaviour for government officials. Some of these are markedly in evidence in other chapters in this work.

In the Anglo-Australian legal tradition the law of breach of confidence (or secrecy) is of relatively recent origin and this is particularly so as it applies to the public sector. It is not founded on the view that information is property – a point worthy of note given the easy assumption made by officials that information received or generated by government is 'owned' by it and is therefore available for use by it as it sees fit. Rather, and accepting that difficult balances must be struck between openness and secrecy, between information sterilisation and information dissemination, the law has taken the view that the nature of the information in question and the circumstances of its acquisition are the factors which govern the degree to which, if at all, information should be protected from use or disclosure. Central in this is the recognition that varying, often conflicting, public interests – privacy protection, state interests, the promotion of candour, etc. – are of vital significance in the determination to be made in a given context. In many instances those public interests themselves are infused with strong ethical considerations. Equally, the manner in which discrete public interests are reconciled affords considerable guidance in resolving ethical dilemmas which may confront an official.

The following brief and somewhat over-simplified account of the law of confidentiality in government draws essentially upon Australian law though it mirrors in general the situation that obtains in countries such as Britain and New Zealand. What, as will be seen, is of importance to civil servants in it is that they must be sensitive to the source from which information is acquired; whether or not it is publicly available; for what purpose it is obtained; and whether a particular official's function is one which necessitates his or her access to that information.

The law's starting premise is that a person who receives information in confidence is not entitled to use or disclose that information without the consent of the person who gave it. To this there is, as noted below, an important exception: use or disclosure is permissible when so to do is in the 'public interest' (and this in this context, is a term of art). Information will for present purposes be regarded as having been received in confidence where (a) the information is not itself public property and public knowledge; and (b) it is provided or acquired for a limited purpose. Translating this to the governmental sector, the following rather complicated picture emerges.

Information voluntarily supplied to government by a citizen or corporation

Here, the orthodoxy is that if confidential information is supplied for a particular purpose, for instance to obtain advice, for the purposes of an application, etc., then that information can only be used for that purpose unless (i) the legislative mandate of the agency receiving the information expressly or impliedly authorises or requires it otherwise to use that information, in which case the information can be used to that extent but no further; or (ii) that notwithstanding the purpose for which it has been given, the 'public interest' justifies its further use or disclosure. I will return to the 'public interest' below.

Information obtained from the citizen, etc. under coercive power

The situation that obtains here is the same as in (a) save that the permissible use that can be made by the relevant governmental agency of the information it obtains is set by the purpose for which the coercive power itself has been given to that agency.

Information obtained from the citizen in the rendering of a professional service to the citizen

With government often providing professional services to the public parallel with those rendered by the private sector, for example health care, legal advice, counselling, etc., the professional nature of the relationship rather than the public employment status of the service provider is regarded as the operative factor governing the protection to be given to information of the citizen in the hands of the professional. Given the generous protection the law gives to information acquired in professional relationships, what this means in practice is that, the public interest exception apart, a government employed professional cannot use or disclose the information acquired in a professional capacity in a way which would reveal at least the identity of the client save to the extent that this is necessary to perform the professional service in question or is otherwise authorised by the client. Important recent examples of this in Britain involving public institutions have been the AIDS (*X.* v. *Y.*, 1988) and prisoner release (*W.* v. *Edgell*, 1989) litigations.

When one considers together the above three situations, it is apparent that rather stringent limitations are placed upon the uses that can properly be made by governmental officers and agencies of information acquired from the public. At the heart of the protection thus given to the public is the acknowledgement that though there may be a legal or practical need to provide government with information, nevertheless members of the public, or for that matter companies, retain a vital interest in the preservation of their own privacy, in the protection of their own trade or commercial secrets, and that that interest should be respected and safeguarded. There is here a very obvious and vital interaction between lawful behaviour and ethical behaviour by an official.

The one major exception to the above is that while information received from the public may be given for a particular purpose it may none-the-less be in the 'public interest' for the recipient officer or agency otherwise to use or disclose it. For the purposes of Australian law this will be so (i) where the information relates to serious wrongdoing; or (ii) where use or disclosure of the information would avert an apprehended serious harm to the community or to members of it. Here, in so far as the recipient is concerned, one's 'higher duty' to the State and the community overrides one's duty of confidentiality to the member of the public who supplied the information. Here again the law goes some distance in solving the ethical dilemma that an information recipient may find himself in given the nature of the information acquired by him.

One additional comment should, perhaps, be made. There is an emerging strand in the 'public interest' exception to confidentiality which posits that if a person is to invoke that exception to justify disclosure of serious wrongdoing, the disclosure made should be to 'one who has a proper interest to receive the information' (*Initial Service Ltd* v. *Putterill*, 1968, p.405). The courts have, in consequence, said that the public interest exception does not of itself justify disclosure to the media if in the circumstances there is another appropriate body to receive the information. May not this have some bearing on the contentious topic of whistle-blowing?

Information generated by or within government

This is very much the domain of official secrets legislation. Its effect for most of this century in Commonwealth countries has been to place a blanket prohibition on the disclosure of governmental information (no matter how innocuous or notorious) by officials, unless disclosure is necessary in the course of discharge of official duties. In its temper it was in opposition to the common law. As the current Chief Justice of the High Court of Australia has observed:

> It is unacceptable, in our democratic society, that there should be a restraint on the publication of information relating to government when the only vice of that information is that it enables the public to discuss, review and criticize government action. (*Commonwealth* v. *John Fairfax & Sons Ltd*, 1980, p.493)

This conflict in approach has led to the anomalous result that while it may be a criminal offence under official secrets legislation for a public servant to disclose governmental information to a third party, the courts would not restrain that public servant from disclosing, nor the third party from publishing, the information save where the government could prove – and the onus is on it – that disclosure or publication would be likely to be harmful to the public interest.

The common law attitude, increasingly, has been that

> governments act, or at all events are constitutionally required to act, in the public interest. Information is held, received and imparted by governments, their departments and agencies to further the public interest. Public and not private interest, therefore, must be the criterion by which [a court] determines whether it will protect information which a government or governmental body claims is confidential. (*Attorney-General (U.K.)* v. *Heinemann Publishers Australia Pty Ltd*, 1987, p.191)

Significantly, recent official secrets and freedom of information legislation in some number of countries has moved much closer to the 'democratic principle' of the common law: if governmental information is to be shielded from the public eye, it now more so than previously will be because the information is of a class or type which should be protected from disclosure on public interest grounds.

Official access to governmental information

In the absence of an express limitation on dissemination of information within a department or agency, the right an official has to obtain access to governmental information is set by the 'need to know' principle – that is, does the official require access to that information for the purpose of discharging his or her official function? This restriction, obviously, is of considerable significance where the information in question relates to the affairs of a member of the public or of a corporation. Privacy protection is as important a consideration in the dissemination of information within government as it is in the release of information to the public.

The overall picture I have presented may appear to be one of some complication. My purpose in presenting it is twofold. First, it is not generally appreciated to what extent the law, and not merely ethical considerations or administrative procedures, governs the handling of information in the hands of government. Secondly, the law itself reflects significant ethical concerns and it does in some measure attempt to reconcile those conflicting pressures which, to the conscientious official, are causative of ethical dilemmas.

A v. *Hayden* (1984) 56 A.L.R., 82.

Attorney-General (UK) v. *Heinemann Publishers Australia Pty Ltd* (1987) 10 N.S.W.L.R., 86.

Commonwealth v. *John Fairfax and Sons Ltd* (1980) 32 A.L.R., 485.

Finn, P.D. (1977), 'Official Misconduct', *Criminal Law Journal*, 2, 307.

Finn, P.D. (1987), *Law and Government in Colonial Australia*, Melbourne: OUP.

Initial Service Ltd v. *Putterill* (1968) 1 Q.B. 396.

R. v. *Whitaker* (1914) 3 K.B. 1283

W. v. *Edgell* (1989) 1 All E.R. 1089.

Whitfield v. *Lord Le Despencer* (1778) 2 Cowp. 754.

X. v. *Y.* (1988) 2 All E.R. 648.

Eleven

Trade Unions and Ethics in the Public Service

BARRY J. O'TOOLE

It could be argued that the ethic of trade unionism can be simply stated: trade unions are concerned to improve the living standards and working conditions of those they represent. They do this through a system of collective bargaining, supported by threats of sanctions against the employers of their members. In other words, they are concerned with both the enhancement and the protection of the private gain of their members.

However, such an interpretation would be at best only partial. The history of trade unions clearly illustrates that the ethics of trade unionism go beyond a simple statement of concern with private gain. Trade unions developed from being friendly societies which exercised a collective conscience on behalf of disadvantaged groups and oppressed minorities. Their development, particularly in the latter half of the nineteenth century and the early part of this century, became closely linked with the ventilation of what has come to be perceived as the unethical behaviour of employers, particularly in dangerous industries such as coal mining or oil drilling (for discussions of these aspects of the theory and practice of trade unionism see for example Feather, 1963; Flanders, 1970; Hyman, 1971; Webb and Webb, 1902).

At the more practical level, all unions face ethical dilemmas themselves in their everyday work. Thus, if we return to the earlier statement that trade unions are primarily concerned with the improvement of the private interests of their members, then often truthfulness, an attribute thought to be ethical, can ruin a bargaining position *vis-à-vis* employers. Conversely, truthful accountability to members can ruin the prospects of an agreement being endorsed by them. Given the supposed ethic of trade unionism, it could be argued that in certain circumstances *untruthfulness* would be the ethical course. It may therefore be argued that anything which interferes with the union carrying out its functions in relation to the protection and enhancement of the interests of its members should be set aside. Indeed, we may say that what would normally be considered to be ethically sound behaviour may often be ignored in the pursuit of the ethic of trade unionism. Examples of this, other than untruthfulness, may be strike action by public sector employees in, let us say, the educational or health care systems, where the interests of the beneficiaries of those services may suffer.

However, as noted above, matters are not as simple as this. Using again the examples of health and education, while professionals in those services, nurses and teachers, have taken industrial action over pay, nevertheless the unions representing nurses and teachers have also been concerned with, in the case of teachers, professional standards of teaching and conduct towards pupils, and in the case of nurses, professional standards and patient care. Indeed, it is in the public sector that the conflict between legitimate trade union objectives and what might be considered ethically unacceptable behaviour is at its most acute. How can the unions representing public sector workers such as teachers and nurses argue for industrial action over pay *and* be concerned with professional standards of care when the industrial action they occasionally advocate could of itself be detrimental to those standards? Such dilemmas are as true of the civil service as they are in the education or health care systems or in the provision of social services.

TRADE UNIONS AND ETHICS IN THE BRITISH CIVIL SERVICE

From a general perspective, it may be argued that, traditionally, public servants have themselves believed that they owe their primary duty to the public they serve, through the application of their skills and under the auspices of professional bodies whose codes may be said to encompass ethically inspired standards.

In the British civil service, with which this chapter is primarily concerned, but also to an extent in the public bureaucracies of most democratic societies, this traditional view may be articulated as follows: the civil service is there to serve the public by serving faithfully the Government of the day. In Britain civil servants owe their duty to the Crown (which means, in practice, the elected Government) but express this duty through a commitment to public service (see Armstrong, 1985, 1987; O'Toole, 1990).

Of course, this is neither an adequate nor a universal statement of actuality. For example, some would argue that it may be said to apply to the senior ranks of the civil service only (that part of the civil service which the academic literature tends to concentrate upon); and it may also be argued that it is historically rather than contemporaneously true. This aspect of the argument concerning the ethics of the civil service will be dealt with more fully below.

The corollary to civil servants owing their duty to the Crown, and specifically to the Ministers of the Crown, is that ministers owe an obligation to their civil servants – not just to those with whom they have personal contact, but to all civil servants everywhere. This stems from the nature of the British Constitution, which puts responsibility for the actions of government departments in the hands of ministers, thus allowing ministers to be praised for all that is done well, and to take the blame for all that is done badly. This constitutional position is said to enable civil servants to act anonymously, and thus impartially. Impartiality is one of the hallmarks of the professionalism of the civil servant, and therefore at the heart of the ethics of the civil service. Civil servants are there to serve the public *irrespective* of the Government of the day. By being impartial towards whichever party happens to be in government they are able both to serve the people and the Government which is temporarily in charge of the nation's affairs. Nevertheless, it must be remembered that in a sense ministers are the representatives of the public in the Departments of government, and therefore that, in practical terms, it is the minister to whom the civil servant owes his primary duty. The relationship of ministers to civil servants is therefore of central importance to the public interest, and if it comes under strain then it may be argued that the public interest is bound to suffer (O'Toole, 1990).

In recent years that relationship has become somewhat strained. In the period since the Second World War civil servants may have felt increasingly justified in believing that the obligations which ministers have to them have not been fulfilled. This is particularly true in relation to pay, where civil servants have seen their salaries fall behind those in comparable occupations and where the agreed system of pay comparability was unilaterally abandoned by the Government in 1981. It is equally true in other, perhaps less tangible, areas – especially the esteem in which civil servants are held. That has been going down for more than half a century now, but the decline accelerated with the publication of the Fulton Report, and has been made more apparent by a series of unfortunate lapses, errors and insults on the part of ministers (O'Toole, 1989).

In these circumstances it is perhaps not surprising (though this does not mean that it is either reprehensible or not) that the ethic of trade unionism has come more and more into conflict with the ethic of public service. It is also not surprising that civil service trade unions, including the First Division Association (which represents the most senior grades in the civil service), have behaved more stridently than they have in the past.

TRADE UNIONS AND THE ETHICS OF SENIOR CIVIL SERVANTS

The civil service association which is perhaps most akin to being a professional association is the Association of First Division Civil Servants (FDA). This is the Association which represents the most senior officials in central government in Britain. It represents, in the words of H.E. Dale, 'those men who stand closest to Ministers and exercise a real and constant influence on public affairs' (Dale, 1941). It is with this Association, and these people, that this chapter is now concerned.

First, it is important to say something about the role of the members of the FDA, because this has an important bearing on the way in which the Association carries out its work, specifically on the way in which the Association perceives its role in relation to ethical questions. What do senior civil servants do?

In the words of the FDA itself: the role of administrative civil servants 'is to bring together the disparate issues involved in taking major decisions of policy, to advise on what these decisions should be, and subsequently to put them into effect' (FDA, 1968). These functions, which are more or less universally accepted, involve close contact with ministers. If we make the (admittedly somewhat loose) analogy that civil servants are professionals, in the same way as lawyers or architects, then we may say that ministers can be seen as being the 'client group' of civil servants; that a civil servant has with his minister a similar relationship to that which a lawyer or an architect has with his clients. In other words, ministers are lay people who rely on the advice of their civil servants and issue instructions to them based upon that advice. Of course, this is not by any means a precise analogy. The client relationship for most professionals is a personal and direct one, concerning the private interests of the client; in the civil service the relationship is a collegiate and indirect one, concerning the public interest. In addition, it must be remembered that, in the British civil service, civil servants are 'lay people' too, in the sense that their professionalism consists primarily of knowledge of the machine and only to a lesser extent knowledge of the products of the machine. Politics oils the machine, and politicians are responsible for that process. Ministers have their own part to play in the processes of government which makes them quite different from the clients of lawyers or architects. Nevertheless, just as the ethics of lawyers or architects are primarily bound up with their relationship with clients, so too the ethics of civil servants are bound up with their relationships to their ministers. The question then is, what are the duties and responsibilities of civil servants in relation to ministers? (Armstrong, 1985, 1987; Chapman, 1988)

Of course, this question is not as simple as it may first appear because the ultimate 'client' of civil servants is society itself, and ministers have their duty to society too. The question is thus one of the relationship between government and society. In a democracy the fulcrum of this relationship is accountability and the question of accountability for the actions of government, both ministers and senior civil servants, is thus fundamentally important.

Until relatively recently this relationship between ministers and civil servants was one of constitutional propriety. Civil servants owed their loyalty to ministers and provided them, in theory, with anonymous and impartial advice. Ministers both took the praise for all that was done well by their departments, and took the blame for all that was amiss. Ministers protected their civil servants, who cannot answer for themselves publicly, and received in return complete loyalty. However, changes in constitutional practice, the decreasing morale of civil servants because of numerous problems, and the changing behaviour of ministers in the sense of their being increasingly unwilling to protect their civil servants, have all combined to call into serious question the relationship of ministers to civil servants. The Westland saga and the Ponting case (as well as the GCHQ affair) highlighted the problem and raised the question of codes of ethics for civil servants.

In 1968 the FDA tackled this question, in the context of discussions about codes of ethics, when it set up a sub-committee on professional standards in the civil service. On that occasion the FDA was primarily acting as a professional associa-tion, in the sense that the main impetus for the setting up of the sub-committee was the fact that the Fulton Committee had not considered the question of the relation-ship between ministers and civil servants. The report of the sub committee, published in 1970, was quite a radical report in that it considered that a civil servant's duty went beyond the traditional confines of loyalty to the minister. The report even suggested that there was a duty to the public interest and that there should be a serious attempt at defining what the public interest is (FDA, 1970).

In the 1980s both the stimulus and the response were quite different. The stimulus for the FDA to consider codes of ethics again was a succession of major scandals, usually involving the indiscreet behaviour either of a minister or a civil servant. The FDA's consideration was also a response to the so-called Armstrong Memorandum. The incidents of indiscretion included most notoriously the Ponting and Westland affairs. These two notorious episodes involved ministers misleading Parliament and civil servants having to cover up for them.

The response to the stimulus was the Code of Ethics passed by the 1986 Annual Conference (FDA, 1986). This document was rather more tame than the 1970 report of the professional standards sub committee. However, there are two points about it worth considering. The first is that the code specifically refers to ministers misleading or lying to Parliament (point d, para.2, p.3; point f, para.4, p.3). The second is that the code contains provisions for civil servants to have the right to bring before a body or person appointed for the purpose a situation in which he or she believes that a minister is requiring that person to behave in an unethical manner (point f, para.4, p.3).

In this case the FDA was acting as a trade union. More specifically, it was attempting to provide future protection for its members faced with situations similar to those faced by Clive Ponting and the DTI officials involved in the Westland affair.

Over the two decades that passed between the FDA considering ethics after Fulton and considering the same topics in the aftermaths of the affairs referred to, the FDA itself underwent numerous changes, and became more like a trade union. In 1968 the FDA considered ethics from a professional association perspective; in the 1980s the Association considered ethics from a trade union perspective. In the 1980s the protection of members was uppermost in the minds of the leaders of the Association – and this, paradoxically, may in part explain why the 1986 document was so conservative in character.

TRADE UNIONS AND THE ETHICS OF THE 'OTHER RANKS'

The FDA has about 10,000 civil servants and has a potential membership of not much more. What about the more than 500,000 other civil servants in Britain who are not policy-makers or advisers to ministers? The question of the ethics of these officials has rarely received the attention of academics or politicians or even of civil servants themselves, and it is to this question that this chapter tentatively turns now.

What are the functions of the middle ranking and junior civil servants who are represented by the other constituent unions of the Council of Civil Service Unions? Two rather sweeping generalisations can be made. The first is that these civil servants are primarily involved with the implementation of policies passed down to them by ministers and the other inhabitants of Whitehall (though, of course, policy-making has its bottom-up aspects too); and the second is that vast numbers of these officials have daily and direct contact (either face to face or by post) with members of the public. Using the analogy used earlier it can broadly be argued that the client group of large numbers of middle and junior ranking civil servants is the public at large, not the ministers to whom nominal allegiance is owed. These junior officials deal with social security questions, find people employment, inspect taxes, examine luggage, issue driving licences, give passports, and do thousands of other things with and for the citizens of the United Kingdom.

The corollary of these relationships has been until recently that the ethics of these officials are concerned with justice, fairness, honesty, openness and equal treatment for all those who deal with government departments. Again, this is a generalisation which ignores a large part of the story. In the end, the parliamentary system within which all civil servants work simply cannot be ignored. The redress of political and administrative grievances is one of the *raisons d'être* of Parliament and is almost exclusive to Parliament in the British political system; and civil servants work every day within the confines of parliamentary accountability. However, to argue this is to confirm the reasons why the ethics of executive and clerical civil servants have always been concerned with equity of treatment for the citizen.

Recently, however, the situation has changed radically. Questions have been raised – not just about the doctrine of individual ministerial responsibility, but about the very nature of the bureaucratic system itself and the concomitant system of accountability. The Financial Management Initiative (FMI) and its successor the 'Next Steps' have massive implications for the system of accountability. The 'Next Steps' initiative in particular has set in train a whole range of changes which go to the very heart of the employment matters which are central to the functions of the civil service trade unions. In essence, the new agencies are more or less free to adopt whichever administrative, management and payment structures are thought fit by their Chief Executives, so long as they are operating within a general policy framework laid down by ministers and their policy advisers. Essentially, the concept of a unified career civil service is seen by the unions as being under threat. Furthermore, civil servants are being encouraged to behave in ways which in the past would not have been thought appropriate in the public sector: for example, defending their department's policies, or promoting the activities of their department in a marketing sense. Thus, the implications of the changes concern not just the relationship between civil servants and ministers, but also the relationship between civil servants and Parliament and civil servants and the public. In other words, all aspects of the ethics of middle and junior ranking civil servants are being called into question: on the one hand the FMI and the 'Next Steps', are concerned with the quest for 'efficiency' (which seems to mean cutting the costs of the delivery of services); and on the other hand the programme involves the shifting of responsibility to the shoulders of individual civil servants, and away from the traditional hierarchical and primarily political modes of accountability.

The associations which represent junior and middle ranking civil servants are definitely trade unions in the traditional sense of being protective associations concerned with levels of pay and conditions of service. Naturally, these unions are very worried that the FMI and the 'Next Steps' have witnessed attacks on both the pay and the working conditions of their members. In the words of an article which appeared in *FDA News* commenting on the attitude of the constituent unions of the CCSU, they 'give the impression of being either hostile to the development of agencies or only grudging in their acceptance' (Willman, 1991). What is the nature of the threat the unions perceive? In essence, the unions are concerned that the new agencies will be able to both recruit and pay their employees quite independently of the Civil Service Commissioners (the system of recruitment having been radically altered by the 'Next Steps' programme – see Chapman, 1991). Furthermore, the unions believe it is almost certain that the content of the work will change in consequence of the changes in the accountability structures and procedures.

Civil service unions already perceive morale to be low because of the previous aspects of the FMI, which they see as having lowered the quality of the services that they provide – thus reducing the elements of justice, fairness, honesty, openness and equal treatment for members of the public. They are alarmed by the implications of the 'Next Steps' in terms of the further deterioration, both in these elements and in the accountability of ministers for the actual delivery of services. They are worried that recruitment to the civil service will suffer and that standards will decline even further. They see a threat to the traditional concept of a unified career civil service. In all these ways they are dealing with questions of ethics – because in all these ways they believe that the relationships between their members and the public are being put under serious strain. However, like the FDA's, theirs is a trade union response concerned primarily with the protection of their members.

CONCLUSION: THE ETHICS OF CONSUMERISM?

The latest of the Government's reform proposals for the public service generally and for the civil service in particular is for the introduction of the so-called 'Citizens' Charter'. Essentially this is designed to enable citizens to behave as 'consumers' of public sector services and to allow them to behave in the same way as they would if they were dealing with a private organisation of which they were customers. This means that there is to be a further shift away from the notion of the 'universality' of public services, a situation in which government provides services for society, towards the notion of what might be described as 'particularity', a situation in which the relationship is one of supplier and customer. Civil servants are no longer part of a collective and collegiate whole which caters for society as a whole; they are rather to be retailers of marketable goods and services. They are to be individuals dealing with individuals; not the agents of government.

This shift, which is one of the consequences of the FMI and the 'Next Steps' as well as of the 'Citizens' Charter', raises enormous questions about the nature of accountability in the civil service. Are public servants accountable directly to their 'customers' or are the traditional methods of accountability to be retained? In the case of there being no clear-cut answer to these questions, which set of account-ability procedures will take precedence? What are the implications for individual civil servants in terms of their conditions of service, and even of their pay? Will 'collective bargaining' still prevail in the civil service or will there be further moves toward individual pay structures and the denial of collective responsibility for civil service decisions? All these, and many other, questions can be raised about the Government's reform programme, and none has yet received a satisfactory answer (though many answers there have been). They are questions about ethics, essen-tially because they are questions about the relationships between civil servants and the citizens of the United Kingdom. They are questions for trade unions because they are questions about the relationship between civil servants and their employer.

ACKNOWLEDGEMENT

I am indebted to Peter Jones, Secretary of the Council of Civil Service Unions, for extensive comments he made on an earlier draft of this chapter.

Armstrong, Sir Robert (1985 and 1987), note by the Head of the Home Civil Service, *The Duties and Responsibilities of Civil Servants in Relation to Ministers*, London: Cabinet Office.
Chapman, Richard A. (1988), *Ethics in the British Civil Service*, London: Routledge.
Chapman, Richard A. (1991), 'New arrangements for recruitment to the British Civil Service: Cause for concern', Editorial in *Public Policy and Administration*, 6, 3 December, pp.1–4.
Dale, H.E. (1941), *The Higher Civil Service in Great Britain*, London: OUP.
FDA (1968), 'Memorandum of evidence submitted to the Fulton Committee in the Civil Service', in *The Civil Service, Vol. 5, No.1: Proposals and observations* (Proceedings of the Fulton Committee).
FDA (1970), *Report of the Sub-Committee on Professional Standards in the Public Service*, Filed at A00082 in the FDA's system.
FDA (1986), *Code of Ethics: A resolution passed by the 1986 Annual Delegate Conference*, FDA.
Feather, Victor (1969), *The Essence of Trade Unionism*, London: The Bodley Head.
Flanders, A. (1970), *Management and the Unions: The theory and reform of industrial relations*, London: Faber & Faber.
Hyman, R. (1971), *Marxism and the Sociology of Trade Unionism*, London: Pluto Press.
O'Toole, Barry J. (1989), *Private Gain and Public Service: The Association of First Division Civil Servants*, London: Routledge.
O'Toole, Barry J. (1990), 'T.H. Green and the ethics of senior officials in British Central Government', *Public Administration*, 68, 3, pp.337–52.
Webb, Sydney and Webb, Beatrice (1902), *The History of Trade Unionism*, London: Longman, Green.
William, John (1991), 'Agencies: a challenge to the Unions', *FDA News,* September, FDA.

Twelve

Ethics in Public Service

RICHARD A. CHAPMAN

The focus for most contemporary discussion of ethics in public service is the exercise of discretionary power. John Rohr provides an eloquent justification of this in his *Ethics for Bureaucrats,* one of the most significant books in a rapidly growing literature on this subject. Rohr's book begins with the acknowledgement that 'the bureaucrat's discretionary power has become the pivotal justification for the consideration of public service ethics' (Rohr, 1989, p.ix).

In the western style democracies of advanced industrial societies much of the debate about conflict of interest, in the sense of individual officials benefiting in a material way from their positions at work, has been satisfactorily resolved. Instances of unacceptable practices are dealt with through the courts, with guidance to officials being provided through codes of conduct or other official rules. Individual cases still arise, human nature being what it is, but at least rules to be applied are reasonably clear. In earlier times, or in societies with different political systems, discussion was, and is, about what sorts of behaviour may be acceptable in this context, or even about the meanings of key terms, like corruption. While such discussion may sometimes continue in developed societies, it is no longer the focus for debate about ethics in public service.

As with advancing personal benefits from official positions, much of the debate about the active participation in policy decisions by officials motivated by partisan or ideological commitment is also no longer controversial. In different countries practices vary; indeed, in some countries officials may be elected or selected on a partisan basis; but what is acceptable or not acceptable behaviour in this context has been generally recognised so that officials who know what is and is not expected of them and transgressors are dealt with, if not by the courts then through the political system.

Despite problems associated with the questions of bribery or the ideological commitment of officials having been resolved, there still remains a large area of the work of government where officials encounter ethical dilemmas and where they are responsible for the judgments they make as part of their regular work in government. In this context it should be noted that officials are most certainly taking part in government. As Arthur Bentley demonstrated, the raw material or the real stuff of government can be found 'only in the actually performed legislating-ad-ministering-adjudicating activities of the nation and in the streams and currents of activity that gather among the people and rush into these spheres' (Bentley, 1908, p.180). Of course, in democratic political systems governments.are elected by the people and officials are generally accountable to elected representatives, but it is evident that in the complex experience of life in the modern world the separation of legislative and administrative powers is by no means clear-cut. Politicians can only devote a limited amount of their time to formulating and refining the details of policies because they also have other obligations, including advising and counselling citizens and acting as their representative. Consequently, much of the detail, as well as some of the broad outlines, of public policies has to be filled out by officials. In many cases, it is only the officials who have the expertise and experience who know what is practicable and in these circumstances they have important duties to advise legislators and, on occasions, to persuade them, so that the provisions in legislation can actually be implemented. Without the wise and sensitive contribution of these elements to the process of government, modern democratic political systems would run the danger of being unworkable and/or of falling into disrepute. In this context, liberal democracies are quite unlike the ideal types envisaged in the most elementary textbooks of politics.

There is another way, too, in which officials find themselves exercising discretion in modern democratic systems. The business of government is now so large and complex that even the most skilfully drafted legislation, resulting from inputs by officials as well as politicians, cannot cover every conceivable circumstance. This is well illustrated by the story of Richard Crossman's appointment as Minister of Housing in 1964. He told his Permanent Secretary, Dame Evelyn Sharp, that he would personally approve every decision stated to be authorised by him. Sharp convinced Crossman of the impossibility of his request by having all the files containing decisions for approval on a single day brought up to his room and piled high on every possible surface in his office' (Meynell, 1988, p.92). In practice, legislation has to make provision for unforeseen circumstances and for the application of rules to individual cases, not simply according to mechanistic and thought-less procedures, but according to practice which does not outrage the values of citizens or their expectations of common sense. Therefore, legislation and its subordinate rules must often use qualitative expressions. Various writers have produced lists of terms which are used for this purpose, but Gerald Caiden illustrates this admirably: 'Whenever public laws use such terms as "adequate", "advisable", "appropriate", "beneficial", "convenient", "equitable", "fair", "fit", "necessary", "practicable", "proper", "reasonable", "safe" or "sufficient", or their opposites, they oblige public servants to exercise discretion and make ethical judgments' (Caiden, 1983).

Consequently, as Rohr has shown so well, bureaucrats, through exercising administrative discretion, 'participate in the *governing* process of a democratic regime' (Rohr, 1989, p.4), and it is in this context that ethics in public service and ethics in government are variations of the same theme.

This focus on the importance of administrative discretion as the starting-point of much contemporary discussion of ethics in public service may be the result of two related phenomena. One is the advanced stage of evolution of public administration as a part of the study of politics (or political science, as it is known in some countries). The other phenomenon is the number and variety of cases of ethical dilemmas that have attracted widespread public attention in recent years.

It may be argued that public administration came of age when it developed beyond aspirations to produce a universally applicable administrative science. As Caiden put it in the early 1980s:

> For nearly a century administrative scientists have tried to take public ad-
> ministration out of partisan politics and partisan politics out of public ad-
> ministration. They have sought to create a value-free, neutral, objective science
> of the art of public management, to remove public servants from the corrupting
> influences of the political arena and to transform public servants into profes-
> sional practitioners of nomothetic management principles. They would con-
> cern themselves solely with facts not values, means not ends; they would be
> impersonal but not mindless bureaucrats, administering public policies and
> laws without fear or favour ... [but] public servants ... are not insensitive
> appendages of an administrative apparatus that can do no wrong. They are all
> involved in the exercise of power for good or evil. They are obliged to define
> social objectives, to set social norms, to make tragic choices and to manipulate
> mass behaviour. They shape public policy, select information on which public
> decisions are made, mediate between conflicting interests and impose certain
> values on their clients. (Caiden, 1983)

Some public administration specialists are still working towards developing an administrative science, though generally in a more sophisticated way than in times past, and the point here is not that such approaches are misguided or anachronistic but that they relate to certain aspects of public administration only.

In the past, the emphasis on administrative science may have originated from a misunderstanding or misconception of scientific method. In the early stages of any analysis facts have to be accumulated. However, important though factual knowledge may be, the accumulation of facts is not itself enough. Hypotheses have to be developed and tested to produce theories and so advance understanding. In other words, Aristotle's basic method, that of observation, may be a good begin-ning, but it is only a beginning and other techniques must follow if the subject is to advance. In the specialist field of public administration the subject reached maturity when it involved much more than the application of laws and rules to cases. Such maturity has encompassed the study of the development of the laws and rules; in some cases it has also required analysing the most demanding

administrative judgments, incorporating both the evaluation of particular circumstances and human sensitivity in decision-making.

The other phenomenon contributing to the focus on administrative discretion is
the widespread publicity and controversy associated with cases involving ethical
dilemmas in public service. This unprecedented public attention is not because
comparable cases did not exist before modern times; of course they did. The
difference is that in earlier times citizens generally may have been less interested;
the values of society may have been different; the requirements of national and
international law may have been less sensitive to the human rights of citizens and
officials; in many cases less openness in government meant that details were never
published; modern technologies which both involve the media and are used in
administrative practice were not available; and in some instances individuals (or
their friends and supporters) were less connected with or aware of the potential
value of publicity as a facet of democracy.

THE VALUES OF SOCIETY

Although the specific values of society may change from time to time and from
place to place, the values of society, whatever the precise details may be, are an
important element in guiding discretionary power and influencing particular
decisions in the public service. This relationship of values and ethics was well
encapsulated by O.P. Dwivedi and Ernest Engelbert when they wrote: 'Values are
the ideals, beliefs and attitudes held by individuals which underlie all personal,
social and political relationships ... Ethics are the application of values to individual
behaviour and action' (Dwivedi and Engelbert, 1983). The point is also made by
Rohr that 'bureaucrats have an ethical obligation to respond to the values of the
people in whose name they govern' (Rohr, 1989, p.4). Moreover, the individual
cases which in recent years have received so much public attention have featured
in the headlines largely because they are examples of dilemmas involving values
and are presented in the media from a 'human interest' perspective. This is
illustrated from the United States by such examples as Watergate and the supply
of arms to Iran, and from the United Kingdom by the Ponting case. Each of these
cases involved allegations and discussion about conflicts of values and, more
specifically, lying for the public good, official secrecy, and the expectations that
democratic government should be characterised by openness.

These three themes (lying, secrecy and openness) will be briefly discussed here
for two reasons. One reason is that they represent or are associated with widely
held values and expectations of modern democracies. Other values, including
freedom, fairness and justice, are, of course, also values expected to be found in
democracies, but it has not been the intention to discuss them here. The other reason
for commenting on these particular values is that they have featured prominently
in recent literature on ethics. Moreover, these themes are often interrelated, especially in connection with ethical dilemmas peculiar to the public service.

Lying for the public good has been a matter for discussion since earliest times.
Plato, in *The Republic*, used the expression the 'noble lie' in presenting a fanciful

story to persuade people to accept class distinctions and thereby safeguard social harmony; and Machiavelli's prince was most certainly encouraged to engage in deceit, if it was in his interest to do so. Sir Henry Taylor argued that though the first principles of morality in regard to truth are plain and definite, the derivative principles, and their application in practice are not so: '... falsehood ceases to be falsehood when it is understood at all levels that the truth is not expected to be spoken' (Taylor, 1957, ch.16).

In modern times, the most significant study of this subject is Sissela Bok's *Lying: Moral choice in public and private life*. In that book the author outlined three circumstances which have seemed to liars to provide the strongest excuse for their behaviour: a crisis where overwhelming harm can be averted only through deceit; complete harmlessness and triviality to the point where it seems absurd to quibble about whether a lie has been told; and the duty to particular individuals to protect their secrets. However, Bok commented: 'Where these three expanding streams flow together and mingle with yet another – a desire to advance the public good – they form the most dangerous body of deceit of all' (Bok, 1978, ch.12).

What happens in practice is that moral dilemmas arise for officials, not simply because they have doubts about whether to tell the truth, but because they have to make judgments in particular circumstances about conflicting facets of their conceptions of the public interest. Numerous examples could be given, and, indeed, are given in the literature on this topic (see Bok, 1978, for specific examples and for her extensive notes and bibliography). However, the example which achieved world-wide attention in recent years was the examination of Sir Robert Armstrong, then Head of the British Civil Service, in the Supreme Court of New South Wales, Australia, when the British government was trying to stop publication of Peter Wright's book *Spycatcher*. Armstrong, in answer to questions, explained that though he reckoned telling the truth very high on his list of values, and he would not wish to tell an untruth, he was prepared to make a statement which gave a misleading impression and which, while not a lie, was being economical with the truth (Hall, 1987, pp.88–91).

What emerges from considerations of truth in public service is that situations can often arise where individuals have to make choices which involve deciding what the public interest is, when competing claims are in conflict. Officials have to recognise that truth is a value not only expected in private life but also in public service; it is part of the normal expectations of a civilised modern society, and bureaucrats have an obligation to respond to the values of the people they govern (Rohr, 1989, p. 4). However, for a variety of reasons that may individually be perfectly justifiable, the principle of telling the truth, like other principles associated with societal values, is not an absolute principle that must be followed regardless of circumstances. The last word on lying in public service, or perhaps the taking-off point for further discussion, may be taken from Bok's book. Some lies, she says, notably minor white lies and emergency lies rapidly acknowledged, 'may be more *excusable* than others, but only those deceptive practices which can be openly debated and consented to in advance are *justifiable* in a democracy (Bok, 1978, ch.12).

One of the factors that may constrain truth-telling in public service is the unavoidable involvement of parts of its work with matters that are, equally unavoidably, secret. This legitimate secrecy in public service can become one of the characteristics of administrative practice which give rise to moral dilemmas for officials. Some aspects of public service work have to be secret or the success of particular operations would be jeopardised. This is clearly evident in negotiations, whether they be national, or international, or only domestic and personal. Aspects of public service work also have to be secret when they affect the personal and private circumstances of individuals, because their rights to privacy have to be protected. In addition, one of the most rewarding, demanding and challenging aspects of the work of senior administrators, the development of public policies, can often only be effective if confidentiality is maintained: no policy-maker likes to have preliminary thoughts revealed before they are sufficiently well considered, and premature disclosure can sometimes jeopardise valuable and important intentions.

The differences, from a moral perspective, between lying and secrecy, are, as Bok has outlined in her book *Secrets* (1982), that whereas lying may be *prima facie* wrong, secrecy need not be. There are many good reasons for maintaining secrecy and the examples given here are no more than illustrations of the most obvious. The important point as far as the present discussion is concerned however, is that public servants frequently have to decide matters of secrecy. Someone has to determine what has to be secret first, by developing criteria for general application, then by fitting individual cases or circumstances into the agreed criteria. Someone has to decide what controls should be exercised over secret matters and also how long the controls should continue. However, it is difficult to be effective and efficient in developing and implementing public policies when not all the relevant information is fully available to the officials engaged in those activities, so someone has to ensure that policy-makers in particular areas are kept sufficiently 'in the know'. At the same time, there are also dangers that the rights and interests of citizens may be affected without them being able to influence events or protect themselves.

This means that the problems associated with ethics in public service can be different in both quality and quantity from the problems associated with ethical behaviour in other occupations. In other occupations, customers or clients can often choose to remove themselves from the area of decision-making. Citizens cannot so easily remove themselves, even though they may be personally affected in ways that are of fundamental importance to their quality of life. It is this perspective of public service that often makes the work so worthwhile and intellectually challenging to an official. Nevertheless, it is this very same perspective, with its potential for a high level of job satisfaction, that brings with it dangers. It becomes even more important, in the interests of society as a whole, as well as in the interests of individual citizens, for officials to be trained to recognise the implications of their work, so that they can perform their duties with sensitivity, with regard for the rights of citizens and in accordance with the general expectations that the values of society are upheld and, indeed, advanced.

It is generally believed that in a democracy everything should be done as openly as possible. As Woodrow Wilson once wrote: 'Everybody knows that corruption thrives in secret places, and avoids public places, and we believe it a fair presumption that secrecy means impropriety' (Wilson, 1913). However, even when openness is regarded as generally good, difficulties arise when putting it into practice, and these difficulties give rise to a number of ethical perspectives in public service. Healthy democracy simply cannot exist if government processes err in the direction of too much secrecy, because democracy depends on effective two-way communications between the government and the governed. There are many arguments in favour of maximising openness and there is a large literature that expresses them well (e.g. Chapman and Hunt, 1987; Michael, 1982; Robertson, 1982; Wilson, 1984). However, the point that is being made here is that the extent of openness, its style, and the degree to which it is practised and upheld, are features of the values of particular societies. These features are reflected in constitutional arrangements, including subordinate rules and conventions, but they are also reflected in attitudes of mind. In particular, more danger to the health of a democracy than is easily apparent can result from an over-emphasis in bureaucracies on classifying as secret matters that are better left open, and on over-emphasising the rights of particular bureaucracies to information that they regard as their own. It is only when all the parts of a democratic system are seen to interrelate, in a healthy and effective way, that democracy as a form of government can satisfy the various needs of individual citizens.

THE CONSTITUTIONAL PERSPECTIVE

The values of society are generally reflected in its system of government. The essence of a system of government is reflected in its constitution – that is, the collection of rules which establish and regulate or govern the government, or the framework without which the details would have no form or pattern (Wheare, 1951).

Constitutions, however, consist of much more than ordinary citizens generally realise. Most countries have a written document which is known as the Constitution, and that document reflects the values of the society when it was drawn up, or amended, and indicates that society's expectations in provisions for its government. However, even countries which have such written documents have, in addition, other elements which also contribute to their constitutions in the widest sense. These include sources which, in countries without 'written' constitutions, are the only sources of their systems of government. These include legal precedents or case law; legislation, including subordinate codes and rules; customs and conventions; and statements to be found in authoritative works of reference. In the United Kingdom, which has no written document called a constitution, these sources are of more significance than they may be elsewhere, and much more is assumed in the British constitutional system than in other systems. The important point to note here, however, is not only that all constitutions are to be found in a number of sources (with the relative importance of the sources varying from country to country) but also that, though some constitutions are easier to alter than others, constitutions change from time to time and reflect the values of the societies in which they exist.

In the United Kingdom this is well illustrated in the career of Edward Bridges. By the time he became Head of the Civil Service he was already an acknowledged authority on the practice of the British constitution. As Head of the Civil Service he not only played an important role in ensuring that constitutional propriety was respected throughout the service, he also influenced the development of the constitution by ensuring that, for example, his own expert understanding and interpretation of the political activities of civil servants was reinforced through significant constitutional documents (like the Report of the Masterman Committee on the Political Activities of Civil Servants). Bridges also played an important part in advising prime ministers on such matters as the size of the Cabinet and the organisation and membership of Cabinet committees and subcommittees. Matters of constitutional significance were dealt with by Bridges on an almost daily, routine basis, and even if he was not an innovator in such matters, he brought to his tasks a shrewd appreciation of the constitutional and practical limitations on what was possible, combined with a uniquely relevant practical experience gained over a period of many years. Sometimes his role as a constitutional expert was so strong that he could even call ministers in to tell them when they were behaving badly. Consequently, he made significant contributions to the ways in which the public service worked, especially through the structure of the machinery of government, but he did so in a way which maintained his position of strict partisan neutrality and impartiality. This required a highly developed personal appreciation of ethics in public service, combined with an outstanding command of the constitutional framework within which British public administration proceeds (Chapman, 1988).

Even officials at more mundane levels than the permanent heads of government departments may have important roles to play in this context. In the United States, for example, 'street-level bureaucrats' regularly make routine decisions which in fact have constitutional significance. The policeman who tells demonstrators to 'move along' must interpret concretely the meaning of the First Amendment's guarantee of the 'right of the people peaceably to assemble to petition the government for a redress of grievances'. The social worker who removes a client in the interests of his or her welfare, or a public school principal who suspends an unruly teenager, is taking 'property' from an individual and, under the Fifth and Fourteenth Amendments, may do so only with 'due process of law' (Rohr, 1989).

From the more general viewpoint of ethics in public service, constitutions are important for three reasons. First, they lay down the rules in accordance with which administrators work, including setting down the values and constraints which are important elements in their daily decision-making; in this sense they instruct or guide public servants in what they ought to do and how they should carry out their duties. Secondly, they publicise what is expected of officials, so that citizens also know how the executive or administrative parts of government should work. This publicity and understanding are important parts of the style of government in modern democracies. Thirdly, and at the same time, it should be noted that public servants, who are the most knowledgeable experts on the workings of their particular governments, themselves contribute to the making and interpreting of the constitution. They do this, most obviously, by advising ministers who are considering proposals to change the law and also, sometimes, by proposing changes for consideration by ministers and the legislature. It is often the officials, above all others, who know where the shoe pinches in the actual working of the political system. Constitutions are therefore important for more than one reason at any given time.

It should be noted that all constitutions change. Whistle-blowing, for example, has been regarded by traditionalists as unacceptable in British government, but there has recently been evidence of its acceptability in local government. In 1986 the Widdicombe Report on *The Conduct of Local Authority Business* recommended that the chief executive of a local authority should advise councillors of any action or lack of action that might be illegal (Widdicombe, 1986, para.6.155). More recently, this has been taken further in the Local Government and Housing Act 1989, which legislates for a 'monitoring officer, with the duty to prepare a report on any action or decision that may contravene any enactment or rule of law or ... any code of practice; ... or [that may result in] maladministration or injustice', as is mentioned in the Local Government Acts which created the Commissions for Local Administration (Local Government Act 1974 and Local Government (Scotland) Act 1975). The creation of such a monitoring officer with wide terms of reference is unlikely to have been acceptable a few years ago, but the provisions are now enshrined in law, and constitute a minor facet of the British constitution, with hardly any public attention being given to it.

Numerous themes could be discussed in connection with the importance of the constitutional perspective of ethics in public service, but three will be briefly considered here. These themes relate to codes of conduct; public administration as an institution of government; and the political environment and its interrelatedness with the constitution.

As far as codes of conduct are concerned, one of the most important documents in the British civil service is the Civil Service Pay and Conditions of Service Code. This was the subject of an inquiry by the House of Commons Treasury and Civil Service Committee early in 1990, because of the revisions then being made to it (Treasury and Civil Service Committee, 1990). The Code is an extensive manual covering all aspects of civil service employment, including hours of work, pensions rights, and disciplinary procedures, etc. As British civil servants have no normal contract of service (because of their position as servants of the Crown, with most changes in important aspects of their conditions of service being effected not by legislation but by prerogative power), the Code is generally regarded as, in the words of the evidence to the Committee from the First Division Association, 'the nearest thing to a contract that a civil servant has' – a view with which the present Head of the Home Civil Service broadly agreed. The reason why the Select Committee was considering it in 1990 was that the Code was being amended to bring it into line with the provisions of new legislation, particularly the requirements of the Official Secrets Act 1989.

Two aspects of the new Code are of special interest here. One is the duty of loyalty by civil servants to the Crown, which is stated in paragraph 9904 of the new Code. That paragraph says that civil servants 'owe duties of confidentiality and loyal service to the Crown. Since constitutionally the Crown acts on the advice of ministers who are answerable for their departments in Parliament, these duties are for all practical purposes owed to the Government of the day'. In discussion on this paragraph Sir Robin Butler, Head of the Civil Service, told the Committee that the interests of the Crown and the government of the day were always synonymous; this in practice meant that no civil servant had a separate duty to Parliament. The Committee's Report makes it clear that the words 'for all practical purposes' concerned all circumstances short of 'a rift between the Crown and the government of the day', in which 'the constitution had broken down for some reason'. These important statements, in an extensive manual running to several thousand paragraphs, indicate the very important constitutional status of this Code, which is largely unknown to the general public in the United Kingdom. Moreover, its implications have potentially far reaching consequences in terms of the practice of public administration, and particularly for ethics in public service. It is these implications that constitute the second aspect of the revised Code relevant to the present discussion.

There have always been discussions about the constitutional implications for civil servants of matters which gave rise to issues of conscience. One example of this was the guidance provided in 1980 for officials appearing before parliamentary select committees. This guidance is known as the Osmotherly rules because it was contained in a memorandum drawn up by Mr Edward Osmotherly, the assistant secretary then in charge of the Civil Service Department's machinery of government division. It was to Osmotherly's eternal chagrin, to use Peter Hennessy's phrase (Hennessy, 1989, p.362), that the memorandum now always associated with his name subsequently became a controversial document in British constitutional history. The Osmotherly rules, along with other documents like the Armstrong memorandum on the duties and responsibilities of ministers, were drawn up to guide officials who might encounter doubts about what their duties should be in particular difficult circumstances. The new Pay and Conditions of Service Code makes further provisions in precisely the same direction by drawing attention to details in the Osmotherly rules and the Armstrong memorandum, for civil servants to appeal on questions of conscience right up the formal hierarchy to the Head of the Civil Service personally. Indeed, the Head of the Civil Service told the Committee: 'I would regard a civil servant ... as having a right of appeal to me if they [sic] could not resolve the matter of legality or propriety within their own department'. In practice, however, there is so far no evidence of 'crisis of conscience' cases being referred to the Head of the Civil Service since the new procedure was first introduced.

The important point to make here is that codes may be important for a variety of reasons and their importance may vary from one system of government to another. They are sometimes produced by trade unions as guidance for members; sometimes they may be valued by citizens who, by referring to codes, can learn of their legitimate expectations when being dealt with by public servants. Even more important for the present discussion, there are occasions when working manuals like the Pay and Conditions of Service Code can, even when they are officially classified as confidential documents, have constitutional significance.

This indicates, from a perspective that does not always get much attention, what Rohr has referred to as the significance of public administration as an institution of government, and the importance of constitutional law and history in both academic programmes on public administration and public management training. In this context, 'public administration joins together what constitutional principle keeps apart' (Rohr, 1986, p.x). Indeed, there is a sense in which public administration is not merely a static institutional context where values and formal rules for government converge; it is where the dynamics of government can be seen in practice. Moreover, the practice of public service management has to advance not only according to rules and procedures codified in documents with a constitutional value but also according to the highest standards of professional expertise. These high standards also have a role to play in public service ethics. As Glenn Stahl has put it: 'toleration of incompetence is itself one of the more insidious forms of corruption' (Stahl, 1983). Where administrative practice slips from the highest standards, problems of ethics arise not only because corruption of quality leads to other forms of corruption, but also because corruption of quality is itself a matter of moral concern from the perspective of the decline of professional standards.

When professional standards decline they often become a matter of concern for citizens who have expectations of what they wish to receive in terms of quality of service. It then becomes more difficult for citizens to be realistic about other aspects of the institutions of government. It is, for example, sometimes hard for citizens to know how the institutions of government fit together, and this is especially so where a country does not have a key document known as a written constitution. Written constitutions can become a focus for reference and analysis, but in systems of government without such basic documents it is much more difficult for people to know how the system of government as a whole works or ought to work. This difficulty is magnified (as in Britain) where there is no properly considered or adequate provision in the country's education system for teaching about the system of government and about the rights and duties of citizenship. It is even more magnified where some of the key documents for understanding how the system of government works are classified as confidential and are therefore not easily accessible, even for keenly interested citizens.

The confidentiality of important constitutional documents assumes that they are not matters that citizens need to know about. It is all very well, and indeed true, to say that the socialisation of individuals before they join the public service provides them with a value system which includes beliefs about ethical standards considered generally acceptable in society (Kernaghan, 1983); but widespread ignorance among mature and reasonably well educated citizens about how the system of government works suggests a very uncertain and complacent approach to some of the values usually expected in a liberal democracy. A democracy which has little regard for the citizens' understanding and/or interest in that democracy's own workings, which makes no proper provision for those citizens to understand the essentials of their system of government, and which fails to encourage more than a small minority to be active in more than a few democratic obligations, does not seem to be programming itself to achieve the highest standards of ethics in public service. Let it not be thought, however, that these comments are directed only to the British system of government with its so-called unwritten constitution. Similar points can be made about countries with written constitutions where the constitutional elements outside the key written document are insufficiently appreciated as elements of constitutional significance.

THE QUALITY OF PUBLIC PERSONNEL ADMINISTRATION

While matters of constitutional significance affect the ways in which public officials perceive their work, at the more practical level, day-to-day personnel management also plays an important role; and it is probable that a significant number of ethical dilemmas experienced by officials could be resolved fairly easily by changes in systems of public personnel administration. This may be so in relation to whistle-blowing. One particularly interesting comment on this issue has come from Sir Brian Cubbon, formerly Permanent Secretary to the Home Office (see ch.2). One of his personal performance indicators was that there should *never* be any leaks by officials in his department. He also felt that, rather than rely on guidance to officials from codes of ethics, which can be wooden and inflexible, he preferred to emphasise the benefits of good management and training. Difficulties arise, unfortunately, when personnel management and training in the public sector are less good than practitioners would like them to be.

There are, of course, numerous easily understandable and acceptable reasons why public personnel administration achieves less than the standard of excellence to which it aspires. For example, in times of financial constraint short term economies can be most easily achieved by cuts in training budgets. Cuts can also be made fairly quickly, if they are urgently needed, through economies in staff welfare and counselling provisions. These and other economies may be genuinely regretted, when they are introduced, by politicians and senior officials, but they are nevertheless introduced because of the demands of elected representatives, and often in response to pressures over which government has little or no control.

Whistle-blowing nevertheless occurs from time to time, in spite of rules against it in countries with systems of government involving ministerial responsibility, and in spite of safeguards to enable officials experiencing crises of conscience to resolve their difficulties through hierarchical appeals. What may, in the longer term, be even more serious than failures in the system, but is largely unknown, is the number of crises of conscience that are sublimated or resolved without whistle-blowing. Instances are revealed from time to time, usually without much public attention, because people have simply moved out of public sector employment. This way of resolving such a difficulty may not, however, be either in the best interests of the official, whose conscience may still be worrying, or in the best interests of the public service, which might be richer for the continuing service of sensitive and idealistic personnel.

What is sometimes insufficiently appreciated is that officials contemplating action to resolve their personal crises of conscience may, with a little appropriate help, be able to resolve their difficulties fairly easily and continue to work in the public service. Sometimes problems of this sort arise from misunderstandings or ignorance and, if the official could discuss the situation with someone independent of the formal line of authority, an entirely different perspective may be offered so that the problem disappears. Sometimes these crises may simply be a matter of an official getting some detail out of proportion and this, too, can on occasion be resolved by sensitive counselling. Moreover, individuals facing crises of conscience may have to draw up a sort of mental balance sheet to see whether contemplated action will result in serious consequences quite out of line with the size of the problem at issue. Sensitive counselling by someone who is not a line manager may help by drawing attention to factors overlooked in the balance sheet. At the end of the day, these are the sorts of factors which may have to be considered by an individual genuinely facing a personal crisis of conscience. It is in this context, for problems of a relatively low level of magnitude, and where such problems are likely to be more common and less newsworthy, that suggestions have been made in the United Kingdom for the creation of some sort of independent adviser or ombudsman.

This proposal has not been turned down for reasons of economy but because the case for such a service has not been accepted. The Head of the British Home Civil Service told the House of Commons Treasury and Civil Service Committee that an independent appeals body was unnecessary and impracticable. He argued that 'the importance of an independent person or body ... would be very disruptive of the relationship between ministers and civil servants'. He said that there was no evidence that the present system, whereby officials consult their superiors when facing crises of conscience, did not work. He told the Committee that he had not yet (12 March 1990) had to hear an appeal of this sort and he felt that was because there was not such a widespread demand or dissatisfaction among civil servants that they felt they needed to bring cases to him: 'Such things are easily sorted out lower down. If there was such pent up demand, you or I would have heard about it' (Treasury and Civil Service Committee, 1990, Q.96, 109).

It may well be that these statements indicate that the problem has not yet been fully appreciated by the civil service. The question is not just a matter of dealing with people who have contravened the rules, or are about to do so, to resolve a crisis of conscience. It is a much wider issue than that, because it involves helping officials who are normally rule-abiding, but sometimes also idealistic, to continue to give of their best in their official duties and to maintain their faith in the administrative system within which they work. Like other issues referred to ombudsmen in other contexts, if an individual feels he has a problem, then a problem exists, even if it is the sort of problem that can be simply resolved by providing information, or explanation, or removing a misunderstanding.

Evidence that does exist from the experience of well-publicised cases suggests that existing provisions in public personnel administration are sometimes insufficiently sensitive or not sufficiently prepared to respond at the early stages when individual officials are beginning to experience a crisis of conscience. Clive Ponting, for example, asked to be moved to another job but his request was not granted, and his is not the only case in recent years of an official who asked to be moved and whose request was refused. Reliance on good management practice should, perhaps, only be emphasised when the public service personnel systems are good enough to cope with such problems.

From observation of press coverage of cases of crises of conscience it seems that they are often concerned with conflicts of loyalties. These may include feelings of loyalty to personal standards, to conceptions of the public interest, to superiors, and to clients or citizens. It is unsophisticated and superficial to see them simply as expressions of ideological motivation or behaviour calculated to advance the interests of an individual or group. Often, when cuts are made in training programmes, or when training programmes are insensitively and exclusively geared to specific skills or quantitative elements involving techniques intended to result in measurable improvements in performance, sacrifices are made by cutting courses which emphasise less measurable elements, including developing sensitivity and broadening horizons of employees so that they have new perspectives on the implications of their work. It is therefore sobering to read of the findings of the recent investigations by April Hejka-Ekins, which showed that, as far as ethics courses in schools of public administration in the United States were concerned (i.e. courses emphasising the development of moral judgment) there were more ethics courses taught in 1976 than in 1980 or 1985 and 1986 (Hejka-Ekins, 1988). These findings are, however, quite consistent with the increased emphasis on business enterprise and business styles of management characterised by the governments led by Reagan in the United States and Thatcher in the United Kingdom.

ETHICS IN PUBLIC SERVICE

The personal values of public servants are the most important element in public service ethics. These values have a variety of sources which include the family background and early socialisation of officials; their education; their choice of career and selection at recruitment stage; training and socialisation after recruitment; the continuing changing values in society; influence from the political environment; the embodiment of some of the values and other factors in constitutions, codes and rules; and the requirements of national (and sometimes international) law. Moreover, all these factors change over time – even rigid constitutions have flexible elements; laws, too, can be changed.

The second most important element in public service ethics is to be found in the duties of officials within political systems. Political systems vary in important respects from one country to another, even when constitutions or countries are dedicated to the highest ideals of democracy. In some democracies there are ministers who are accountable to parliaments, while in others quite different arrangements have evolved; consequently officials in different systems have different duties, responsibilities and rights. Whatever the country and whatever the political system, however, public service is firmly based in the constitution – using the term in its widest and most comprehensive sense to refer to non-written elements as well as written elements, even where a so-called written constitution exists. Written constitutions have a certain neatness, finality and logical authority, but do not alone resolve ethical problems. Crises of conscience and ethical dilemmas of various sorts are naturally occurring phenomena in public service. Successful public servants may only rarely find them burdensome, but that does not mean that they do not exist at all or are not more burdensome to others.

A third important element in public service ethics is the expectations of society. This is, perhaps, the facet which is most amorphous. Social values and expectations can be volatile; indeed, it is because of such volatility that people are protected by constitutions and laws, otherwise their basic expectations to a good quality of life may be jeopardised by the talents of orators and the political acumen of extremists. Nevertheless, the expectations and general values of society can be important in influencing behaviour and guiding it into what is well illustrated in Britain in the class system, and in other patterns of behaviour characterised so perceptibly by George Mikes (see Shils, 1956; Mikes, 1946).

Nevertheless, if a democracy is to continue in a healthy condition these features of public administration, features that are developed beyond elementary understandings of administrators implementing laws laid down or approved by legislators, should be recognised as much more than the private domain of officials and/or ministers. They should instead be seen as matters for public education, public discussion and informed opinion. Perhaps the healthiness of modern democracy can be gauged by the quality of its public debates about important details of how public administration actually works and, prior to debate, its educational provision to ensure that citizens are fully aware of their system of government, how it works, and what its problems are.

Arthur Bentley made valuable points about this in the early years of this century, but insufficient attention has been paid to what he and others have said. Bentley emphasised that the raw material of government cannot be found in law-books because these merely state the method by which certain participants in government proceed, or claim to proceed in their part of the work. It cannot be found in the 'law' behind the textbooks, except when this is taken to mean the actual functioning of the people – in which case law is an important aspect of the raw material, but by no means a complete statement of it. It cannot be found in the proceedings of constitutional conventions, nor in the arguments and discussions surrounding them. Hints and hopes are there, but only minute fragments of the raw material. It cannot be found in essays, addresses, appeals and diatribes on tyranny and democracy. All that the world has ever produced in this way cannot do more than point out to us where the raw material can be found. It cannot be found in the 'character of the people', in their specific 'feelings' or 'thoughts' or their 'hearts' or 'minds'. All these are hypotheses or dreams. Whatever truth or other importance they may possess, they certainly are not 'raw material' but instead highly theoretical.

That is why public administration in its most general sense is so important as an activity and as a study. It is, in fact, what Bentley saw as a large part of the raw material of government. All the other elements may be significant, but public administration is at the centre of this vital sphere of activity. Furthermore, in that sphere of activity ethical problems for officials arise from time to time. Their existence should not be cause for undue anxiety because they are a natural phenomenon. Unthinking, dehumanised officials would not experience such problems, but they are not the sort of officials appropriate for modern liberal democracies. To pretend that there are or should be no ethical problems in public service would be myopic and unhelpful. To try to remove them or prevent them arising at all would be unhealthy.

At the end of the day, ethics in public service is an issue of crucial importance. In the modern world much of life, both qualitatively and quantitatively, depends on government. Because government is now so big and deals with more than basic needs and elements of protection, the professionalism of public servants is even more important than in the past. Consequently the qualities of individual public servants are also important. Public servants must be trusted to exercise judgments wisely, and they must be carefully selected for that trust. It is in their crucial work involving discretion and advice, as well as policy-making, that the ethical standards of public service are evident. Nevertheless, it remains the ultimate responsibility of citizens, through their governments, to ensure that all the structures and procedures of government are best suited to their purposes, in good working order, continuously reviewed, and positively supportive to public servants when they carry out their satisfying and demanding, but also very responsible work.

ACKNOWLEDGEMENT

I wish to thank John Rohr of Virginia Polytechnic Institute and State University for comments on an earlier draft of this chapter.

Bentley, Arthur F. (1908), *The Process of Government: A study of social pressures*, Evanston, IL: Principia Press.

Bok, Sissela (1978), *Lying: Moral Choice in Public and Private Life*, New York: Pantheon.

Bok, Sissela (1982), *Secrets: On the ethics of concealment and revelation*, New York: Pantheon.

Caiden, Gerald E. (1983), 'Public Service Ethics: What should be done?', in Kenneth Kernaghan and O.P. Dwivedi (eds), *op. cit.*

Chapman, Richard A. (1988), *Ethics in the British Civil Service*, London: Routledge.

Chapman, Richard A. and Hunt, Michael (1987), *Open Government*, Beckenham: Croom Helm.

Dwivedi, O.P. and Engelbert, Ernest A. (1983), 'Education and Training for Public Service Ethics', in Kenneth Kernaghan and O.P. Dwivedi (eds), *op.cit.*

Hall, Richard V. (1987), *A Spy's Revenge*, Ringwood, Victoria: Penguin Australia.

Hennessy, Peter (1989), *Whitehall*, London: Secker & Warburg.

Hejka-Ekins, April (1988), 'Teaching Ethics in Public Administration', *Public Administration Review*, 48, pp.885–91.

Kernaghan, Kenneth (1983), 'Public service ethics in Canada', in Kenneth Kernaghan and O.P. Dwivedi (eds), *op. cit.*

Kernaghan, Kenneth and Dwivedi, O.P. (eds), (1983), *Ethics in the Public Service*, Brussels: International Institute of Administrative Sciences.

Meynell, Dame Alix (1988), *Public Servant, Private Woman: An autobiography*, London: Gollancz.

Michael, James (1982), *The Politics of Secrecy*, Harmondsworth: Penguin.

Mikes, George (1946), *How to be an Alien*, London: Deutsch.

Robertson, K.G. (1982), *Public Secrets: A study of the development of government secrecy*, Basingstoke: Macmillan.

Rohr, John A. (1986), *To Run a Constitution: The legitimacy of the administrative state*, Lawrence, KS: University Press of Kansas.

Rohr, John A. (1989), 2nd edn, *Ethics for Bureaucrats*, New York: Dekker.

Shils, Edward (1956), *The Torment of Secrecy*, London: Heinemann.

Stahl, O. Glenn (1983), 'Public service ethics in the United States', in Kenneth Kernaghan and O.P. Dwivedi, (eds), *op. cit.*

Taylor, Sir Henry (1957), *The Statesman*, Cambridge: Heffer. [First published in 1836.]

Treasury and Civil Service Committee (1990), Session 1989–90, Fifth Report, *The Civil Service Pay and Conditions of Service Code, together with the Proceedings of the Committee and minutes of Evidence*, HC 260, London: HMSO.

Wheare, K.C. (1951), *Modern Constitutions*, London, OUP.

Widdicombe, David (Chairman) (1986), *Report of the Committee of Enquiry into the Conduct of Local Authority Business*, Cmnd 9797, London: HMSO.

Wilson, Des (ed) (1984), *The Secrets File: The case for freedom of information in Britain today*, London: Heinemann.

Wilson, Woodrow (1913), *The New Freedom*, New York: Doubleday, Page and Co. Quoted in Sissela Bok (1978), *op. cit.*

Index